Private Benefits

Material Assistance in the Private Sector

This is a volume in the

INSTITUTE FOR RESEARCH ON POVERTY
MONOGRAPH SERIES

A complete list of titles in this series appears at the end of this volume.

Private Benefits

Material Assistance in the Private Sector

MICHAEL SOSIN
School of Social Work
and Institute for Research on Poverty
University of Wisconsin–Madison
Madison, Wisconsin

1986

ACADEMIC PRESS, INC.
Harcourt Brace Jovanovich, Publishers
Orlando San Diego New York Austin
London Montreal Sydney Tokyo Toronto

This book is one of a series sponsored by the Institute for Research on Poverty of the University of Wisconsin.

ACADEMIC PRESS, INC.
Orlando, Florida 32887

United Kingdom Edition published by
ACADEMIC PRESS INC. (LONDON) LTD.
24–28 Oval Road, London NW1 7DX

Library of Congress Cataloging in Publication Data

Sosin, Michael.
Private benefits.

Bibliography: p.
Includes index.
1. Charities–United States. 2. Social service–United States. I. Title.
HV91.S627 1986 361.7'0973 85-26665
ISBN 0–12–655320–3 (alk. paper)

PRINTED IN THE UNITED STATES OF AMERICA

86 87 88 89 9 8 7 6 5 4 3 2 1

The Institute for Research on Poverty is a national center for research established at the University of Wisconsin in 1966. Its primary objective is to foster basic, multidisciplinary research into the nature and causes of poverty and means to combat it.

In addition to increasing the basic knowledge from which policies aimed at the elimination of poverty can be shaped, the Institute strives to carry analysis beyond the formulation and testing of fundamental generalizations to the development and assessment of relevant policy alternatives.

The Institute endeavors to bring together scholars of the highest caliber whose primary research efforts are focused on the problem of poverty, the distribution of income, and the analysis and evaluation of social policy, offering staff members wide opportunities for interchange of ideas, maximum freedom for research into basic questions about poverty and social policy, and dissemination of their findings.

Contents

List of Tables

Foreword

Do private charities to aid the poor represent the remnants of the era before the growth of the welfare state, or do they provide a modern alternative to the welfare bureaucracy? The complex history, present efforts, and likely future of the private not-for-profit sector in distributing material aid to the needy is the theme of this monograph. The research is timely because in recent years there has been increased interest in the privatization of public programs.

Michael Sosin's study uses organizational theory to focus on the goals, structures, and operating procedures of numerous private agencies. His empirical results are based on an extensive questionnaire administered to public welfare officials, a detailed 12-county survey of all social agencies, both private and public, and intensive case studies of material aid programs and important community institutions in four counties located in the Southwest, Southeast, Midwest, and Northeast. He addresses such questions as: What proportion of private philanthropy is devoted to aiding the needy? What is the relationship between private assistance and need? How do agencies respond to increased need? Do they fill gaps in public programs? Or do the public and private sectors overlap? Where do private agencies get their funding? What are their goals? How do they treat their clients?

At the turn of the century private agencies were considered the primary agents for dealing with the problems associated with poverty. The Great Depression demonstrated their inadequacy. Since then, responsibility for alleviating poverty has rested with the public sector. In the last 30 years the private sector has grown more slowly than the public—as government spending on social welfare grew from $32.4 billion to $532 billion, philanthropy grew from $1.7 billion to $17.3 billion. Furthermore, most philanthropy today is devoted to support of educational and medical institutions, not direct assistance to the poor.

Sosin analyzes not only why private philanthropy has grown so slowly but why aiding the poor is rarely seen by many private-sector agencies as an appropriate function. In competition with one another and with government for legitimacy and funds, organizations have sought sheltered niches (the Red Cross, for example, concentrates on disaster relief) or have channeled their services in what they judge to be a more professional direction (providing family counseling, for example). A few, such as the Salvation Army, continue as they have since the nineteenth century, offering shelter to the homeless—some in the hope of encouraging religious conversion.

According to Sosin, the private sector nevertheless plays a significant role:

> . . . private agencies exist in every community and save many from starvation and homelessness. Often they provide the only source of shelter to hundreds of thousands of people—some the victims of disaster, other facing a sudden loss of income or a change in family circumstances, still others chronically homeless for a number of reasons. Private food programs provide for many who would otherwise go hungry. General programs cover utility payments, rent, and needs for furniture; side programs cover important health-related expenses; and single-mission agencies provide what they are organized to distribute, whether shoes or shelter. Although public programs may in theory meet the same needs, overlap is only theoretical, owing to limited budgets; the private agencies indeed fill needs.

Sosin finds that in some respects the private sector operates more effectively than does the public sector: It can respond more rapidly and with greater flexibility, it may be more compassionate, and, with first-hand experience of the needs of the poor, it is in a position to advocate for them.

Though increasing dissatisfaction with government policies and programs has been voiced recently, it is inconceivable that private agencies can ever replace public income maintenance programs. Indeed, the private sector, as described by Sosin, cannot even fill the gaps created by recent budget cuts.

Yet Sosin, drawing on the research reported here and in his earlier book, "Last Resorts,"* does envision an increased role for the private sector. He points to a new outlook on the part of social workers, who see material assistance as a necessary adjunct of counseling. He suggests a greater advocacy role for the private sector and favors increasing the percentage of United Way funds allocated to material aid. In the long run he sees the possibility of the private sector taking responsibility for those public programs, such as Emergency Assistance, that require discretion and a quick response. He also endorses public sector funding for certain private agencies to enable them to deal with the immediate

* Joel F. Handler and Michael Sosin. *Last Resorts: Emergency Assistance and Special Needs Programs in Public Welfare.* (Orlando, Fla.: Academic Press, 1983).

pressing needs of the poor. He is hopeful that "by creating a division of labor between the public and private sectors, it will be possible to meet more fully the needs of the impoverished: to combine humane treatment, equity, and a potential for social change in a complex, impersonal, persistent social order."

SHELDON DANZIGER
Director, Institute for Research on Poverty

Acknowledgments

All research projects depend upon the voluntary efforts of many people; this project is no exception. Not only am I deeply indebted to all of those anonymous individuals who agreed to be interviewed or to otherwise share information–from those working in social service organizations and other community agencies to those who have received material aid from the agencies–but I also owe thanks to many who helped support the research, collect and analyze the data, and comment on earlier drafts of this book. The research could not have been completed without the financial support of the Graduate School of the University of Wisconsin–Madison and of the Assistant to the Secretary for Planning and Evaluation, U.S. Department of Health and Human Services. Also vital were the facilities of the Institute for Research on Poverty at the University of Wisconsin–Madison and the encouragement offered by the Institute's director, Sheldon Danziger. Individuals to whom I owe thanks include Jon Bartells, Steven Cole, Joyce Collins, Michael Daley, Sandra Danziger, Eileen Doyle, John Flesher, Ann Killen, Mark Kleczewski, Chris Linse, Patricia McLaughlin, Suzanne Rinaldo, Judy Rose, Elaine Staley, Bernard Stumbras, Jody Taschwer, Joseph Volk, and Daniel Weinberg.

Special thanks are due to two individuals. One is Joel Handler, who read and criticized an earlier draft of the book, and whose encouragement was important throughout the project. The other is Liz Uhr, whose editing helped me turn my manuscript into a finished book.

CHAPTER 1

Private Social Welfare and Public Social Welfare

Growth of Government Bureaucracies

Since the New Deal reforms of the 1930s, public bureaucracies have greatly expanded their efforts to ameliorate individual economic distress. Government programs, while perhaps inadequate, now insure many of us against adversity arising from unemployment, illness, or old age. They also provide a financial cushion for many of the most needy families whose members cannot find work. Some have claimed that alternate strategies might have been more effective, but it is clear that the reductions in poverty that have occurred over the last two decades are largely a result of public transfer programs (Plotnick and Skidmore, 1975; Danziger, 1982; Danziger and Smolensky, 1983). Many even believe that the gap in the marketplace between the rich and poor is widening and that only governmental programs stand in the way of increasing inequality (Taussig, 1976; Sosin, 1979).

The growth of these programs implies large levels of governmental control over public resources. Benefits are dispensed through such U.S. Department of Health and Human Services programs as Aid to Families with Dependent Children (AFDC), Supplemental Security Income (SSI), and Social Security. The Department of Agriculture administers Food Stamps, while the Department of Housing and Urban Development controls housing allowances. Some of these programs are partly supported by state funds, and in any case, state and local governments dispense a wide range of benefits of their own. The proportion of the gross national product devoted to the federal share of social welfare, minuscule before the New Deal, has thus increased from 4.0% in 1950 to 11.4% in 1979, while state expenditures over the same period expanded from 4.9% to 7.1% of the GNP (Lampman, 1983).

The growth of large-scale public bureaucracies is part of a massive expansion in the size of social organizations in general, a trend that has received a good deal of attention from scholars for a century (Weber, 1947; Jacoby, 1973). Criticism has accompanied growth. Many are concerned that large organizations develop standardized rules that limit their responsiveness to individuals with particular problems (Coleman, 1974; Katz et al., 1975), that they serve the interests of some at the expense of others (Michels, 1915; McNeil, 1978), or that they reduce political and cultural pluralism (Kornhauser, 1959; Janowitz, 1976).

In public welfare, such criticisms have a good deal of justification. As public benefit programs have expanded, responsiveness has become limited. The degree of standardization in the welfare system, for example, has increased. Most programs now calculate benefits on the basis of a rather strict set of eligibility criteria. These criteria are enforced by strict quality-control standards (Brodkin and Lipsky, 1983; Mills, 1981). Many individuals might not meet the criteria and still experience need. Further, special problems that might make for additional resource deficiencies for those already aided are seldom addressed (Handler and Sosin, 1983). Ironically, while a classic criticism of a nonstandardized system is that it allows inequities to occur, substantive inequities arise from standardization (Moynihan, 1969; Handler and Hollingsworth, 1971; Handler and Sosin, 1983).

The other side of the problem is that, while the way grants are calculated is generally standardized, there are differentials in coverage. In AFDC, and to some extent in other federal benefit programs, the standard grants vary in generosity across states and even across counties within states. Further, benefits for those considered more deserving, the poor elderly or the disabled, are often larger under Supplemental Security Income than are grants for families under AFDC. And those who are considered least deserving (individuals living alone and couples without children) are not served by most federal programs (except Food Stamps) and must rely on very uneven benefits provided by state and local governments. In Janowitz's (1976) terms, "equity claims" for benefits are unevenly distributed.

Another complaint—one that is a bit more speculative—is that the public bureaucracies stand in the way of further improvements in the lives of the poor. Officials committed to expanding benefits of their particular programs may tend to deny claims of groups not served, or groups served by other agencies. The very existence of bureaucracies may even symbolically indicate to many that no further reforms are needed—whether this is the case or not (Edelman, 1977). The reliance on transfer programs in which powerful bureaucracies have a stake may also reduce support for other strategies to reduce poverty.

Private Alternatives

There are many ways of checking the problems generated by large government bureaucracies dispensing aid to the poor—such as by legislation and political party activism, by interest-group advocacy, and so forth. Another countervailing force is private philanthropy and the private social welfare agencies it spawns. The interest in philanthropy cuts across much of the political spectrum, because complaints about the operations of government are also widespread. (Friedman, 1962; Harrington, 1976; Janowitz, 1976). Some believe that the private sector now plays an important role in curbing the excesses of the public sector; others believe that there is a high potential for a contribution (Manser and Cass, 1975; Grønbjerg, 1982).

Of course, the private network is much smaller than the public. Public expenditures on social welfare have been estimated to be seven times those of the private sector (Kramer, 1981), even taking private in-kind donations into account. Indeed, the proportion of the gross national product devoted to private philanthropic expenditures, 0.8% in 1979, is only a small proportion of public expenditures, 18.5%—even though measures of philanthropic expenditures include donations to arts and education as well as to social welfare, considered narrowly. Unlike public welfare, private philanthropy has been a stable, not growing, percentage of the gross national product since 1950 (Lampman, 1983). It thus can be argued that private agencies are like David taking on a series of Goliaths.

Nevertheless, private agencies may still be a vital force in social welfare. One primary responsibility of private organizations is to dispense services that the public sector cannot, or will not, provide (Kramer, 1981). Some localities, for example, rely totally on private agencies to make foster-care placements (Werner, 1976). More commonly, private agencies supplement services provided through government, counterbalancing the rigidity of public programs.

Private agencies may also be prime forces for social change. The smaller part of this role involves the ability to innovate programs and treatment technologies, though the utility of the private sector in program change has often been questioned (Kramer, 1981). More central to the present discussion, private agencies can directly advocate with government to improve the well-being of clients (Epstein, 1981).

Because private agencies are often recipients of financial aid from the government (Terrell, 1979) or are composed of individuals who are potential beneficiaries, self-interest may dictate that they support new legislation for some specific groups, such as the handicapped or the mentally ill. They may also have ethical, religious, or political goals to advocate (Manser and Cass, 1975).

At the same time, doubts may be raised over the extent to which agencies advocate. Private agencies, for example, might not advocate for new programs that are not in their interest. Epstein (1981) notes that most advocates work for a specific population group; 12% focus on children and youth, 27% on the physically disabled, and 32% on the psychologically disabled. One might suspect that agencies advocating for one group of clients may do so at the expense of other clients.

Private agencies clearly have an ideological impact that may also reinforce problems in the public sector. There is strong distrust of government and a "slight preference" (Kramer, 1981) for private welfare agencies in the United States. A common assumption is that they will be repositories of "grass-roots democracy" (Manser and Cass, 1975) as they meet many needs for services. Even if facts diverge from theory, demands to increase public services can be rejected using the claim that the responsibility is already met by the private sector.

Private agencies are also likely to have distinctive missions. Rather than dispensing benefits or advocating on the basis of some type of legally legitimated rule, some of these agencies dispense benefits and advocate on the basis of their own beliefs. This may limit the extent to which they meet the most severe needs.

Furthermore they may demand that clients behave in specific ways to obtain benefits. They may expect clients to convert to Christianity, to apply for a job, or to refrain from what is deemed amoral sexual behavior. As a result, private agencies may carry out some of the onerous "social control" functions that actually support the status quo against change (Cloward and Piven, 1971, 1974; Galper, 1975). At least in theory, they may force clients to adopt a passive demeanor in order to obtain benefits, or to search for jobs that do not exist in an uncomplaining fashion. Private philanthropy may therefore be a force for progress or reaction, a meaningful adjunct to our social welfare effort or an excuse for limiting assistance to the needy. What purposes does it in fact serve?

Focus of the Book

This book examines the roles of private agencies in providing material aid to the poor—the support they make available, the extent to which they advocate for clients, and the extent to which they are used to support the status quo and resist social change. The book also suggests their potential role. In part, the study is meant to point to the role these agencies generally play. But in documenting the characteristics of private aid, the study also by contrast points out those types of aid and services that will be delivered by the public system (and monitored through public mechanisms) or not at all. Thus the study touches on the entire interplay between public and private welfare and the social and political context that affects the way we serve those in need.

In this analysis, the focus is on one function of the private sector that is most closely bound up with financial support—the provision of material assistance in the form of cash, vouchers, or in-kind services. Generally, this aid is meant to deal with such pressing problems as a lack of money for food or a lack of a place to live. This focus excludes many other services that might be important to individuals, ranging from child care to medical attention. To cover these services would invite expanding the book to an analysis of the entire private sector. The focus on material needs, narrowly defined, clearly directs us to an area of important practical concern.

Conceptually, the need for assistance can be divided into three parts (Handler and Sosin, 1983). First, there are one-time *emergency needs,* which are clearly beyond the control of individuals, such as need generated by a fire or flood that destroys a family's home, leaving them without housing, food, and clothing. For those who receive benefits from the government, a lost or stolen check is a borderline need in this category.

A second category involves *special needs,* caused by chronic deficiencies or circumstances affecting only some individuals. Most obvious is a health-related need for a special diet, appliances, or special furnishings. Needs for clothes for school and special medical equipment are also included.

Finally, there is the emergency *need for basic goods* such as food, clothing, or fuel. In theory, such needs should be covered by an individual's salary from work or regular benefits from the public system. However, often individuals do not have salaries or benefits from government, or they find that their assets have been depleted in a given month.

One of the characteristics of the need for basic goods is that it involves agencies in moral issues. Administrators of public programs assume that individuals receiving benefits should budget properly to avoid running out of basic goods (Handler and Sosin, 1983). Therefore, although some public programs have emergency components (which are described later), these are seldom used to provide basic needs. The private sector faces the same moral question: Does the need represent poor budgeting, a dissolute life-style, or outright fraud? And they face an additional one:

Should the private agencies be forced to pick up the slack when government benefits are not sufficient, causing many individuals chronically to run out of cash? As we shall see, the largest component of private material aid covers basic goods. Decisions over basic needs represent the clearest point at which the interplay between the two sectors and the effects of other social constraints can be observed.

The examination of the private effort to meet material needs is particularly important today. Changes in federal laws have greatly reduced public financial support. Along with increased rhetorical claims about the utility of the private sector, the changes result in a higher level of need than private agencies might be expected to meet. To what extent do private agencies rise to the challenge? Are they useful in pressuring public officials for changes in policy? Does the very existence of the private agencies allow reductions in public support to occur and be rationalized, even when they result in serious, life-threatening problems for some individuals?

Methods of Study

A number of research strategies were developed to explore the role of the private sector in meeting material needs. Of course, part of the inquiry involves a careful analysis of existing information in historical studies, an examination of the role of the private sector in general, and a study of largely unpublished reports about the contemporary private material assistance system and its clients.

In addition, independent research was undertaken. Some data stems from a previous study, an examination of public emergency assistance programs (Handler and Sosin, 1983). This study sampled public welfare agencies in 1979. The sample used a stratified, random design. States were randomly selected from six cells, and counties were randomly selected within states, provided that their population was at least 25,000. The stratification criteria for the states included the size of the AFDC program, the extent to which AFDC grants were standardized (flat grants), and the existence of public emergency assistance programs.

This data source contains a small number of questions about the private sector, along with a good deal of comparative information on public emergency assistance programs. Its most important advantage is that it is a random design (each county actually ended up having approximately equal likelihood of entering the sample). There are 240 counties in the sample, representing 61% of all questionnaires sent out. In comparing counties that responded with those that did not, no significant demographic differences (size, urbanization, income, etc.) were found.

Unfortunately, this source of data did not directly sample private agencies; it merely contains some information on the way these agencies are perceived by public welfare officials in the AFDC system. Therefore, additional information was obtained from 12 counties–two in each of the six cells mentioned above.

The main sources of data for the 12 counties were the directories of social agencies, which are published in most moderate- and large-sized cities in the United States. Directories contain lists of public and private agencies, descriptions of their responsibilities, and something about their patterns of funding and social organization. It was possible to code information about the public and private sector for the directories, including the problems covered, population served, services rendered, sources of funds, and so forth. The directories also provided a guide to the role of providing material assistance in the private network. Data were coded for 1250 agencies—excluding legal aid clinics, public schools, and other programs that are not a part of social welfare as it is usually defined.

When one uses directories, one is dependent upon the accuracy of those who have tabulated the directories. There is some possibility of unevenness in coverage or inaccuracy of the descriptions. Indeed, because information on sources of funds is so uneven, in this book only one directory in each cell—the one that had complete financial information on each agency, or the one randomly selected among the two if they both had useful information—is used in analyzing the role of sources of support.

Most of the analysis in this book that uses the directories compares private agencies that deliver material assistance to other private agencies. In this case, biases in the sample may be less critical, unless agencies that deliver material aid are selected for inclusion in the directories in a different manner from other agencies. There is also a possibility that relations between demographic characteristics and agency characteristics are biased, if demographic characteristics determine the extent to which items are included in the directories. Such a bias is unlikely, however, because results of the 12-county study matched results obtained from the study of public emergency aid. And, when information in the directories was compared with data from case studies of emergency aid, the directories were found to be highly accurate.

Intensive field trips were made to four counties to gather detailed information on the way agencies deliver material aid. These counties were selected for variation in the size of public welfare benefits (low or high) and the size of the private material assistance effort (a high or low number of agencies compared to the population, according to the directories). Three of the field visits were made to counties in the 12-county survey. However, the counties with high public welfare benefits and high private benefits were very small—too small to provide useful information. To increase the relevance of the research and to ensure that a large city was included, the last visit was made to a larger community not in the original sample.

The field study obtained a wide range of information. To gain a general background, interviews were conducted in each county with representatives of the United Way and public welfare officials. In addition, except in the largest city, virtually all private agencies that dispensed material aid were visited. The head of the agency, or occasionally the head of the material assistance program, was interviewed in depth. Information was collected on the benefits the agency dispensed, the organization of the agency, its relation to the public sector, its source of funds, and the pressures it faced. Annual reports and other sources of statistical information were collected, whenever available. Approximately 60 interviews were completed.

This research design focuses attention on formal agencies, or at least on programs attached to formal organizations (such as local church programs). It can be argued that informal material assistance is thereby ignored. We do indeed eschew an analysis of informal giving between individuals; this is a separate topic that demands a different theoretical and methodological focus. "Informal agencies," which arise and vanish as demand for them alters are rarely mentioned here because they do not systematically provide material aid. One guess is that these informal associations, which have received a good deal of recent attention (Berger and Neuhaus, 1977) more commonly address issues involving threats to local neighborhoods or cultural needs than material want.

Finally, to gain insight on the world view of clients, intensive interviews were conducted with a small number of clients. Information was gathered on the personal backgrounds of the clients, their reasons for using private agencies, their other experiences with the public and private sector, and their evaluations of the benefits received. About one-third of the interviews were in the largest city in the four-county sample, and the others were conducted in a moderately sized, but convenient city not in the sample.

Plan of the Book

The remaining chapters present evidence and arguments on the research questions that have been raised—insofar as evidence could be gathered from the available sources. Chapter 2 places the discussion in historical context and presents a theoretical perspective. Chapters 3, 4, and 5 attempt to document the factors affecting the size and distribution of private agencies that meet material needs. Chapter 3 places them in the context of the other private and public welfare agencies in the community, and Chapter 4 presents a descriptive picture of the community and internal factors that support or hinder the material assistance effort. Chapter 5 looks for statistical determinants in the nature of the community and the missions of the agencies. Building on these chapters, Chapter 6 documents the specific procedures by which private agencies meet needs, and Chapter 7 reviews the overall level of benefits, the nature of the clients, and their perceptions of the agency. Chapter 8 turns to an examination of advocacy and protection of the status quo, and the concluding chapters review the themes and present some policy suggestions.

CHAPTER 2

Background and Theory

Providing Material Aid before the New Deal

The key period for private agencies occurred after the Civil War (Swift, 1934; Abbott, 1941; McMillen, 1945; Bremner, 1960; Axinn and Levine, 1975; Leiby, 1978; Trattner, 1984). With increases in urbanization and immigration, many major cities faced new demands. Some responded by briefly expanding public welfare departments (Alexander, 1980), but this trend did not continue. During the 1880s private philanthropists claimed that the private sector was more appropriate as a vehicle for helping the poor and that public welfare was too corrupt, generous, and haphazard.

Gradually private agencies expanded and managed to take financial support away from public agencies. They forced many public relief-giving agencies to close down. For example, in New York City in the 1870s, public outdoor relief (relief delivered to people in their homes) was attacked by a group of private reformers, the Association for Improving the Conditions of the Poor. They claimed that public relief was expensive, and that relief-giving was tainted with Boss Tweed politics. Accordingly, the responsibility for outdoor relief was passed on to private agencies, who dispensed public funds. But distrust of the government remained, and the 1898 Charter of Greater New York banned all public support for outdoor relief (Kaplan, 1978).

The private welfare effort of this period was not based on any single theory of community responsibility. Rather, the agencies generally had particular missions, goals, or methods that might further one view of society and the characteristics of the poor over another. By examining four social movements that included relief-giving as an important responsibility, it is possible to trace some antecedents of contemporary themes and ideologies in the private sector.

Private agencies that engaged in either dispensing material aid directly or advocating for the needy fell into four broad categories according to their primary objectives. Religious fundamentalists sought to convert the poor to Christianity. Secular Charity Organizations, imbued with the spirit of the age of laissez faire, sought to reform the poor, to turn them into industrious, moral, and tidy members of society. A third group aimed at ethnic and religious solidarity. The Catholic Charities, in particular, attempted to set examples of moral rectitude through good works and tightknit religious communities. Although Catholic Charities and even the secular Charity Organizations sometimes turned to advocacy to accomplish their goals, advocacy was the principal approach of another group of organizations, the settlement houses. Concerned with integration in the United States of the poor and disoriented immigrants who poured into the cities, these organizations fought for, but did not furnish, material assistance. Instead they provided a range of cultural activities such as reading clubs, crafts, adult education classes, and social centers for youth.

THE SALVATION ARMY: RELIGIOUS FUNDAMENTALISTS

The early Salvation Army represents a prime example of the tradition of Protestant conversion (Colier, 1965; Lavine, 1970). William Booth, the British founder of the Salvation Army, desired to spread the fundamentalist Protestant message to the East London slums. In 1865, after failing to find support in traditional sects and falling out with a donor who temporarily supported his preaching, he established the Salvation Army. He envisioned it as a group of well-disciplined individuals who would spread the Gospel to the down-and-out.

The Army was not designed to be part of any particular sect—it simply favored conversion to Christ. However, its philosophy was clearly more in keeping with Protestant fundamentalism than with Catholicism or more moderate sects. Its aim was to bring "human souls to God through Prayer and Good Works" (Colier, 1965, p. 19). And it believed that conversion would come from a one-to-one experience in which a member of the Army convinced a down-and-out individual to accept the Gospel.

Although only interested in prayer meetings at first, the Army soon began to add services that would meet material and social needs. As brought to the United States in 1880 by George Railton, and later administered in America by Friedrich Booth-Tucker, the Salvation Army particularly stressed "good works" along with the social solidarity and religious fundamentalism of the actual members of the Army. The earliest American Salvation Army missions included soup kitchens and shelters, which are still core activities of many local offices.

Booth-Tucker soon dropped out to begin Volunteers of America. He was replaced by William Booth's daughter, Evangeline Booth. Her influence was central to the formation of the American Salvation Army model. She was even more interested than Booth-Tucker in good works and the internal solidarity of the Army. Reforming the poor seemed to be secondary to her; as she told a potential contributor, "You must realize that the down and out want food and comfort, not reform and 'God will make you happy in the next world'" (Colier, 1965, p. 70).

Her decisions in organizing local Army chapters were consistent with this less strident tone. She relied heavily on donations from business and installed local boards of directors composed of community leaders. The Army became quite localized (and to some extent remains so today). While there were national programs, local Army offices needed to adopt only some of them and had a good deal of discretion over which programs to offer. There were some centralizing forces—rules, a regional organization, and most important, central training for Army officers—but there were counteracting local pressures. Beyond strong commitments to reduce alcohol consumption, proselytize, and help individuals to establish a stable residence, no national pattern favoring any one lifestyle or set of values developed.

The Salvation Army was typical of many fundamentalist organizations in that it never directly challenged the role of the public sector in offering relief. Rather, the Army saw itself as an alternate, morally superior organization that would attract those in need by its superiority.

Like most fundamentalist agencies, the Salvation Army played only a very small role in attempting to advocate for social change or other support from the government. Its only major effort at social reform since the turn of the century was support for Prohibition. In general, the Salvation Army has gone its own way, mixing conversion and good works and largely ignoring larger political issues.

PROTESTANT SECULAR REFORM: THE CHARITY ORGANIZATION SOCIETIES

Charity Organization Societies claimed that fundamentalist groups were too "liberal," and viewed their task as organizing and reforming the many private agencies that developed in cities after the Civil War (Watson, 1922). The Charity Organization Societies, a lay group, believed that there was too much waste, overlap, and duplication of services in existing urban charities, and that the public system also provided aid indiscriminately.

Indoctrinated with the belief that class differences reflected innate talents as well as application, the Charity Organization Societies introduced a system of charity that was aimed at dealing with personal deficiencies. They based their system on principles of what was called "scientific charity." Under this system a scientific investigation of any applicant would take place before relief was dispensed, to determine which individuals could benefit from aid and thus should be served. It was expected that public or private charities would rely on the Charity Organization Societies for a determination of who was "deserving" and who was not.

The standards for dispensing assistance clearly reinforced industrial values of work, obedience, and thrift, along with some of the tenets of Calvinism. Charity Organization Societies normally considered the deserving to include those not expected to work, such as women with small children. But even here aid would be denied to those who led an immoral life or appeared to misuse funds, and to those who drank, kept an unclean home, engaged in any form of vice, or were lazy. Aid was only given to those who seemed to accept the advice dispensed by middle-class "friendly visitors," who were expected to help deal with the problems that gave rise to poverty—intemperance, laziness, and vice. Based on what the friendly visitor thought was warranted, average grants were low.

In keeping with the idea of maintaining the work force, Charity Organization Societies believed that "charity should never deal with the able-bodied unemployed," who could be saved from laziness only if forced to seek a job (Watson, 1922, p. 108). A severe work test resulted in a propensity to deny aid quite often. Selectivity was thus high; the New York Charity Organization Society aided only 36% of applicants in 1886 (Kaplan, 1978).

The Charity Organization Societies claimed to provide for basic material needs, and they believed it was unnecessary for the public sector to supplement their benefits. They accepted only the need for public almshouses for those who could not provide for themselves. At the very least, they expected to have control over which clients were served by the public system, claiming that a greater degree of efficiency in services would result.

Although advocacy was not their primary activity, Charity Organization Societies supported slum clearance and other reforms of the physical environment, while advocating a decrease in government services. They were instrumental in eliminating police-run shelters for single men, who, they feared, would use housing to idle away their time; the organizations preferred to help pass laws against vagrancy. And, of course, they helped bring about the turn-of-the-century reduction in public relief.

Over time, Charity Organizations appeared to moderate their approach and eliminate some of the more onerous conditions for receiving aid. Moreover, they actually came to support certain types of governmental programs for the poor. As early as 1922 one authority noted:

> Because of the rising standards of adequacy in relief, the budgets of many societies have increased at an unprecedented rate during the decade. Many societies have been forced to face constant deficits. This, along with other reasons, has led more than one society to work for such measures as Workman's Compensation and Health Insurance. (Watson, 1922, pp. 169–170)

During the 1920s Charity Organization Societies turned to family problems, and the organization eventually grew into the Family Service Association of America. While not all local agencies shared this position, the Family Service Association during the mid-1930s officially favored the public provision of financial benefits (Swift, 1934). The family agencies realized not only that the problems of poverty were too large for them to handle, but also that they could achieve professional status most easily if the public sector took over relief and allowed them to deal with family matters. Thus, there was some pressure from internal and external sources to advocate. However, one result was a separation of relief-giving from professional services and a claim that these private agencies should not be heavily engaged in distributing monetary awards (Cloward and Epstein, 1967). Furthermore such advocacy supported government responsibility without seriously considering its nature and never addressed the larger issues of income distribution or working conditions. It was limited to a response to economic conditions of the 1920s and 1930s. The Family Service Agencies have only recently renewed their interest in advocacy.

ST. VINCENT DE PAUL AND CATHOLIC CHARITIES

Charity Organization Societies were staffed primarily by middle-class, white Anglo-Saxon Protestant women, whose philosophy stressed hard work and middle-class morality. It is no wonder that, although Charity Organization Societies perceived themselves as universal and capable of organizing all charities in the cities, other religious and ethnic groups did not share their opinion. Catholics (O'Grady, 1931), Jews (Lurie, 1961), blacks (Ross, 1978), and various other ethnic groups developed separate agencies that shied away from a formal association with the Societies.

Catholic agencies had a large, direct impact on urban life. At first, they organized along ethnic lines, but this changed. The first organized effort to cut across such lines was the Society of St. Vincent De Paul. Like the Protestant reform groups, this Catholic lay group desired to spread its religious philosophy. But it did not focus on individual face-to-face conversion. Rather, the Society was premised on the assumption that a highly respected religious community would serve as a moral model and thus would attract converts. The founder of the society, Frederich Ozanne, believed that a focus on good works would ensure the legitimacy of the organization:

> The chief explanation for the success of the Church in times past was charity and the willingness of its members to sacrifice themselves in the interests of their fellow human beings. . . . He visualized the practice of charity spreading from one man to another until the world was reorganized on the basis of Christian law. (O'Grady, 1931, p. 236)

The Society of St. Vincent De Paul in the United States engaged in many social tasks, including developing schools and tuberculosis sanitariums. Local societies began to engage in charity work after the Civil War. Often a central society would coordinate Catholic charities in a city, acting as a clearinghouse and catalyst. Local volunteers to the society in parishes would actually dispense the material goods. For the times, support was fairly generous; the New York organization reported expenditures of $235,205 for 19,193 clients in 1905, not including in-kind benefits (O'Grady, 1931).

During the first two decades of the twentieth century, societies of St. Vincent De Paul lost some of their charity-dispensing responsibilities in certain cities. The diocese itself, headed by an ordained priest, replaced the central organization. The priest helped administer Catholic Charities, which became the central Catholic relief and service agency of a city. Some St. Vincent De Paul networks continued to have primary responsibility for providing material relief, but beginning in the 1920s many became more involved in providing services to Catholics in institutions or establishing second-hand clothing and furniture stores.

Like the Catholic Church in general, Catholic agencies were receptive to using public funds (Coughlin, 1965). In fact, members of the Society of St. Vincent De Paul organized the National Conference of Catholic Charities in 1911, and this organization eventually supported the minimum wage law, social insurance, and unemployment compensation. Advocacy was in the spirit of an organization that upheld the interests of Catholics, many of whom were factory workers, in a society in which Protestants were generally the wealthier owners of factories. But such advocacy was clearly limited in scope and did not challenge income distribution or other basic tenets of society; Catholic religious groups seemed to be asking to join society, not to change its general tenor.

Beginning in the 1920s, another group, the Catholic Workers, carried the program much further and advocated for much more radical change (Miller, 1973). Under the philosophy of Peter Maurin and the administration of Dorothy Day, the movement shared some of the philosophy of the Society of St. Vincent De Paul and stressed conversion by the establishment of a religious community. The Catholic Workers believed that their own organizations were attempts to create the ideal, timeless society that would grow and dominate. However, a social restructuring was a key part of the assumed ideal society.

The Catholic Workers were heavily involved in material issues. They lived in settlements and opened them up as "hospitality houses." Presumably, each guest was a potential contributor to the religious community. At the same time, feeding the poor was viewed as part of the attempt to create an ideal society. This double mission of conversion and good works was unstable. The focus on the internal organization and dispensing good works have taken precedence over the idea of actually inviting guests to join the movement.

While the inward tendency of the movement has become dominant in recent years, the Catholic Worker organization was, and to a certain extent remains, committed to social change through government legislation. Believing that their perfect society was an alternative to capitalism (and communism), workers became involved in the labor movement, welfare reform, and pacifist activities. Indeed, Michael Harrington, whose book *The Invisible Poor* played a large role in the development of the War on Poverty during the 1960s, gathered his information while involved with a Catholic Worker settlement.

SETTLEMENT HOUSES

The settlement-house movement had its origin in England (Davis, 1967). Established in 1889, the first settlement was Toynbee Hall. Many American settlements were established soon after; there were 74 by 1897. Some were basically conversion-oriented, dedicated to reforming the religious habits of the poor through the proximity the urban settlements offered. More relevant are the settlements in the United States that developed along more secular lines. Jane Addams, the head of Chicago's Hull House, felt that such settlement houses served the purpose of "mutual adjustment." She believed that Eastern European immigrants had much to offer the United States; their folk culture and style of life could add depth and interest to what she believed was a "sterile" middle-class American culture. The purpose of Hull House was to encourage an interaction of immigrants with the middle class so that a new, more complete cultural life could be developed.

Politically, nonreligious settlement houses seemed to represent a philosophy of progressivism (Rochefort, 1981), whereby the social structure would take into account the needs and desires of a pluralistic society.

Settlement houses were involved in material and financial issues in indirect ways. They advocated changes in social policies that would improve the lives of immigrants; for example, they encouraged research into the problems of urban life. One notable product of the cooperation of settlement-house workers and outsiders was the Pittsburgh survey, completed in 1914, which described slum housing, child-labor practices and sanitation difficulties.

Contacts with immigrants led settlement-house workers to understand the very important role of local government. Accordingly, during the first decade of the twentieth century the urban settlements often engaged in local politics and advocated for improved sanitation, housing, and recreational facilities. They also became involved in electing aldermen and mayors in some of the major cities, and in organizing labor unions. Leaders of the movement occasionally took part in larger social causes, successfully lobbying for child-labor laws and the 1912 formation of the Children's Bureau. Settlement-house workers were part of the political coalition that fought for unemployment compensation and mothers' allowances, and their activities were closely linked to the reforms of the New Deal.

There were limits to the reforms in which settlement-house workers engaged. They shied away from confrontational tactics or from basic issues of income distribution (Trolander, 1982). And as the middle-class volunteers came to be replaced by full-time professionals in the 1920s, the movement lost some of its zeal (Lubove, 1980). Social reform often gave way to an emphasis on group work with inner-city youth.

Nevertheless, settlement-house workers left their mark on social welfare. Their ideas were influential in the New Deal and even in the later War on Poverty. The Mobilization for Youth, for example, which was an effort during the 1950s to build local, community organizations for the young, was located in settlements in New York. The mobilization model eventually was adopted by the War on Poverty in its Community Action programs.

New Deal to 1980

Conversion, individual change, ethnic and religious solidarity, and advocacy have continued to play a role in private charities, but they have been challenged by other trends. Private agencies faced a crisis after the 1930s. Their role in providing financial support came into question. Many of the new government programs the reform-minded groups desired had been implemented as part of the New Deal. In addition, under the growing central fund-raising campaigns that collected donations from the public at large, agencies that dispensed material aid were often relegated to a second-class position. Material assistance had become a public responsibility, and private agencies that dealt with the poor were not held in high esteem. They seemed merely to duplicate public functions. Professionalism also arose and seemed to call for an emphasis on individual counseling. Working one-on-one with clients and concentrating on psychological issues seemed to bring social workers closer to the model practiced by the scientific professions such as medicine (Cloward and Epstein, 1967). Charity Organization Societies, having turned to family counseling, lost interest in financial issues; groups such as Catholic Charities often became broader social service agencies that focused heavily on child welfare and family problems; and the settlements became much less powerful.

Certain private organizations retained a commitment to material aid. Some, such as the Salvation Army, found a special niche. The Salvation Army focused largely on single men who were not covered by most governmental benefit programs. Another example is the Red Cross, whose disaster services (along with programs for veterans) had a middle-class flavor that retained popularity and did not seem to overlap with public responsibilities (Berens, 1967). Many traditional agencies, such as Catholic Charities (which changed its name in many localities to Catholic Social Services) and a number of religious missions also continued to dispense material assistance. Others focused on specific problems, such as medical expenses.

The War on Poverty renewed interest in the needy, and an additional small number of private agencies began to provide material aid. More important, public funds were dispensed to agencies that were not under governmental auspices, to provide both services and support for the poor. Community Action agencies, the most noteworthy example, were intended to serve as vehicles for political participation of the poor, and also to act as employment agencies, employers, legal aid counselors, and social service agencies. They also attempted to develop political coalitions that are vital if lobbying is to be undertaken for further political reforms. As a result of their goal of serving poverty-area communities, Community Action programs also often tended to provide specific goods to meet material needs. Nonetheless, it is unclear whether many other private agencies also returned to focus on the poor. Most now believe that their ceding of material aid to the public sector during the New Deal was irreversible (Grønbjerg, 1982).

Current Issues

A major focus of this book is an examination of the extent to which historical trends have affected private agencies. Are the claims about their loss of interest in material problems valid? Are new pressures altering the commitment of these agencies to poverty?

A decrease in public aid, which reverses a generation of advances, began in in 1970s and continues. As recessions have become deeper and more frequent, more and more individuals have been in need. At the same time, benefits from every level of government have either failed to keep pace with inflation or have been cut back. Calculated for a family of four, benefits in the Aid to Families with Dependent Children program were reduced (controlling for inflation) 22% during the 1970s, a reduction that was felt in 47 of the fifty states (Handler and Sosin, 1983, pp. 10–11). This occurred while the unemployment rate doubled. Further, while not all of the evidence is in yet, the loss of income to the needy seemed to be greater in the first half of the 1980s. New legislation has reduced benefits and tightened eligibility requirements for many programs. The total assets a family can have and still receive AFDC was reduced from $3000 to $1000; and, after 4 months of employment recipients can no longer keep part of their earnings from work in addition to their benefits. Reporting requirements, such as the requirement that welfare recipients must report their income monthly, promise to discourage many from claiming benefits to which they are entitled. It has been estimated as a result of changes in law and the economic conditions, that the percentage of the population in poverty has increased dramatically, from 11% in 1979 to over 15% in the mid-1980s (Danziger, 1982). These changes certainly put more pressure on private agencies to deal with financial issues.

At the same time, the Reagan administration has touted the ability of private agencies to take over some public responsibilities. In his 1982 State of the Union Address, President Reagan talked of a private sector and volunteerism initiative that is intended to increase the use of volunteers and private agencies. He stated that these agencies "are almost invariably more efficient than government in running social programs." His aim has been to encourage private sources to make up the decrease in federal participation and to again assert a dominant role in welfare. Even if the increases do not occur, the message seems to be that the very existence of private agencies indicates that need is being met even as government benefits decline.

Such events may increase the extent to which private agencies meet material needs, or they may lead to an increased utilization of the private sector to legitimate a decrease in public benefits. A third possibility is that economic conditions and governmental priorities are leading to increases in advocacy. Private agencies may advocate for a restoration of public assistance benefits. More radical agencies may even look toward overhauls in the distribution of income, the allocation of employment, or even the ownership of property.

Private agencies that choose to advocate can also deal with the specific problems that clients face as their economic situations deteriorate. Housing appears to be a prime example. As rents rise, those who have fixed incomes have a more difficult time paying their bills. The failure of AFDC clients to meet rent payments is now a major problem. When surveys were completed about the rent-paying capability of AFDC clients in 1974, it was demonstrated that only 7% were behind in rent. By 1980 the average recipient was a full month behind (U.S. Congress, Subcommittee in Public Assistance, 1977; Platt, 1980). Some believe that urban renewal and renovation projects have created serious problems by decreasing the number of units available for low-income tenants. As a result, even though the total vacancy rate rose between 1970 and 1980, the proportion of income paid as rent increased from 20 to 27% (U.S. Department of Commerce, 1970, 1980; U.S. Department of Labor, 1981). Indeed, there are no limits to other income-related social issues with which private agencies might concern themselves. These range from racial discrimination to the special problems of inner-city youth.

How, then, have traditional approaches and current issues affected private charities? To what extent is material assistance presently stressed? Does its provision still depend upon ideologies such as conversion or "good works"? Have these philosophies been modified over time, as is the case in the Salvation Army and Catholic Worker Movement? Has interest in the needy heightened as a result of economic problems? Do programs vary in whom they serve and how they grant aid, depending upon the underlying philosophy? If so, how frequently are the philosophies that support material aid present, and to what extent are they modified by an interest in professionalism in the private sector or a belief that the public sector should deal with material needs?

What is the role of social activism in private agencies? These concerns form the core of this book.

Theoretical Perspective

In assessing the many factors that bear on private agencies, a theoretical perspective serves to define the inquiry in detail and suggest appropriate avenues for study. In fact, a study of private agencies providing material assistance is in essence an exercise in applied organizational theory, which looks at the behavior of private organizations.

Many of the earliest organizational studies were accomplished by adherents to the "institutionalist" approach, who insisted that organizations must be viewed in the context of the society in which they operate (Selznick, 1949; Zald, 1970). Institutionalists are partly interested in any one group of organizations because of the way they may inform us about more general social trends. Thus, a study of the change in the YMCA is also an examination of pressure to centralize and to deal with inner cities (Zald, 1970).

The institutionalists rely largely on examinations of the values and goals of organizational members and interested parties. Accordingly, they have been severely criticized for a "functionalist" bias that seems to imply that all social institutions are inevitable products of an interrelated social structure. The possibility of conflicts among subgroups or the effect of individual predilections or actions is overlooked. In recent years, organizational theorists have attempted to deal with this criticism by relying on "open systems theory" (Katz and Kahn, 1966; Buckley, 1972). From this perspective organizational behavior is a product of the forces in the environment, the operation of the agency, and the interaction between the two.[1] It stresses the more specific interchanges that develop in the competition for resources and the attempt to provide services that attract the public.

This book adopts and tries to integrate both perspectives. The institutionalist model is followed in examining the private sector in a manner

[1] One caveat should be mentioned. In its extreme form, open systems theory has been known to be as limiting and infused with biased assumptions as the institutionalist view. Some open systems analysis practically implies that all systems come to a steady state or that the results of the interplay of forces is inevitable, so that whatever exists cannot easily be changed. This book adopts a more contingent view, in that it notes that there are strains toward existing practices, but it does not claim inevitability. As one proponent of "modern" systems theory proclaims, human purposes must be considered in social analyses along with impersonal forces (Buckley, 1972).

that also keeps an eye on social patterns in social welfare and thus on broader goals and values. The open systems model is adopted in looking at both the organization and the environment in light of specific causal arguments concerning resources exchanges. However, the real key to the study of any social institution, no matter which model is used, is the choice of precisely what environmental elements constrain the behavior of the organization. For this book four categories of forces will be considered: the general environment, the role of funding agencies, the role of the internal operation of agencies, and the role of clients.

GENERAL ENVIRONMENT

Open systems theorists and some institutionalists see organizations as partly a product of a general social structure; they are part of a larger social world and must be analyzed as such. At the most general level, private agencies dispensing material aid must be viewed as a function of the capacity of the community, in that they only form if there are sufficient resources to enable them to exist. Not only does this involve finances, it also involves knowledge and skills needed to coordinate activity. It is clear that the large growth in industry at the end of the nineteenth century, combined with the formation of a new class that did not have to work for basic subsistence, freed resources that helped form agencies (Wilensky and Lebeaux, 1958). Urban areas also witnessed a growing sophistication about organization, which was derived from industry. It is important to consider the current role of such resources. It may very well be that wealth, sophistication, and professionalization contribute to the form of the present private agency network (Stinchcombe, 1965; Brittain and Freeman, 1980; Pennings, 1980, 1982; Freeman and Hannan, 1983).

These resources, however, may not always be the tangible ones many open systems organizational theorists generally consider. Historically, the disbursement of material aid has depended upon community values as well. Therefore one must consider the community forces that give rise to an interest in serving those in need. Later chapters of the book will consider forces as varying as ethnic solidarity, community homogeneity, community income distribution, and religious sentiments.

A key concept to consider in understanding the changing role of external forces is that of legitimacy. Dependent on financial contributions from others to survive (unlike a business), private agencies that dispense material aid must be able to legitimate themselves to the broader public. This legitimacy often depends upon what Wilson (1973) calls purposive incentives—that is, ideological or moral goals that convince individuals to donate their time or resources. Before the New Deal, typical incentives included the desire to convert individuals to Christianity, the wish to aid immigrants to adapt to a new country, or the desire to inculcate middle-class values in the poor. There were also some solidarity incentives: Individuals may have donated funds to the diocese, for example, to be used to meet material needs, in order to remain in good standing in the Church.

Do these incentives still provide enough legitimacy to enable private agencies dispensing material aid to survive? One of the issues this inquiry explores is whether a new legitimacy has grown out of recent changes in government policy and economic conditions. If so, how are the new incentives translated into activities by private agencies? Through the provision of more benefits, through advocacy, or through support of the status quo?

An insight gained from open systems theorists is the role of competition for resources. Even if support and expertise are plentiful, they can be used in varying ways. Agencies dispensing material assistance, therefore, compete for resources with other private agencies, and differences in legitimacy in the community may result in more or less emphasis on material assistance as compared to other activities. An analysis of these agencies depends on an assessment of the motive for contributing to material assistance as opposed to other private activities—such as family counseling, child welfare, or dealing with drug abuse.

This competition may also occur between sectors, as private agencies may compete with public agencies for support. It has been claimed, for example, that since the New Deal, the public sector has taken over the provision of income maintenance and private agencies cannot compete for funds to engage in this activity (Grønbjerg, 1982). But this argument assumes that the two sectors are in direct competition; it may also be that the private sector receives funds from sources that are not so sensitive to public priorities and activities.

Beyond these overall patterns, one must also be concerned with variation across communities. Those who support greater use of the private sector claim that the private sector would become more involved in economic issues if the public sector reduced its role. This argument may be translated into an examination of the relationship between the two sectors in each community. Can private agencies mobilize legitimacy to a greater degree in communities in which there is a reduced public assistance effort? Or do other constraints, such as the capacity to organize, play the dominant role?

Variation may simply demonstrate that particular patterns of services reflect particular communities. Most generally, it may very well be that concern with material needs, and the willingness of members of the community to support agencies that provide material aid, varies with the legitimacy with which clients are viewed. Ethnic differences between those in need and the rest of the community may reduce interest in providing material support; religious or social solidarity may have the opposite effect. Concerns over fraud and abuse may also vary. Indeed, as discussed later, such concerns may affect very specific eligibility rules and procedures as well as the overall size of the network.

FUNDING AGENCIES

Open systems theory also stresses the importance of the manner in which organizations are related to one another. Any one organization may receive its resources, such as capital, workers, or clients, from other organizations (Evan, 1966; Thompson, 1967; Jacobs, 1974; Pfeffer and Salancik, 1978; Aldridge, 1979). Useful insights into organizational behavior have been developed by the focus on the more specific interorganizational relations.

To what extent does a reliance on specific funding sources affect the character of the delivered services? Open systems theorists often claim that the more dependent an agency is on an outside force, the more it must cede to the demands of that force. It may very well be therefore that reliance on government reduces the ability of agencies to challenge government and thus advocate; and reliance on the United Way may cause an expanded interest in social services (a United Way priority), along with the provision of material aid. Similarly, it may be that those who are less dependent upon such sources retain the traditional patterns of services to the largest degree.

But one must not take this open systems perspective too far. Agencies need not completely adjust to those they depend on. Even organizational theorists admit the possibility of mutual dependency in which groups share power. And funding agencies may be unconcerned with or fail to monitor the activity of the agencies they support. Indeed, a "loose coupling" of organizations and a resultant freedom to act is a current concept of organizational theorists (Weick, 1976).

For private social welfare agencies, financial support from other organizations is a particularly important factor. The United Way, a combined, once-a-year fund-raising campaign, is one very important potential source of funds. United Way organizations often have a monopoly or near monopoly on fund-raising through the workplace; agencies not in the United Way network are thus at a fund-raising disadvantage. However, it may be that few agencies providing tangible assistance are funded by the United Way—partly owing to the religious nature of many of the agencies, and partly owing to the importance in United Way of corporate leaders who do not favor material assistance.

An alternate source of funds is government itself. However, some barriers to government support stem from the New Deal philosophy that material benefits are a public responsibility. Perhaps only certain private agencies that deal with special minority populations may be able to obtain funds from the government that are used either to meet material needs or to advocate for change.

INTERNAL OPERATIONS

Missions

Organizational theorists have debated the importance of organizational goals—or missions, as they may be referred to in private agencies. A typical argument is that, because agencies respond to their environment, their goals are merely a product of what is demanded of them (Simon, 1964; Yuchtman and Seashore, 1967; Gross, 1968; Young and Finch, 1977). But a perfect correspondence between the environment and each organization is unlikely. Organizations may exercise some choice in their dealings with their environment for the reasons mentioned in the last section. Missions therefore deserve separate attention.

The traditional range of missions of private agencies have led to very different types of aid and levels of advocacy and support for the status quo. Historically, one important strain toward change emanated from the contradictions in missions within agencies as they interacted with a changing social structure. Some gave up supplying material aid to the poor when the task proved greater than their ability to cope. Some responded to organization pressure to stress forms of charity that provided more status. Others had to choose between internal cohesion and the support of a wide range of social issues.

These types of contradictions may be quite important at present. There may continue to be a limited number of types of relevant missions, centered on conversion, religious good works, ethnic solidarity, social change, or specific social problems such as health issues. Perhaps the movement toward less tangible social services has indeed altered the perception that material aid is a legitimate private function.

Private agencies are under no legal constraint to serve all in need. Rather, given limited resources, they are under some constraint to limit aid. Naturally the selection process will be consistent with the goals of the agency. The extent to which they adopt procedural rules to direct their aid to certain sorts of clients in certain situations will be a reflection of their moral stance, their distrust of individuals, their limited funds, or their desire to bring about some sort of behavioral change: sobriety or the saving of souls.

Agency Decision-Making

Various forces are being played out in the everyday decisions of those who control private agencies. Resources must be balanced against demands from clients, and the resulting policies must face some scrutiny by funding agencies and individual donors. Historical commitments and thus past decisions are also important factors.

Organizational theorists claim that the logic of decision-making can be conceptualized on a constraint model in which decision-makers attempt to establish procedures that satisfactorily balance goals and pressures. The decisions will tend to be compromises, neither optimal nor totally objectionable. When the situation is more conflictual, decisions will tend to reflect to a greater degree the desires of the more powerful participants—the funding agencies, employees, or other individuals on whom the agency head is most dependent (March and Simon, 1958; Cohen et al., 1972; Starbuck, 1983).

Decision-making may be proactive. Agency administrators may anticipate criticism and respond in advance by going out in the community and managing commitments, forming alliances, or publicizing, if not dealing with, the situations that create problems for the agency. Or it may be reactive. This book assumes that agencies dispensing material aid are more likely to be reactive. There are more perils to taking a public stance and actively attempting to change the environment than there are rewards. With reduced legitimacy and conflicting pressures upon them, private agencies tend to make the decisions that give them a low profile. This means that they respond to the community's demands. The type of aid they deliver and the problems they address appear to be more influenced by the community environment than by the needs of clients. Even advocacy may be viewed as a reactive decision. Most agencies choose to advocate only when demands from clients are irreconcilable with services available. Advocacy can serve to deflect criticism that an overburdened agency is not doing enough, and it may engender additional public resources and reduce the agency's burden thereby.

Some organizational theorists may insist on measuring the power of various interest groups and ascertaining whether power completely dictates decisions. However, such a calculus is not the prime concern of this policy-oriented study. Indeed, I do not believe that constraints can be viewed in such a tight, linear manner. Rather, I believe that each agency has a number of choices, and that the constraints are only loose guides. Past work on other organizations implies that decisions depend upon agency commitments to protect staff from external pressure—as filtered through external demands—the ability to resist demands without sanction, and the views of the individuals outside the agency with whom key actors prefer to associate. Each agency's response is variable and contingent. The most important task is thus to comprehend the patterns across agencies and the various causes for them, not to assess the exact determinants of individual action.

CLIENTS

The most crucial consideration in examining private agencies is the way in which they interact with clients. In theory, clients are an "input" and can affect agency operations. With reductions in welfare benefits, long, recurrent recessions, the reduction in the housing stock, and rising costs, new groups of individuals are now making demands upon private agencies. The stereotype of the alcoholic transient is being replaced in many agencies by the young male or young family that has recently become poor. How do agencies respond to these new poor? How do clients use, and view, the help they receive? Private agencies may be a way of life for some individuals; the trip to a food pantry may be a weekly event, or a couple may simply travel around the country, collecting whatever resources private agencies will dispense. Or private agencies may be a last resort that involves a clear loss of dignity. These differences may of course reflect agency policies as well as individual characteristics.

CHAPTER 3

The Organization of Private Welfare

Most private agencies that dispense material assistance (63% according to the 12-county study) are also involved in other activities, ranging from family counseling to coordinating blood banks. Material assistance competes with these other tasks for resources—staff and financial support—as well as with such other private concerns as the local Family Services Agency and the local branch of the American Cancer Society. In short, the quest for legitimacy is partly a competition between agencies that dispense material aid and other types of agencies, and an examination of the material aid network must begin with an overview of its relation to the entire social welfare system, private and public.

Comparing Private Agencies

SOCIAL PROBLEMS OR ISSUES COVERED

What is the distribution of activities in private agencies, and where does financial assistance fit in? Central to the missions of private agencies is the social problem or issue covered. Table 3.1 summarizes the problems covered in private agencies using data from the 12-county survey described in Chapter 1. The first column (Rank) ranks the problem according to the frequency with which it is covered, and the second column (Frequency) gives the percentage of private agencies dealing with the problem. (Agencies may, of course, deal with multiple problems.)

A preliminary inspection of the table reveals that the range of problems is indeed large. There seems to be a social agency that in theory can deal with practically any social problem. Agencies may help with legal issues such as landlord–tenant problems, they may help with personal or family problems, or they can be involved in various health activities.

TABLE 3.1
Problems Covered in Private Social Welfare Agencies, by Rank and Frequency (N = 1024)

Problem	Rank	Frequency
Individual and family life	1	28.2%
Health	2	16.1
Need for day care	3	10.8
Financial emergency	4	10.7
Physical handicap	5.5	10.2
Unemployment	5.5	10.2
Aging	7	9.0
Mental health	8	8.6
Alcoholism	9	7.7
Developmental disability	10	7.6
Nonfinancial emergency	11	6.5
Need for family planning	12	5.7
Homelessness	13	4.2
Criminal justice	14	3.2
Drug abuse	15	3.0
Continued financial need	16	2.4
Dependency and neglect	17	2.3
Natural disaster	18	1.9
Need for transportation	19	1.1
Discrimination	20	0.8
Protection and care	21	0.6
Consumer complaint	22	0.3
School problem	23	0.2
Landlord–tenant problem	24	0.1

Note: Ranks are averaged in the case of ties.

Some rough patterns do, however, appear. The two social problems most stressed are individual and family life, and health. Although the same agencies may provide for both types of need (one cannot simply add the figures together), it is clear that well over one-third of all private agencies are engaged in these activities.

The agencies that focus on these two problems include the numerous and well-known family agencies—such as the transformed Charity Organization Societies—various ethnically oriented agencies, and those, such as Girl Scouts and Boy Scouts, that provide recreation or other "noncorrectional" services.

Health agencies, too, are quite well known. Many national organizations, such as the American Cancer Society and the March of Dimes, have offices in nearly every community. These agencies raise money to promote research, but they also provide some local services. Nursing services for cancer victims and donations of major equipment to hospitals are two cases in point.

The popularity of these two issues is no surprise. The general public has a high degree of sympathy for problems related to individual and family adjustments and to health. They are problems that affect many "average" people and seldom raise concerns over fraud, laziness, or abuse.

A second group of items might extend from the third rank through the twelfth. Items in this group are covered in about 5 to 10% of the private agencies. These problems tend to be more specialized. Mental health clinics, day care, and family planning are not required by everyone, despite the fact that professionals have long claimed that these problems are indeed quite common in American society. The general public might be less willing to support these tasks because they recognize themselves somewhat less often in the group of recipients who might need specialized services.

Moral stigma is also attached to some of the problems in this category. Alcoholism and unemployment have traditionally less than favorable images, and family planning has always been controversial. But other problems in this category do not entail stigma. Those who are developmentally disabled or physically handicapped are not normally considered to be members of the undeserving poor, and were not so considered even by the early Charity Organization Societies. Thus, while moral stigma may play some role, it is not of overwhelming importance in the ranks of items in this group.

It should be noted that the need for material assistance for emergencies falls within this second group. In this sample, a financial emergency is the fourth most commonly handled problem. Clearly, emergency assistance does not have as great a role to play in private agencies as individual and family life or health problems, but it is dealt with as frequently as a number of other specialized problems.

A rough third group of items appears to extend from the rank thirteen through nineteen. These problems, which only between 1 and 5% of agencies handle, include such specialized problems as drug abuse, and dependency and neglect (which is normally handled by agencies that dispense foster-care and adoption services).

While these items appear to be heterogeneous, they have a few traits in common. Generally, they appear to involve problems that are highly stigmatizing, or that are also dealt with by the public sector (or both). Services to criminals and drug abusers obviously deal with populations that are far from the purview of the typical donor of funds. Problems of dependency and neglect are usually handled by public foster-care and adoption programs. They are solely a public responsibility in some communities (Werner, 1976). Perhaps support for some of these problems is limited by a perception that the clients are not as deserving of support, either owing to their own moral failings or because public social services are available to them.

Three problems that are related to material assistance are in this third category—homelessness, the need for continuing financial aid, and natural disasters. Meeting these material needs is clearly not a popular function of private agencies. Disaster services, however, are probably more adequate than these ranks indicate, because the well-funded Red Cross has a near monopoly on dealing with these relatively uncommon events in each community.

Problems dealt with by less than 1% of all private agencies rank below nineteen on the list. For the most part, they are new to the private social service sector. Landlord–tenant problems, consumer complaints, and discrimination and protection and care (such as provision of a guardian) are normally dealt with by legal agencies (not included in our data), not social agencies; school problems are dealt with by the schools or redefined as family problems.

SERVICES RENDERED

Additional information is found on Table 3.2, which presents the services rendered by private agencies—that is, the way in which they deal with social problems or issues. Four services seem to be particularly common among private agencies—education, counseling, recreation, and information and referral. All are utilized by at least 20% of private agencies, and each of the first two are used by at least a third of the agencies.

Many of these services are means of dealing with the most common problems. Education is a case in point. Education of children is usually part and parcel of the provision of day care, and health-related agencies often also consider education a primary activity. The American Heart Association, for example, reports on the symptoms of a heart attack, and the Red Cross provides classes in pulmonary resuscitation. Education is a readily accepted activity. It does not imply blame, either of the social structure or of individuals.

Counseling is also quite common. It often may be based upon the "medical model" in social work, which encourages individuals to change their mode of functioning. Implicit in counseling is the assumption that problems are a result of individual failures, not social condi-

TABLE 3.2
Services Rendered in Private Social Welfare, by Rank and Frequency (N = 1024)

Service	Rank	Frequency
Education	1	37.2%
Counseling	2	34.3
Recreation	3	21.6
Information and referral	4	20.2
Material assistance	5	13.5
Medical care	6	13.4
Day care	7	12.5
Employment and training	8	11.5
Advocacy	9	11.2
Transportation	10	7.4
In-patient rehabilitation	11	7.1
In-patient maintenance	12	3.7
General social services	13	3.5
Rehabilitation-day	14	3.2
Adoption	15	2.5
Chore	16.5	2.2
Foster care	16.5	2.2
In-patient educational	18	1.5
Community organization	19	1.3

Note: Ranks are averaged in the case of ties.

tions, and this appears to be popular; counseling (according to statistical tests not reported in a table) is more common in agencies that stress individual and family life problems, health, mental health, alcoholism, neglect and abuse, and family planning.

Recreation, the third most common service, has characteristics intermediate between education and counseling. It can be used to promote a traditional life-style, but it seems to blame the victim less than counseling. For example, inner-city recreation programs offer an alternative (many believe) to life on the streets, and programs such as the Girl Scouts are supposed to help children develop appropriate sets of values.

Information and referral services are not similar to other popular services. However, the services are often used by agencies with waiting lists to refer clients they cannot, or will not, handle (Teele and Levine, 1968). They normally are supplementary services that protect an agency from outside demands, rather than a core agency activity.

Five services are rendered in 10 to 20% of the agencies; day care, medical care, material assistance, employment and training, and advocacy. Three of these seem simply to reflect social problems directly. The rank of material assistance reflects the moderate rank of the four problems related to it (financial emergency, homelessness, continuing financial need, natural disaster); day care services generally match up with day care agencies; and medical care is provided by agencies dealing with health problems.

Advocacy is an interesting addition to this list. It does not just rely on changing individuals, but instead actively attempts to improve their lot. Nor is advocacy limited to attempting to obtain changes for individuals. According to a further breakdown, almost 9% of all agencies are engaged in attempting to change laws and policies; 6.4% attempt to change administrative rules; and 7.8% are interested in changing decisions for specific individuals (not shown in table).

Advocacy is particularly common in agencies dealing with the handicapped, the developmentally disabled, and those suffering from discrimination. (See Chapter 8 for details.) Perhaps it is common when agencies perceive increasing governmental benefits and gaining an acceptance of their clients by others as important to their own survival.

A large number of services are dispensed less than 10% of the time. These services are typical for agencies that deal with specialized problems, although there is not a one-to-one correspondence. Rehabilitation, for example, can be used to deal with the physically handicapped, and adoption and foster care are the prime services for children who are neglected. Material assistance is more common than these specialized activities.

POPULATION SERVED

Are there demographic patterns among the clients that private agencies serve? Most experts believe, as Grønbjerg (1982) notes, that the key trait of contemporary society is a universalistic orientation, which means that ascriptive characteristics should not be stressed too much. Therefore, although private agencies are free to be selective, one might expect that the use of such criteria as race, religion, and sex would be rare.

Table 3.3 confirms this expectation. Universalism is clearly the dominant mode in the private sector. Just 5.8% of the agencies serve only males, and 2.5% serve only females. Very small percentages rely on racial or religious selectivity. Even the means test is uncommon; only 5% formally exclude clients on the basis of income.

Only when it comes to age is there selectivity. Even here, 45% of the agencies claim that their services are available to all clients, and every age group is served by a majority of agencies. Basically, the older the

TABLE 3.3
Populations Served in Private Social Welfare Agencies (N = 1024)

Population served	Frequency
Population group	
Males only	5.8%
Females only	2.5
One religious group	1.2
Below a given income (means test)	5.0
Race	
Whites	99.2
Blacks	99.2
Native Americans	99.6
Asian Americans (various groups)	99.5
Spanish-speaking (various groups)	99.1
Age	
Less than 5	58.7
5–12	57.2
13–17	68.9
18–21	71.8
22–54	69.9
55–59	74.3
60–64	74.9
65 or over	74.7
All ages	45.0

clients, the more often they are served by any agency—although teenagers and working-age adults are minor exceptions to this pattern.

This age selectivity seems closely tied to the specialization of problems and services in many private agencies. Employment services, counseling, foster care, and adoption tend to be directed to specific age groups. The problems of aging obviously demand selectivity. At present one of the main ways of organizing specialized services thus seems to be to focus on specific age groups.[1] Agencies dispensing material aid must also feel pressure to avoid particularism except perhaps in concentrating on one age group.

The Private Sector and the Public Sector

Competition is not only internal. Private agencies may also compete with the public sector. Such competition may breed a division of labor,

[1] As in all cases in this chapter, mentioned differences are statistically significant at the .05 level and were tested by cross-classifying the mentioned variables.

whereby private agencies shy away from areas in which the public sector is dominant and instead provide complementary services (Kramer, 1981; Grønbjerg, 1982). But if community sentiments are important in dictating the way an agency covers various issues, it may be that the community demands similar areas of concentration in both sectors.

Table 3.4 presents some data that compare the two sectors, focusing (for the sake of brevity) only on problems. It presents the ranks of problems in the private sector, and compares the ranks of these problems in the public sector. In addition, it presents the frequencies with which each problem is handled by private and public agencies.

TABLE 3.4
Comparison of Problems Covered in Private and Public Social Welfare Agencies, by Rank and Frequency

	Private agencies (N = 1024)		Public agencies (N = 226)	
Problem	Rank	Freqency	Rank	Frequency
Individual and family life	1	28.2	5	9.3*
Health	2	16.1	10.0	4.9*
Need for day care	3	10.8	14	4.0*
Financial emergency	4	10.7	3	21.3*
Physical handicap	5.5	10.2	7	7.6
Unemployment	5.5	10.2	2	22.7*
Aging	7	9.0	8	7.1
Mental health	8	8.6	14	4.0*
Alcoholism	9	7.7	10.0	4.9
Developmental disability	10	7.6	6	8.0
Nonfinancial emergency	11	6.5	17.5	3.1*
Need for family planning	12	5.7	17.5	3.1
Homelessness	13	4.2	14	4.0
Criminal justice	14	3.2	4	14.7*
Drug abuse	15	3.0	12	4.4
Continued financial need	16	2.4	1	34.7*
Dependency and neglect	17	2.3	10.0	4.9*
Natural disaster	18	1.9	22.5	0.4
Need for transportation	19	1.1	22.5	0.4
Discrimination	20	0.8	19	2.7*
Protection and care	21	0.6	16	3.6*
Consumer complaint	22	0.3	21	0.9
School problem	23	0.2	20	1.3*
Landlord–tenant problem	24	0.1	24	0

Note: Ranks are averaged in the case of ties.
$r(s) = 0.68$ (rank-order correlation).
* $p < 0.05$ (comparing frequencies).

Comparing the two sectors is much more tricky than might be imagined. For example, comparing frequencies, alone, may be misleading. While the typical private agency handles 1.5 problems, the typical public agency handles 1.7. In a sample of 1250 agencies, small differences that reflect the larger size of public agencies may lead to statistically significant differences in frequencies.

It is best, therefore, to concentrate primarily on the ranks. To determine the extent to which private and public agencies focus on different problems, in general, a rank-order correlation is useful. If the two sectors differ greatly in the problem covered, then there should be a negative rank-order correlation between them. A positive rank-order correlation indicates similarities.

Differences in ranking indicate the extent to which individual problems receive different stress in the two sectors. Somewhat arbitrarily, a cutoff of a difference of over five ranks is used as an indicator of a different stress for a particular problem in the private and public sectors.

To ensure the accuracy of this approach, differences in frequencies are also presented and analyzed to a limited degree. These are computed using *t*-test comparisons of the frequencies. The tests rely on the pooled estimate of variance, the .05 level of statistical significance, and a two-tailed test. Results of the tests are included in the table; very large differences in frequencies will also be discussed.

In Table 3.4, there are nine instances in which differences of ranks of problems between the two sectors are greater than five. In five cases, problems are ranked higher by the private sector. Health ranks second among private agencies and tenth among public; day care ranks third as opposed to fourteenth; mental health ranks eighth, as opposed to fourteenth; nonfinancial emergencies rank eleventh as opposed to a tie for seventeenth; and family planning, which ranks twelfth among private agencies, ties for seventeenth in rank among public agencies.

In four cases items receive a higher rank among public agencies. Continued financial need ranks first among public agencies but sixteenth among private; dependency and neglect ranks tenth, opposed to seventeenth; criminal justice ranks fourth, as opposed to fourteenth; and protection and care, which ranks sixteenth among public agencies, ranks twenty-first among private agencies.

Many similarities in ranks are also apparent. A number of items share the middle ranks in both sectors. Financial emergencies rank fourth among private agencies and third among public agencies; physical handicaps tie for fifth among private agencies and rank seventh in the public sector; aging ranks seventh in the private sector and eighth in the public sector, and so on. There are also similarities among the lowest ranks; the items ranking nineteenth through twenty-fourth in the private sector rank no higher than sixteenth in public agencies.

There are many more differences between the sectors when frequencies are compared—13 altogether. With the exception of family planning, all items ranked differently also demonstrate significant differences according to the frequencies. Additional differences also come to light. According to the frequencies, private agencies are more likely to deal with individual and family-life problems. Public agencies seem more likely to handle discrimination, school problems, unemployment, and financial emergencies.

It should be noted that some of the differences in frequencies are quite large. In particular, the larger stress of the public sector on unemployment and financial emergencies, along with the stress of the private agencies on individual and family life, involves differences of over 10%. These differences seem to need to be explained along with the differences in rank.

PATTERNS OF SIMILARITIES AND DIFFERENCES

Some of the patterns of similarity and differences contribute to understanding the role of material assistance agencies in the system of services. One anticipated finding is that government agencies are much more likely to deal with basic material needs. This is in keeping with the historical picture. Since the New Deal, the expectation has grown that material assistance is primarily a public activity.

This expectation may have extended to emergency assistance, which is also more frequently provided in public than private agencies (although the differences are small). Homelessness and disaster problems are evenly distributed across public and private agencies. These results lead us to the possibility, as history suggests, that private agencies that provide emergency aid or continuing assistance still must face the issue of legitimating a service normally provided—and perhaps expected to be provided—by the public sector. Later in this book we will have much more to say about the issue.

Another notable difference is that public agencies appear to deal more often with what might be called "social control" issues, issues that are dealt with by applying pressure on individuals to change their behavior. Clear examples of public dominance in social control are the more extensive role of the public sector in criminal justice, discrimination, and school problems. It is even possible that the relatively heavy stress on unemployment in the public sector is part of a social control concern; the historic belief that many individuals do not want to work and must be forced to do so.

These trends are only matters of degree. There are some agencies in both sectors involved in all problems, and social control issues are not popular problems in either sector. Nevertheless, they suggest the possibility that private agencies may not be expected to act in control capacities. (If this is so, it would represent a change from the times of the Charity Organization Societies.) It also may imply that there are few pressures on private agencies dispensing material aid to control their clients.

Private agencies are more likely than public agencies to stress individual and family life, health, the need for day care, and mental health. It has been mentioned that these problems can affect a large segment of the population. Public activity might be relatively limited in these areas partly because private agencies are plentiful.

A final, and perhaps surprising, point is that similarities between the public and private sectors generally outnumber differences. There is thus a positive rank-order correlation between the two sets of problems. The correlation is fairly large, .68, and is statistically significant. Only a small minority differ greatly in rank, while only about half differ to a statistically significant degree in frequencies. The two sectors tend to cover similar problems much more often than they cover different ones. And the problems they choose to cover are those of the so-called deserving groups. It may very well be that the public demands similar, not different, services from the two sectors, viewing only some problems as legitimate.

Organization and Funding Patterns

The description of the domain of the private sector presents only part of the context for agencies that dispense material aid. Another part involves patterns of organization and funding. Private agencies may operate under differing auspices: religious or secular, national or local. The sources of funds the agencies utilize also differ. By overviewing the range of options and types of domains on which each focus, one can obtain an understanding of the possibilities for organization and funding faced by agencies that provide material aid.

Unfortunately, one cannot use data from all 12 counties to understand patterns of organization and funding, because some of the directories do not contain complete information about these issues. Thus, in the examination of organization and funding—summarized in Tables 3.5 and

TABLE 3.5
Patterns of Organization and Funding in Private Agencies (N = 570)

Pattern	Percentage of private agencies
Religious auspices	15.4%
National organization affiliation	20.2
United Way funding	10.2
Federal funding	19.0
State funding	18.1
County funding	13.1
City funding	3.7
Religious funding	4.4

3.6—only six directories (one for a county in each of the six sample cells) are used.

SECULAR VERSUS RELIGIOUS ORGANIZATIONS

As we have seen, religious sentiment played a very important role in many of the private social agencies that developed during the nineteenth century. Moreover, many agencies were directly under religious control. But the control of private agencies by formal religious groups is not now common. Only 15.4% of private agencies in the county sample are under formal religious control. This small percentage probably is the result of a number of changes in the private sector since World War II, when areas that were their special province were taken over by public services, and when other private agencies developed to dwarf the number of preexisting religious agencies. Residential-care facilities for children, for example, are mostly in public hands, because private institutions have been largely replaced by public training schools (or by secular residential treatment centers).

The proportion of religiously dominated organizations may also be small because of a relative increase in the number of private agencies that are supported by other sources of funds. Only 5% of all private agencies report receiving funds directly from church groups (though, presumably, most religiously affiliated organizations rely heavily on individual contributions). Recent years have witnessed great expansions of United Way funds and government grants and contracts. Religiously affiliated agencies, though potentially eligible for these funds, tend not to receive them. Cross-tabulations of auspices and funding demonstrate that religiously affiliated agencies are, to a statistically significant de-

TABLE 3.6
Frequencies and *T*-Tests Concerning the Domain of Private Agencies: Public Funding and No Public Funding ($N = 570$)

	Frequencies	
	Public funding ($N = 183$)	No public funding ($N = 387$)
Problem		
Individual and family life	27.3%	25.1%
Health	8.7	21.2*
Day care	11.4	17.8*
Continuing financial need	3.3	3.4
Employment	15.3	1.6*
Mental health	12.6	5.7*
Drug dependency	3.3	2.3
Criminal justice	4.3	1.3*
Service		
Counseling	27.5	27.9
Rehabilitation-day	3.8	1.8
In-patient rehabilitation	14.8	5.4*
Medical care	10.4	13.4
Employment and training	18.6	3.1*
Day care	14.8	18.1
Advocacy	12.0	10.3
Continuing financial support	0.0	2.2*
Ages		
Under 5	47.5	64.9*
6–12	39.9	55.8*
13–17	56.8	65.6*
18–21	63.4	67.7
22–54	61.8	65.9
55–59	72.1	69.0
60–64	73.8	69.3
Over 65	73.2	69.5
All ages	30.1	44.2*
Males	94.5	96.4
Females	97.8	97.9
Whites	96.2	100.0*
Blacks	96.2	100.0*
Asiatics	97.8	100.0*
Hispanics	95.6	100.0*
Native Americans	98.4	100.0*
All religious groups	100.0	99.7*
Means test	5.5	4.4

* $p < .05$.

gree, less likely than other agencies to obtain federal, state, and county funds, but are more likely to rely on direct donations and fees from clients.

An analysis of their domains not reported in a table reveals that religious agencies cover all problems, services, and client groups. But they are more likely than other agencies (to a statistically significant degree) to focus on problems of individual and family life, and day care. These are activities that influence life-style, and religious groups may have a strong desire to teach one style over another. They can help create a religious atmosphere for children in a Baptist day care center, or counsel against divorce or abortion in a Catholic Social Service agency. Most relevant to this study, they also are unusually heavily involved in giving financial assistance, an activity that thus appears to have a high ethical content.

NATIONAL VERSUS LOCAL AFFILIATION

Kirsten Grønbjerg (1982) argues that the tendency for organizations to affiliate with a national group has been a very important factor during the last half-century. According to her, national organizations tend to exercise at least some control over most local units, and to maintain their legitimacy and ensure consistency across jurisdictions, they tend to be particularly universalistic, serving all in need who ask for service. She also argues that they focus on "soft" services and "quality of life" problems such as counseling services to families. She lists health, family problems, and education as three highly stressed problems.

As Table 3.5 notes, national organizations are indeed a powerful force. Fully 20% of the agencies in the six counties are so affiliated. These organizations have a great range of services. Many are among the agencies that one most commonly considers as part of the private sector. The Red Cross, Salvation Army, American Cancer Society, Boy Scouts, and YMCA are typical representatives.

While one might hesitate to use her exact terms (for example, it is difficult to call health services part of "quality of life," which, Grønbjerg claims, does not include life-sustaining needs), there is a good deal of support for Grønbjerg's (1982) characterization of the areas on which national organizations focus. Looking at their domain, they are more likely to serve all age groups. In fact, 58.3% of them serve all such groups, as opposed to 35.2% of other agencies. And no national organization has any formal ethnic or racial criteria.

As expected, national organizations focus largely on individual and family problems (such as in the YMCA) and health matters. Family planning is also a common activity. In keeping with these problems, information and referral, counseling, and health services are more common in nationally affiliated organizations than in other private agencies.

National organizations seem to offer some immunity from the need for government funds, and, to a statistically significant degree, nationally affiliated organizations are less likely to receive support from government agencies. On the other hand, they are somewhat more likely to obtain support from the United Way. The significance these patterns have for dispensing material assistance will be shown in later chapters.

FINANCIAL SUPPORT FROM UNITED WAY FUNDING AND FEES FOR SERVICE

United Way of America grew out of the perceived need of private agencies to raise funds jointly. Its supporters point to the advantages of joint action. Rather than inundating the community with innumerable pleas for support, agencies join United Way and launch a combined yearly fund-raising operation. In theory, this saves considerable time in fund raising and makes year-to-year support more certain. In addition, in theory, the United Way employees can direct funds where they are most needed and thus support some causes that would not obtain sufficient funding otherwise.

Despite these possibilities, the United Way has been heavily criticized for its concentration on services for the middle class. The manner in which funds are raised is said to generate biases. The yearly United Way campaign focuses largely on the workplace. Workers can voluntarily (although pressure may be exerted) use a payroll-deduction plan to support United Way. One alleged result of this type of fund raising is that the United Way is dependent upon the good will of the heads of large corporations, who permit the payroll deduction campaigns to take place.

Many claim that the United Way is dominated by corporate executives. This domination is apparent in the board of directors, which establishes general funding priorities and also reviews the budgets of applicant agencies. Agencies requesting funds must therefore provide services in keeping with the priorities of the corporations. For example, a United Way survey points out that businesses view the United Way as useful in providing services to the employees of the corporations (United Way of America, 1977). Thus one might expect that services that help keep working families together would dominate over unemployment services, material assistance, services to the handicapped, and so forth. In addition, corporate leaders may prefer to support large, stable, well-known, conservative national organizations. Indeed, if the United Way were to slight powerful national organizations, these groups might establish competing fund-raising campaigns. Organizational sociologists have pointed out that the United Way is particularly sensitive to the interests of organizations that have some independent power (Pfeffer and Leong, 1977).

Bakal (1979), one of the severest critics of the United Way, offers evidence for these points:

> More than one-third of the 27 members of the Stamford United Way board in a recent year were senior representatives of such major corporations as Xerox, Olin, Continental Oil, and General Electric Credit. Sitting on the 63-member board of San Francisco's United Bay Area Crusade one year were 26 top officials of such enterprises as Bank of America, Standard Oil, Kaiser Industries, Transamerica, and Southern Pacific. Of the Minneapolis United Way's 57 board members, a majority are from business. . . . (p. 406)

> Today local affiliates of just 15 or so large national charities (such as Red Cross, YMCA, YWCA, Salvation Army, Boy Scouts, and Girl Scouts) receive about half of all the monies the United Way raises . . . small struggling agencies, particularly those representing black and other minority groups, receive only a fraction of the United Way allocations—only 2 percent according to the leader of one group. (p. 411)

Our data also offer some support for the criticisms. As claimed, United Way only supports a small proportion of all agencies—10.2% in our sample of six counties (see Table 3.5). And when United Way support is cross-classified with the types of domains of the agencies (not in a table), clear patterns develop. Individual and family life problems, for example, and foster care and recreation services are (to a statistically significant degree) more likely to be offered by agencies obtaining funds from the United Way. Nationally affiliated agencies (as has been mentioned) are also more common. Services to children are also stressed more in United Way agencies than in others.

Nevertheless, the United Way appears to be more progressive than some alternatives. One alternative to United Way funds is fee for service, which is used in 140 of the 570 organizations (not in a table). Agencies relying on fees clearly must serve the middle class. They are statistically significantly more likely than other agencies to stress mental health, day care, and individual and family life; they are less likely to engage in advocacy, provide information and referral, or give material assistance.

Indeed, a mixed record is apparent in United Way support for material assistance. This funding unit supports material assistance agencies more than do any other sources of funds tested (to a statistically significant degree). Most of this money, however, goes to the Salvation Army and Red Cross. Thus United Way support, focusing largely on middle-class concerns, offers only ambiguous support for material aid efforts.

GOVERNMENTAL SUPPORT

Many surveys indicate that perhaps one-third of the budget of an average social agency comes from government sources. Some programs, like the old Title XX of the Social Security Act (1975–1981), dispensed half of their funds to private agencies (Filer Commission, 1977; Terrell, 1979). Indeed, as Table 3.5 makes clear, fairly large percentages of the private agencies in the six-county study receive support from at least one public level. What types of problems, services, and populations do such private agencies fund, and what are the implications for material aid programs?

In theory, it is possible to develop some understanding of the issue by relating the acceptance of governmental support by private agencies to all of the variables described in Tables 3.1, 3.2, and 3.3. Unfortunately, the tables provide too much information. Such an extensive series of comparisons would be too confusing to discuss. As an alternative a few variables that seem to represent the range of private responsibilities are analyzed.

As Table 3.6 points out, 183 of the private agencies in the sample receive public funding from one or more levels of government. Those that receive public funding are more likely (to a statistically significant degree) to cover unemployment or criminal justice problems and less likely to be involved with health or day care problems.

Public funding is consistent with the provision of employment and training, and with in-patient rehabilitation (that is, rehabilitation in an institution). It is inconsistent with the provision of continuing financial support.

Agencies receiving public funds are less likely to serve those under 5 years old or between 6 and 12, and they are also less likely to serve all age groups without restrictions. Governmentally funded agencies are more likely to serve all religious groups, but are less likely to serve a listed ethnic group.

The implication of these relationships is that public agencies are more likely to fund private agencies that share some of the special concerns of the public sector. Unemployment is a public agency responsibility more frequently than a private one (according to Table 3.1), and private agencies receiving public funds focus on this problem more often. Criminal justice follows the same pattern. In contrast, when issues involve areas in which private agencies are more active than public agencies, such as individual and family life, health, and day care, public support does not relate to a private emphasis on these problems.

Relations involving services are rare, demonstrating no particular large-scale pattern. In-patient rehabilitation seems more common when there is public funding, and a specific hypothesis seems likely; these rehabilitation services are probably largely supported by state and federal health and rehabilitation funds. The reliance in the United States on public support of private providers rather than on a national health care system seems to explain the relation best (a reliance that seems to be due to lobbying from various medical groups).

Employment and training services are more common when there is public funding. As mentioned with respect to the problem served, this may indicate that public agencies fund services that are public priorities.

The common pattern, however, does not fit our core concern. Agencies receiving public funds are less likely to focus on continuing financial need than are other private agencies, although this activity is normally stressed in the public sector. Why is this so? Perhaps because since the New Deal, the notion has grown that financial problems are a governmental responsibility. Furthermore, contracting out financial services to private agencies is usually illegal (in order to maximize equity and ensure equal treatment). This differentiation appears to make material aid unique.

Many believe that agencies that receive public funds are more universalistic because public funds do not usually go to specific interests (Grønbjerg, 1982). Even confining the discussion to statistically significant differences, the results are unexpected. Public funding seems to encourage particularism, not universalism. Thus, in terms of age, private agencies receiving public funds serve "all" age groups less often and focus on the young to a slightly smaller degree than do other private agencies.

Perhaps the relation occurs because public agencies are under legal constraints to avoid specializing in an age group. Accordingly, when services to a specific age group are required, public agencies tend to contract the services out to a private agency. Combined with information concerning the problem and service offered, the data appear to suggest that public agencies often rely on the private sector to handle problems and services that are in the public domain, but encourage private agencies to limit the ages of the population served. Unfortunately, such categorization runs counter to requirements to provide material assistance to all of those in need.

The use of private agencies to provide particularized services is also apparent in the relations involving race. In direct opposition to the claim that public funding promotes universal coverage, private agencies that receive public funds are somewhat more likely to exclude some ethnic group. Again, this appears to be a function of the way public agencies use private agencies to be more particularistic than public agencies can be. Government officials may at times believe that certain ethnic groups, such as Native Americans, need a separate service. It is not appropriate for public agencies to have ethnic criteria; rather, they apparently rely on private agencies to provide such services. Publicly funded private agencies are the only organizations in our sample that have formal racial criteria. In short, private agencies appear to be valued by the public sector for an ability to specialize, not for an ability to reach broad sections of the community.

The only relations that are consistent with the common claim involve religion. Literally all of the publicly funded agencies serve all religious groups. There is a strong constitutional mandate, backed by many years of public discussion, that the government cannot support sectarian causes. This mandate seems to be carried out in public dealings with private agencies.

These relations demonstrate the unique situation faced by private agencies that dispense material assistance. In general, the public sector appears to fund problems and services that it also focuses on, encouraging further development in areas that are deemed to be the province of government. Material support is the exception. It is rarely supported by public funds. It appears that the general philosophy is that the public sector should directly deliver the financial services it supports. Private agencies that dispense material assistance are thus on their own.

Conclusion

This overview of the private sector begins to reveal some of the difficulties private agencies have in dispensing material aid—difficulties that will be apparent throughout this book. Material assistance is not among the very top priorities of the private sector. Private agencies prefer to provide services that deal with large segments of the population and have low levels of stigma. In addition, the most popular services are those that attempt to change individuals, provide services for personal growth, or provide information. Material assistance, while an activity of many private agencies, clearly is not designed for very large segments of the population, may involve stigma, and implies some criticism of the ability of the economy and public welfare system to provide for people's needs.

Material aid is a special case in the division of labor between the public and private sectors. Material assistance is one of the few needs that public agencies provide but do not fund heavily in the private sector.

While evidence is limited, patterns of organization and funding seem to indicate some of the same phenomena. The common and powerful national organizations are not apt to support material assistance programs. Although United Way funds a significant number of private agencies that dispense material assistance, that support is often limited to affiliates of a few well-known agencies, notably the Red Cross and Salvation Army. Obviously fees for services cannot be collected from those needing financial aid.

Yet material assistance is provided. Barriers are overcome. As we will see, religious funding, some support from the United Way, and some direct donations are used to support agencies dispensing material aid. But agencies providing material assistance face an uphill struggle, and the existence of these agencies, the generosity of benefits, and the nature of groups assisted must indeed be affected by the constraints.

CHAPTER 4

Agencies and Their Communities

All welfare programs are defined in part by the support they receive in the community. Chapter 3 suggests that private efforts to provide material assistance receive comparatively moderate backing. They are ranked in the second and third most popular groups of private programs and receive somewhat limited financial aid from the major funding sources. What is the nature of the material assistance network in this environment? To what extent are private agencies shaped by the communities in which they function?

Presumably moderate backing puts agencies in a threatened position in which agency heads must accept the secondary status of their agency, obtain support from the key sources that fund material assistance efforts, and pay attention to those who might threaten agency survival (see Chapter 2). As our application of open systems theory suggests, such decision-making may respond to four sets of factors: the community, other organizations with which private agencies that dispense material aid may interact, the missions of agencies, and the nature (and needs) of the clients.

This chapter examines the community programs within the open systems framework with the aid of data from the four case studies described in Chapter 1. The case-study approach has important advantages. In providing specific information about agencies as well as the concerns of local communities, the case studies illuminate the very intricate interactions between the community, funding mechanisms, levels of need, and agency missions. Because the gathered insights are only suggestive, Chapter 5 tests many of them with statistical data and also adds some insights that can only be gleaned from a statistical approach. Subsequent chapters use other techniques.

Texas County

COMMUNITY CHARACTERISTICS

"Texas County"[1] is a county of contrasts. It is a resort community with many wealthy part-time residents and large oil and chemical employers offering good jobs. There is however little employment for the unskilled; the unemployment rate was about 8% in 1982. And there is a high degree of need. Average family income is nearly $2000 below the figure for the typical county in the 12-county study, and 17% of the population (or above the national average) were in poverty according to the last available information (1977).

Poverty here is not mitigated by generous state welfare programs. In fact, the state AFDC program is one of the least generous in the nation. In 1980 the average monthly grant for all aided families was $108. The state also refuses to fund a centralized General Assistance program to meet needs of nonfamilies, nor does it participate in programs that deal with emergency or special needs (AFDC–Special Needs and AFDC–Emergency Assistance, to be described in connection with other counties).

The only available public resource for many emergencies is the City County Welfare Office. This office, supported by local government, is primarily designed to meet emergency needs. It provides food, shelter, utility allowances, and a few miscellaneous items. Often aid is limited to a 30-day period. Aid generally is in the form of vouchers rather than cash, and cash assistance never exceeds $10.

Benefits are quite small. The maximum food allowance for a family is $15 weekly for the first person, and $5 weekly for each additional family member. The maximum for rent for a family of any size is $120 a month. Although the agency tries to do everything it can and approves some form of aid for 70% of those who apply, regulations keep the caseload down (in May 1982 it handled only 863 cases). Families receiving AFDC are largely ineligible for county aid, since they can receive only one emergency grant in their lifetime. Transients who do not have a promising job lead are not aided either, except through the provision of bus fare back to a hometown.

The county is about 40% Hispanic and 5% black. Much of the poverty is concentrated among members of these groups. The quality of life is quite low for many of the poor. For example, a number of Hispanics live

[1] The names of the counties and of some individual agencies have been altered to protect the confidentiality of the interviews. These names are in quotes the first time they are mentioned.

in urban shacks—one-room wooden buildings that may not even have running water.

Transients are another major problem. As economic conditions deteriorated in the late 1970s and early 1980s, a large number of single individuals and families headed for Texas County and other communities in the South. Some believed that jobs were available; others were forced out of northern communities during the winter because of high utility bills.

It is impossible to establish how many transients are in Texas County at any one time, but the county is the site of a beach "tent city" of between 2000 and 3000 tents. For those on the beach, showers are available at a city park, at a cost of fifty cents. The police periodically evict these transients. One agency head told us: "the police go from tent to tent, questioning people. If they find that the people are tourists, they will be allowed to stay. But if they have no place to go, they will be evicted from the beach." The weather and insects make tents far from an ideal habitation.

Transients have so few resources that they cannot accept many jobs that might be offered, since for a typical job there is a 2- to 3-week waiting period before a first check is received. It is even difficult to obtain public welfare, because a permanent address is required. Private agencies commonly provide temporary aid when transients are waiting for a first check or wish to move on.

PRIVATE NETWORKS PROVIDING MATERIAL ASSISTANCE

In Texas County, few resources and a lack of interest result in a small number of material assistance agencies, despite high need.

United Way, which one would expect to be interested in local poverty and minority problems, seems relatively detached. Fewer than one-fourth of the members of the board of directors were Hispanic or black. Their philosophy appears to represent that of the white middle-class power structure. Economic issues are not a major interest. Instead they stressed disaster aid, in an area frequently visited by hurricanes. The Red Cross is the prime beneficiary of United Way support for disasters. Outside of the Red Cross, the only other agency funded by United Way to provide material aid is the Salvation Army. This connection is not unusual. Nearly all United Ways support the Army as a result of agreements made decades ago when the Salvation Army joined United Way. The other high priorities of United Way do not include material assistance. Rather, much stress is placed on services to children, including recreation and counseling programs and Big Brothers and Sisters.

The director of the United Way exemplified the agency's philosophy. He agreed that public funds were being reduced during the last few years, but he stated that private agencies should not replace them. He argued that, for too long, the United States has been moving toward a welfare state; the United Way should not support the welfare state. He claimed that the philosophy of the United Way is to dispense "charity, not welfare." To him charity connotes services rather than financial support.

It is no surprise that a large proportion of the agencies deal with problems normally identified with the middle class, and that the number of agencies dispensing material aid is unusually limited. Many of the agencies that dispense material aid are traditional ones with high levels of legitimacy, historically, and thus some distance from community pressures. These agencies have an ability to survive in a relatively indifferent community.

The Salvation Army is one such traditional agency. It is of moderate size in Texas County, with a budget of about $270,000 in 1981. Of this, roughly half comes from the fund-raising activities of the agency, such as the Christmas campaign, while 16% comes from program fees. The United Way contributes the remaining 34%.

The traditional mission of the Salvation Army is to deal with transients, and the large number of transients in the community call heavily upon the Army's services. One of the main services is emergency food, and on a typical day there will be 40 men and 5 women served. A men's shelter has 12 beds, although the facility has handled up to 38 men in a night. Women who need shelter might be put up at a motel for a few days. Food vouchers in small amounts might also be provided to 4 or 5 nonresidential families per day.

The agency's unusually negative views of recipients reflect the community. Although 80% of those who come receive at least some aid, the agency stresses selectivity. Single transients, in particular, are distrusted. As the head of the agency told us, "We don't spoil them just because the government does." The philosophy is to "help a man and not just give a handout." Aid is refused to those who refuse to look for work, and to those who do not look "desperate enough." Believing that welfare recipients already receive sufficient support, the Army does not aid them.

In part because of the visibility of transients and in part because of the predominance of Protestant fundamentalism, Texas County has an unusually high number of other shelters, primarily for single men. For example, the "Truth Mission" has facilities for men and a meal program for men, women, and families. It does not receive United Way funding. It is supported by churches and religious individuals.

Similar is the "Religious Help Mission," which has an unusual source of funds. Most of the budget comes from the residents. Although the charge is $5 nightly, no one is turned away for lack of funds. The director of the agency, through his connections in the community, is able to find jobs for most residents. This enables them to pay the fees. The mission allows individuals to stay as long as they desire. Some have stayed a year, the director proudly pointed out, and have left with over $1000 in savings to start a more permanent life.

The shelter is quite large, with an average population of over 100 per month—mostly men—and a staff of 11. It is funded on a budget of only $125,000 yearly. Individual contributions are a large part of the budget. But as the director noted, "It burns me up that everyone sends people here, and then the United Way won't give us a dime."

Despite the need, especially among Hispanics, agencies that do not offer shelter are small and specialized. A rural church-related program offers $5–10 for travelers as part of a general social services program, the Association for Retarded Citizens has a small food and clothing program, and the Jewish Community Council provides small amounts of cash to Jewish travelers who are in temporary need.

There is only one major agency to serve residents within the limits of the central city, Catholic Charities. This agency is primarily oriented to meeting material needs, eschewing the family-oriented services found in many other Catholic charity agencies. However, even here migrants are the chief beneficiaries. In 1981 the agency served 5287 people. Of these 1522 were single males, and the director believed that "99% of these" were transients from the North. Only 157 clients were single women. Families served included 1625 adults and 2384 children. Here, too, recent migrants were said to dominate.

Even though resources are limited, the agency does everything it can to cover needs. Almost no one is turned down. Few receive exactly what they want however. There has to be some evidence that the situation can be resolved before aid is furnished. For example, some part of the rent deposit can be paid for a family who receives some support from the local welfare department and also receives food stamps or AFDC. Individuals are expected to attempt to obtain resources from the public sector first. (Yet the public sector expects private aid to be given first.)

The agency uses its funds ($13,700 in 1981, plus an equal amount of in-kind donations) to cover a wide variety of needs. Each need is dealt with in a different manner and thus with slightly different rules. Clothing requests are normally referred to St. Vincent De Paul, where a letter from the agency guarantees that clients will receive goods. The agency also dispenses clothing and furniture from its small supply of donated material.

The largest four items in its budget are furniture, food, rent, and utility payments. Groceries consumed over $5000 during 1981, not counting in-kind donations and the federal cheese-distribution programs. Typically Catholic Charities dispenses 3 days' worth of staples along with vouchers for $5.00 or less to cover such perishables as milk for infants. Rent payments normally cover security deposits and are made for clients who will also be aided by city/county welfare, and utility deposits are also dispensed in cooperation with government. Combined, the two sets of items consume about $3000. Yet many transients receive only a 1-day food basket. Another $3000 is spent annually on gasoline, transportation out of town, and temporary shelter.

Although there is a great need for this focus on material concerns, the agency succeeds only owing to the high status of the charismatic director, who is granted autonomy to do whatever he wants. He is aided by the fact that those who contribute to the organization are not necessarily aware that material assistance is dispensed. The vast proportion of the funding comes from the Diocese, and thus indirectly from the parishioners. The agency was in the United Way, but it withdrew; the United Way provided only "nominal" support of a few thousand dollars, and "red tape" was too great a burden. The agency thus relies mostly on cash and in-kind donations. But the Catholic Church does not advertise for donations. Tellingly, the director is worried that a campaign attracts clients as well as donors.

To sum up, in Texas County, though there are many needy local residents (especially Hispanics) and their needs are great, the focus of most private agencies that dispense material assistance is on the transient population. The community clearly views transients as the major poverty-related problem and supports some services for this group. There are four local shelters that provide temporary housing for transients. There are also many facilities designed to ease transients out of town.

The community has many traditional, religious values that support conversion-oriented agencies that have a historic interest in providing material needs. Key agencies include the Salvation Army, three local conversion-oriented shelters, and Catholic Charities. The proportion of agencies that provide for material needs may thus be high, in part because an unusually large proportion of agencies in a resource-limited network must be supported by direct religiously based contributions. Such agencies have many rationales for serving the poor. The services for the needy who are not transients depend largely on the ability of agencies to find resources that do not reflect the community. (Within the community but not part of it are generous military programs tied to the military bases. These are discussed in Chapter 6.)

West Virginia County

COMMUNITY CHARACTERISTICS

"West Virginia County" has a level of need somewhat similar to that of Texas County. It is relatively small, with a population of about 110,000 people, and is a bit less urbanized than Texas County, 67%. Thirteen percent of the population were in poverty according to the most recently available figures (1977), and the average family income is about equal to that of the Texas example.

State benefits for the AFDC program are also within the same range. The average monthly benefit for a family in 1980 was $182, among the lowest in the nation. This partly reflects the low average income in the state and a resulting state budget that is not sufficient to meet many problems.

There is, however, a deeper desire to meet needs of the poor in West Virginia. Perhaps because the population is less stratified, the poor are seen as typical citizens who happen to be needy. As a result, a statewide program meets emergency needs of families: AFDC–Emergency Assistance. In addition, the state supports a General Assistance program for individuals who live alone and couples who do not have children.

AFDC–Emergency Assistance is a federal program that deals with emergencies. Funded half by state funds and half by the federal government, the program is restricted to "families." A family can only use it once, for 30 days' worth of goods, in any year. In West Virginia County there usually are about thirty Emergency Assistance cases each month, costing $8000 in assistance funds. But in 1982 the number was triple that total.

The program will pay for almost anything if there is an emergency—utilities, housing, food, medical expenses, transportation, and so forth. However, an emergency is defined as a situation beyond the control of the individual—simply running out of cash is not sufficient for eligibility. And the family must explore private sources first. Perhaps owing to these requirements, the county rate of approving aid, about 25%, is unusually low.

Because there is a statewide General Assistance program, a similar set of emergency rules applies to single individuals and couples without children in the county. Transients, however, are only given up to $50 to move on. Very few transients come to the agency—perhaps 15% of the caseload. Few transients pass through West Virginia.

The low benefit levels for AFDC (and gaps in other programs) indicate the existence of need, but compared to the remainder of the state, the major city in West Virginia County has been relatively free of the worst economic problems. It is a manufacturing center, and about one-fourth of the population of the county were employed in manufacturing in 1977. But economic times deteriorated by 1982 because of layoffs at the major plants. The unemployment rate rose from 7.6% in 1980 to 10.9% in 1982.

Rural poverty is also a problem in the county. Throughout the mountains, small, isolated poor families live in hollows. In fact, this general area was a site of earlier Senate hearings about rural poverty. In the overwhelmingly white, Protestant county, special concern over the problems of minorities is rare. Blacks make up only 4% of the total, and many respondents insisted that the black community was middle class and had few special needs.

PRIVATE NETWORKS PROVIDING MATERIAL ASSISTANCE

The dominant ideology of West Virginia County appears to be a belief that it is not unusual to be poor and those in need deserve assistance. In keeping with this philosophy, the United Way has some interest in serving the poor. One of its seven service categories is "family assistance," which includes material aid and budget counseling. The United Way has also established a centralized food bank. Funding for material needs is granted to the Salvation Army and Red Cross (as is typical) but also to two other agencies that deal with emergency financial needs—a rural Rescue Mission receives a small grant (of about $3000), while a local settlement house receives over $30,000 of the less than $1 million which is the total United Way budget.

Part of the support for material aid in West Virginia County comes from traditional sources, particularly religious ones that tend to support shelters. West Virginia County has one major shelter, the City Mission. It is supported chiefly through appeals to religious sentiment, though some money comes from a federal grant for a program that deals with domestic violence, and $3 daily fees are charged residents after the first 2 nights.

Perhaps owing to community expectations, the shelter demonstrates little selectivity. The emergency shelter is thus often occupied by single men and women as well as by families. The shelter can house individuals for up to 2 months. In general, people are turned away only when it is full or when drug use or intoxication threatens the safety of others. (A separate rehabilitation program provides shelter to alcoholics and drug abusers.) The shelter is often full; many who need shelter do not receive aid in this county.

Most agencies serve AFDC recipients heavily, reflecting community sympathy for the poor. Though there is no equivalent to Catholic Charities in the county, a number of agencies are moderately involved in meeting the basic needs of those who live in their own homes. Central to this network is a unique arrangement for controlling the material assistance efforts. A central intake agency, Information and Referral, interviews all clients, and decides on eligibility for any other program.

Information and Referral is basically a public program, supported from the federal Social Services Block Grant and matched through in-kind contributions of the library (the contribution is the building in which the agency operates). When the public AFDC-Emergency Assistance program began, in 1979, to mandate that private resources be exhausted before public aid could be given, Information and Referral became a key gatekeeper. Desiring to stretch aid as far as possible and sharing a common culture, agencies accept its role. At present, the agency has the power to turn individuals down, to obtain agreements with private agencies, and even to make aid conditional on budget counseling, applications for food stamps, or attempts to obtain a job.

In keeping with an interest in meeting needs, the main strategy is to *package* aid, using a combination of resources to meet whatever needs can be met. If clients are from out of town (a fairly rare occurrence), the agency might set up a $50 grant from public welfare, additional travel money from the Salvation Army, and a special agreement with Greyhound for a reduced fare. Agencies are used for different things. The small local Salvation Army, for example, covers small utility bills, travel expenses, and food. It dispenses about $30,000 in benefits yearly, largely to the working poor (532 clients were served in 1982). Welfare recipients are given emergency aid only until the next check arrives. A program run by the local paper covers larger needs, but only for special, heart-rending cases.

One of the key organizations in the network is the "West Virginia Settlement House," a local settlement house that services only those receiving public welfare. The agency receives $32,000 from the United Way and about an equal amount in donations. It is also able to mobilize a huge amount of in-kind contributions from the community, and thus is not completely dependent on United Way. It appears to have strong public legitimacy.

The agency has its own priorities concerning what goods to dispense, which reflects its unique sense of self and the community-wide desire (perhaps fostered by the public sector) to serve AFDC clients. It claims to give out 225,000 garments a year, while also serving about 700 transients and an equal number of families in more substantial ways. About 2000 food baskets are dispensed yearly.

The agency will also pay shelter costs for a day or two, provide food vouchers for a week, and pay small utility bills in the $25 range. It carries out a massive yearly clothing drive for school clothes. The agency also dispenses furniture, but only to those who live in the neighborhood. West Virginia Settlement House appears to be a community tradition, legitimated by the good works of the founder, who began to help the poor in 1916 and also instituted the religiously oriented service program.

"Christian Food Bank," another agency, is the centralized food bank in the area. It serves the traditional church function of granting in-kind aid. Established with the help of United Way, it is supported largely by churches and is the central location for dispensing virtually all food and clothing that churches provide. Using Information and Referral for intake, the agency deals largely with recipients of public assistance grants who are facing "true" emergencies. Indeed, before March 1982 about 500 individuals used the agency monthly; then, new, tighter policies cut the number of cases by two-thirds. The average food basket is worth about $30, and repeaters can receive benefits as long as Information and Referral sends them. The number of blacks who use the food and clothing bank and other agencies is negligible.

One of the interesting facets of the county is that many agencies that do not normally provide material aid do so locally. The Red Cross, for example, has expanded beyond its normal disaster and military-service emergency program, dispensing a small number of grants to individuals facing private emergencies. The March of Dimes also has a small program for those families whose children have birth defects. Thus, while money appears to be tight within this community, there are pressures to meet needs.

There appear to be few direct pressures on agencies concerning *what* material needs to meet. West Virginia Settlement House places its highest priority on clothing, followed by food; the March of Dimes only dispenses aid within its area of interest; the Red Cross is primarily involved with veterans; and a newspaper program is committed to extreme cases. As for whom to serve, community pressures work against selectivity, because it is assumed that nearly anyone can end up needing material aid at one time or another.

Pennsylvania County

COMMUNITY CHARACTERISTICS

"Pennsylvania County," a community slightly under 300,000, appears to have been less needy, historically, than the two examples just discussed. Only half urban, the community has an average income of slightly above the average, and a poverty rate of 5.6% as of 1977. The county is an industrial community with over half of the labor force employed in steel mills and other heavy industry.

Pennsylvania is one of the richer states in the nation. AFDC benefits are therefore unusually high. The average grant for a family in Pennsylvania was $279 a month in 1980, in the top third of the nation. The state has a relatively strong historical commitment to social welfare, demonstrated by its participation in AFDC–Emergency Assistance and the existence of a statewide General Assistance program.

Even so, the extent to which special, emergency needs are met by the public system is small. The state's version of the AFDC–Emergency Assistance program defines emergencies narrowly and includes only situations over which an individual "has no control." This includes burnouts or results of violence. Given the current economy, the county considers a sudden loss of job as constituting eligibility, because "to lose a job is a catastrophe in today's economy." The program can dispense up to a full month's worth of needs in an emergency situation, but the limits on eligibility keep the program small.

This is the major public program, although there are a few others. For example, under a state program AFDC applicants and recipients, along with General Assistance cases, can receive a payment to cover one month's shelter in an emergency situation—although the limit is $100. There is also an emergency medical program that is used chiefly for transients who are not eligible for Medicaid. Transients can also receive transportation allowances to enable them to interview for a job or move some place where they have a proved source of support. There also is a small, federally funded AFDC-Special Needs program, used largely to cover work-related expenses.

Obviously, there are large gaps in the public system, such as those that occur when an emergency does not fit the agency's definition. And General Assistance benefits are being cut back. The program used to be available for indefinite periods; it has been shortened to 90 days for those who are "employable" and under 45 years of age.

Pennsylvania County also appears to contain some communities in which poverty is a continuing problem. The central city contains an urban slum, populated largely by blacks, who make up 3% of the population of the county. Respondents believe that this community has all of the "typical" urban problems: one-parent families, high reported crime rates, dilapidated housing, and so forth.

Another problem is rural poverty. Many poor older people live in the small towns, and some farms are barely surviving. However, in general, the rural attitude appears to be that people should take care of themselves and that social services are not needed.

The community has an increasing unemployment rate as well. Beginning in 1980 the larger industrial plants began to lay off workers. In a short time, those who were not used to poverty became members of the "new poor." The unemployment rate rose from about 6.5% in 1980 to over 10% in 1982.

PRIVATE NETWORKS PROVIDING MATERIAL ASSISTANCE

Traditionally, an unusual amount of financial support might be expected to come from religious groups, because this is a Pennsylvania Dutch community with over 250 local churches. Indeed, there appears to be a good deal of homogeneity in the community in general, and homogeneity results in a tendency to centralize services when they are offered.

Even though the community is three times the size of West Virginia County, for example, the United Way here supports the same number of agencies with slightly more than three times the budget. The United Way is strongly committed to efficiency and to combining services where possible—thus, a Voluntary Action Center, staffing volunteers for local projects, was recently cut out of the budget, and the functions were transferred to an agency that could operate the program more efficiently. In fact, when programs are added they often are administered by existing agencies. The United Way, for example, has increasingly become interested in "women's issues." A new rape crisis center was added, but to save administrative money, it was made part of the existing YMCA.

The United Way historically paid little attention to material needs, dispensing funds only to the Salvation Army and the Red Cross. While this has not changed dramatically, there has been an attempt to increase the funding of the former agency. In 1981 it was decided that a food bank was needed; the Salvation Army was given some funds and aid in starting the program because it already had a "good reputation."

Because this community has had low levels of perceived need in the past, few private agencies deal with material needs. And of those that do, a small number are most active—mirroring the centralization of United Way. The rest are quite small or dispense material aid as a sideline. For example, the local Red Cross, similar to most, has a small program for veterans in addition to its program to meet disasters. The federal energy program is administered by a private agency: the Community Action project. And the March of Dimes distributes some assistance to those in its domain.

There are difficulties in serving the rural population, as demonstrated by the Community Action agency in a small town. Much of its support comes from the public programs it administers—for example, it dispenses emergency energy funds for the area (serving slightly over 100 people a year) and also runs the cheese-distribution program. However, the federal funding for the agency will soon end, and local funding is scant. The mayor believes that people should be able to make it on their own. Soon the agency will go out of business.

The agency has not received much aid from the city. A few years back, when emergency food was required, Community Action raised money through walkathons, recycling, bake sales, car washes, and church donations.

In keeping with the degree of centralization, three agencies that meet material needs are unusually large. Two are religiously affiliated and appear to obtain much support due to the religious nature of the community and the special characteristics of the heads of agencies. (Both agencies have grown rapidly over the last 8 years under new directors.) The agencies are so different in philosophy that they present a clear example of the discretion private agencies have when they receive funding from direct, religiously oriented donations.

One such agency is the "Rescue Mission," one of the largest religious shelters in the nation. The agency has a total budget of about $450,000 a year, not including in-kind contributions. It receives its funds from many of the 250 Protestant churches in the area and raises special funds for buildings and other major needs.

The Rescue Mission receives no support from the United Way, and the director does not desire such funds. He believes that the program has a religious emphasis that the United Way could not support: a compulsory prayer program.

The agency supports programs it believes best encourage fundamentalism. Among them are a children's emergency shelter and a boys' club to foster religious growth as well as a shelter for adults. The adult shelter of 16 beds demonstrates a strong conversion-oriented mission. It houses only men, and there is the compulsory religious service. More important, this program is basically a hook into a second program. To stay more than 2, or on occasion 3 days (in a 30-day period), men must enroll in a religious rehabilitation program. The program includes alcohol counseling, individual counseling, a devotional session, special chapel services, and Christian education services every day. Perhaps for this reason the shelter is seldom more than half full. Even so, the longer program generally has a full house, and half of those who enter the mission remain for this program.

The Salvation Army is the primary program for nonresidential needs, one that seems to serve all comers. Like the Rescue Mission its budget is unusually large, about $425,000 a year. Of this amount, $90,000 comes from the United Way, and much of the rest stems from donations from individuals and church-related groups. The funding assures autonomy.

Although the Salvation Army has many programs for the general community, such as intramural sports leagues, classes, and other recreational activities, material assistance seems to be one of its prime functions. A rather large amount of aid is dispensed in the Human Services program. For example, in June and July of 1982 the agency dispensed short-term aid to about 1300 families. Short-term aid includes vouchers for fuel, utilities, food, rent, and shelter. Due to the relatively large budget, the agency will serve individuals multiple times a month and perhaps up to nine times a year. In 1982, 3375 families received food, 319 families received utility vouchers, 4400 families got furniture and clothing. "Transients or single men" served numbered 1940.

The vouchers are dispensed without any conditions—religious or otherwise. Nevertheless, in keeping with its religious philosophy, the agency has a relatively large service staff for those who wish to use it. Homemaker services, budget counseling, and advice are offered. The head of the agency said that he operates like "the welfare agency should" if it had the time.

The Salvation Army has also been a driving force behind a new food bank, funded partly by the United Way. The food bank is quite large; it handled over 300,000 pounds of food in a 5-month period in 1982. Families can come up to two times a month and four times a year. Given the growing unemployment rate it is no surprise that the caseload tripled between 1979 and 1982. This program was established for the new poor and represents the only clear link between community special demands and services.

A final component of the program is an emergency shelter, which may hold up to 10 people a night. The program is similar to that of the Rescue Mission in that individuals can only stay 2 days without special approval. But no religious services are required, and there is no rehabilitation program. In fact, while the Army seems to have a strong religious program in general, it is separated from the services program in the sense that the former is not a requirement for the latter.

The third important agency in Pennsylvania County is the "Benevolent Society." This is one of the few agencies in our sample that is primarily the product of a benefactor. As such it also goes its own way and does not reflect special community concerns. It was founded in 1874, during an era of expanding private programs, by a civic leader who believed that post–Civil War needs should be met by private philanthropy. The program continues to receive some support from a foundation and also undertakes a small, fund-raising campaign to major benefactors. A religious order administers the funds.

The society provides what the benefactor had in mind: food, shoes, and utility payments to approximately 225 clients per week during the winter. (It is not open during the summer.) The bulk of aid is in the form of small vouchers for food or shoes; about 25 clients a week receive aid for utility payments. Although the amounts distributed for food and shoes are small (enough food for about five days, for example), the utility program can dispense $200 to those in need.

The society has relatively rigid requirements. A formal interview and a home study are conducted to determine need. Elderly clients are given priority, and young applicants are refused assistance when work—such as shoveling snow—is available. On the assumption that welfare benefits are sufficient for them, welfare recipients are also refused aid.

Comparing the three core agencies, a huge variation in the degree of selectivity is apparent. Priorities are set by private agencies in Pennsylvania County without much interference, although the United Way has encouraged some response to increasing unemployment, a problem seen as the core issue by the agency.

Midwest County

COMMUNITY CHARACTERISTICS

"Midwest County" is a typical large, urban, industrial county in the Midwest. Its city population of about one-half million and county population of slightly over one million rank it somewhere in the second ten in the United States. It is basically a manufacturing center that is closely tied to large heavy industry such as assembling heavy machinery. Its average income was slightly above average, while its 1977 poverty rate was also near average at 6.4%.

The public welfare system is state supervised but county administered. Perhaps to make such an unusual combination manageable, the system is rigid. General Assistance is a local, not a state responsibility, and few provisions are made to meet emergency needs. The average monthly benefit for an AFDC recipient is fairly generous: $439 per case in 1980.

Four crowded and busy offices administer the county welfare program, which includes a county General Assistance program, Food Stamps, Medical Assistance, Aid to Families with Dependent Children, Supplemental Security Income, and a range of smaller service and income maintenance programs.

The AFDC–Emergency Assistance program in Midwest County is a limited one. It only covers fires, floods, and natural disasters. In 1981 it provided $150 grants for about 200 families. In other emergency cases, families are totally dependent upon the private sector. The main welfare office is mazelike, and workers operate with a constant background of noise. Visitors are greeted by signs like "Stop. Pick up an application form. Take 12 steps forward. Turn right. Be seated." To avoid possible violence, workers do not have names on their offices and seldom divulge them; it is quite difficult to find out where any specific individual is located.

Part of the problem of need stems from the difficulties of obtaining a quick response from this overworked department. A supervisor said that even for fire, "Overworked workers refuse the extra work of emergencies when they can. They give them [the clients] a quick shuffle out the door." The wait to apply for assistance can last 2 days, and the processing time for applications is also lengthy. Private agencies are clearly needed to provide temporary aid.

Local General Assistance cases exploded between 1979 and 1982, from 3000 to nearly 10,000, and continued to grow at a slower pace through 1984. The benefits for General Assistance, while small (under $200 a month for a single individual) are at least available to many individuals and help mitigate some of the worst financial problems of the needy.

The city clearly has its share of urban problems. Most notable is unemployment. Traditionally, the city has had an average unemployment rate. It was 6.4% in the beginning of 1980. But its heavy industrial base has been hit most severely by the recent recession. As of the end of 1982, the unemployment rate was 11%, and it is not likely to fall quickly as the economy improves. (The city has much outdated heavy industry.) Rather, there will continue to be a large group of the new poor who might receive AFDC benefits or AFDC–Unemployed Parent benefits (when the family is intact), be dependent on General Assistance, or turn to private agencies.

As in all major cities, some inner-city poverty problems exist. The inner city in Midwest County is not particularly large, nor is it unusually heavily composed of minorities. Roughly 11% of the population is black, the average for the county as a whole. Perhaps due to its size, the minority community has a somewhat lower visibility than it has in other major cities.

The county is predominantly an Eastern European ethnic community—Poles, Russians, and many other slavic groups—and prides itself on a strong work ethic. Also important are members of the German community.

Given the work ethic, one powerful political strain is the urban labor democrats, who might vote for civil rights and high unemployment benefits, but who are very concerned about crime and skeptical of welfare benefits. But the city also has a strong socialist tradition in some sections. And there are many active progressive liberals with more pro-welfare attitudes.

PRIVATE NETWORKS PROVIDING MATERIAL ASSISTANCE

As a heterogeneous urban area, Midwest County displays a range of private agencies that far outstrips that of any other county in our case study, but no centralized structure of private services appears to exist. The central city seems to have separate north, south, east, and west sides, with distinct ethnic mixes and social classes. Because neighborhood control is so strong, separate private agencies exist to meet similar needs in different parts of the city.

The United Way (which includes Midwest County and some smaller counties) exemplifies the heterogeneity of the community. In 1982 it funded over 120 different agencies. Many are county-wide units, but others are local and have names that begin with "west side" or "south side."

The United Way generally has not been highly interested in meeting material needs. Material assistance was not a priority until 1981, when emergency food bank coordination, an increase in support for shelter beds, and increased accessibility to the emergency energy program were instituted. This new commitment has led to funding for a Salvation

Army emergency lodge and the allocation of funds for another emergency shelter and two food coordination programs.

The United Way divides its programs into five areas: Health and Mental Health, Individual and Family Life, Social Development, Justice and Employment, and Neighborhood Development. Emergency aid, part of Individual and Family Life, received only a small sum, not including the Red Cross—less than $200,000 of a budget of about $10 million. The Red Cross, a separate priority not included above, received over $1 million, partly for disaster aid.

More typical of the agencies that provide material aid in this community is a committed, progressive group of Catholic activists in the central city, who deal with problems of the poor in the classic Catholic Worker tradition. Most notable in this network is "Catholic Meal Program," a Catholic community of Capuchin priests (a branch of the Franciscan order). The stated mission of the group is to work with the poor, and the organization espouses values of community, sharing, caring, and hospitality. It currently provides an evening meal for approximately 500 "guests" a night. There is no charge for the meal, no one is asked to prove need, and no other conditions are imposed on the guests. According to the director, "We assume that anyone who will wait for an hour in the cold to get a meal is really hungry. . . . Anyone who is hungry—but not drunk—is welcome."

Catholic Meal Program receives no funding from any level of government. Nor does it receive support from the Catholic Church, the Capuchin order, or the United Way. Support is actually refused from any source other than individual contributions. Cash contributions are kept to a minimum, and no fund-raising campaign is carried out. The emphasis, rather, is on support through participation in the meal program. Each night 33 out of a total pool of 5200 sponsoring families deliver the food to the meal program, serve the guests, and dine with them. The head of the meal program believes that most of the sponsors are themselves on the verge of poverty.

Catholic Meal Program is a legitimate organization, known to nearly everyone. It receives a good deal of support from the community but is intentionally kept small. The director told us that there was some consideration given to expanding the meal program to more meals a day or covering more needs, but this would create a "bureaucracy" and spoil the community atmosphere. The other services of this agency, such as a food pantry and housing vouchers, are also kept small. The director speaks out on such needs more than he provides for them.

Because of the severe crisis in housing, some public attention has recently been given to that problem. The largest shelter, the Rescue

Mission, is a religiously oriented shelter for men only that is filled to near capacity (200 a night). Its religious goals and refusal to join with other agencies make it an outsider in the network. When the need for shelter became apparent, the United Way looked elsewhere. A small group of limited-size shelters is being organized.

One agency that is important in this movement is the Salvation Army, housed in what was until recently an inner-city motel. The Army did not have a shelter until 1978, focusing instead on recreation, clothing, and food. The commitment of the Army to furnish shelter depends on outside support and requires the Army to reserve most of its beds for those referred from government agencies.

Only six beds are discretionary, available for "off the street" clients. They are used for a wide range of individuals such as battered women, the elderly, the chronically mentally ill, displaced families, and so forth. Housing is relatively long-term, lasting on the average from 6 to 8 weeks. Residents are encouraged to independently pursue solutions to their problems, although counseling is offered and is sometimes mandatory. The staff also advocates for clients who are having difficulties with public welfare.

The Salvation Army provides emergency food, clothing, and counseling to the general public with its own funds. This aid is distributed without a detailed set of eligibility criteria. We were told that the Salvation Army "will be taken every day, but we must continue." The agency dispenses food to about forty individuals or families a day, two-thirds of whom receive public welfare benefits. Small amounts of aid are dispensed, averaging $10 to $15 for a food voucher. Generally, individuals are limited to one visit a month, and those who make use of the agency frequently are expected to accept budget counseling. The Army desires to "go beyond putting a band-aid on the problem."

While the receipt of funds from general sources seems to have reduced the discretion of the Salvation Army in providing shelter, other agencies have used United Way funds to broaden their missions. One example is "Advocates Incorporated," an agency that began with a religiously oriented framework and moved on, changing funding sources as the mission changed. The head of this agency, then a Catholic priest, began an advocacy program in the belief that a "successful religious ministry must attempt to address the material as well as spiritual needs of the community." But soon the religious affiliation was dropped. Currently, the agency receives much of its funds ($40,000) from the United Way. The support is used for the local Travelers' Aid program, and for an advocacy program for health care for public aid recipients. The agency also has a contract with Community Corrections and advocates for the elderly. The agency has $80,000 in contracts with county government, for which it coordinates emergency shelters. As will be described in more detail in Chapter 8, the agency has begun an Emergency Shelter Task Force, designed to act as an intake agency for all of the small shelters. It controls 140 beds in seven shelters, and serves to ensure equity in treatment and to document the need for additional shelters. A statewide coalition to increase shelter care is under way.

The agency also runs one of the seven shelters. The shelter has 14 beds for single individuals who have the ability to become self-sufficient within 2 to 3 weeks. Half of the residents are in this category, and half are permanent residents. The permanent residents pay small daily fees (which usually come out of a public assistance check) and thereby support the whole facility.

Along with shelter and meal programs, Midwest County has a network of agencies that provide tangible assistance to individuals who live in their own homes. There are a number of food banks. One coalition (funded through the local Community Action agency) holds massive food drives through the local baseball team (fans bring food with them) and dispenses the food to many local agencies.

Some of the established agencies seem to have special sources of funds and much more discretion in Midwest County than elsewhere. St. Vincent De Paul Society, for example, tries to refer individuals to other community agencies and resources and to act only as a last resort. For those who are not referred, volunteers assess need and make a recommendation for further action. Aid—food, clothing, furniture, grants, loans, and counseling—is usually given to "those who are in trouble for reasons beyond their control." There are no written policies, but a strong distinction between the deserving and undeserving is apparent: 75% of those who apply are flatly denied. Robbery victims, elderly people needing special medication, those who are in a sudden crisis are typical of clients the agency helps. About half of the aid goes to those who are currently on welfare. In 1982 the agency distributed $414,000, about a third of which was for food.

The agency has a curious structure. Local parishes take most of the requests and dispense most of the aid from local donations. The central office, however, advises local volunteers on each case and keeps records. In addition, when there are large needs, the central office may contribute additional support.

The funding for the agency makes a discretionary policy possible. Most funding for the central office comes from yearly appeals to the congregations of the member churches. In addition, St. Vincent De Paul operates four resale stores for furniture, clothing, household goods, and so forth. The resale value is part of the budget. Twenty percent of the donated furniture is given, free of charge, to the needy.

A small number of private agencies are "self-help" groups run by members of ethnic minorities. One popular black radio personality runs his own material aid program, which provides housing improvements and winterization for a small group of families. The major source of funds is a federal grant. Generally the number of such agencies is limited to those that are tied to Community Action projects or other public initiatives.

Discussion

To compensate for potential lapses in public programs, private agencies would have to be quite sensitive to community needs. They would need to focus on the most serious material problems in the community and would require sufficient resources to do so. Judging from the case studies, however, one must wonder if the agencies can, or even intend to, successfully take on the compensation role.

The case studies suggest that individual agencies are autonomous from pressures relating to the level of need. Instead they are directed toward very special purposes. The fact that agencies have this type of autonomy is demonstrated in dramatic form in Pennsylvania County, where two religious agencies differ in the extreme. One focuses on meeting many needs and responds to a very large number of requests without question. The other conditions aid on religious conversion and serves very few for more than a few days.

In general, in religiously affiliated agencies, donations emanate from churches or parishioners who are relatively distant and uninvolved in the dispersion of funds. Such autonomy implies that certain agencies can indeed respond to a wide variety of need, but it also means that the agencies need not. Contributions are often given without a clear purpose (they tend to be given to a sect rather than to a program), resulting in no necessary relation between funds and community social problems.

Although autonomy can help ensure that the agencies survive and do not face close scrutiny, there is still a need to develop a philosophy to legitimate services to the staff and to those nearby who provide financial support. Whether because they lack imagination, or respond to the expectations from supporters, or are limited by their religious values, religious organizations tend to provide limited responses. Thus, the missions of religiously affiliated agencies vary along a dimension from "good works" to "conversion." The Pennsylvania Salvation Army exemplifies "good works," providing aid that is not conditioned on religious conversion or even on accepting counseling, though counseling is offered. Conversion-oriented agencies, such as Pennsylvania's Rescue Mission, make aid conditional on at least listening to a religious service. This mission may even demand conversion as the price for continuing aid.

The stress on transients, AFDC clients, and so forth seems to depend on the perception by "good works" agencies as to who is needy. While often serving a range of the needy, many such agencies dispense limited types of goods that match agency philosophies. Conversion-oriented agencies select individuals on the basis of whom they may "save," not who most needs tangible aid. Both types of agencies tend to view the poor as morally inferior, in need of more than material aid. Officials in many religious agencies attributed poverty to personal failings, and aim aid at groups that fit this label.

A few religious agencies focus on building a religious community rather than either conversion or good works. Catholic Meal Program is the prime example. But interest in a religious community also constrains the program. The material assistance effort must not be too large, lest it injure the religious community.

Some religious agencies do take a broader view. Catholic Charities in Midwest County and West Virginia Settlement House are examples. But these are limited-budget agencies that cannot meet all demands and instead provide only a few dollars at a time. Simply put, sufficient community support cannot be found even when an agency can retain a large following. With rare exceptions (Pennsylvania's Salvation Army), religiously affiliated agencies perceive only a slice of the poverty problem as important or have funding limits that make them stay away from attempts to deal with the whole pie.

The nonreligious organizations providing material assistance also have a limited view of the problem. Some programs, such as the March of Dimes and the emergency energy programs, focus only on one specialized need. Others, such as the Red Cross, have a variety of services, but only to meet specific problems such as disaster needs or needs of veterans. Not only are the programs limited, they also focus on clients or problems that appear to be particularly "deserving." In all cases the material aid program is clearly dependent on and a function of the other services offered by the agency.

The main exceptions to the secular pattern appear to be agencies supported by the government under a community action philosophy. The old Community Action programs appear to attempt to mobilize the community and provide new resources, apparently without guidance from the funding agency one way or another. The mission of community involvement may be the incentive.

Ethnic agencies seem to accept need as an inevitable part of ethnic life and therefore meet need.

Central funding sources fail to contribute to a close correspondence between needs and resources. For example, the United Way appears to devote little attention to material aid issues. And when it is involved, the extent of interest relates more to community values than to the level of poverty. Texas County is at least as needy as West Virginia County, but the United Way in the former has a much more limited interest in providing material aid.

When it does provide support, the United Way seems to apply some pressure to meet needs fairly. For example, in all communities studied, support would be withdrawn if an agency conditioned help on religious conversion. Nevertheless, this pressure is limited in scope, not affecting the goods dispensed or the general population group served. The United Way may occasionally focus its support on aid to particularly needy individuals, such as the new poor in Pennsylvania County, but the financial contribution of the United Way is small and does not radically influence the community network. The paucity of support is such that many religious agencies feel free to eschew a few dollars and retain freedom to make religious demands on clients.

Because most governments prefer to dispense cash assistance themselves, few private agencies receive funds from the government for meeting material needs, and thus few are affected by demands of public agencies. This is the prime limit to a governmental role in matching needs to resources. There are some exceptions, like the federal energy program, which is often handled by Community Action projects (in three counties). In this case there are strong federal regulations, very little discretion, and some attempt to meet severe community needs. The Community Action agencies are highly dependent on federal funds and must accede to the conditions if they are to continue to exist in an era in which many sources of funds for them have been cut off. Another example of strong control is presented by the Midwest County Salvation Army, which accepts clients on contract in its housing facilities and seems to have little discretion over these beds. But this type of control is rare.

There are some pressures on individual agencies that stem from the broader community. To a limited degree, community perceptions of core problems affect who is served. In Texas County transients receive a large proportion of the available aid, and in Midwest County services to the homeless have increased as the problem has become more evident.

In West Virginia County low AFDC benefits result in a focus on meeting material needs of current welfare recipients. In Pennsylvania County, a focus on the newly unemployed exists and reflects the special economic conditions of that county. However, the weakness of the relation between needs and resources is apparent. Few agencies alter the *type* of aid dispensed as need emerges. And the core problem of the agency may not reflect the degree of poverty in the community—as is the case in Texas County, where Hispanics receive little aid.

From a simple counting of agencies, it is clear that both community resources and community values may limit interest in services in general and in material assistance in particular. Thus despite high need, Texas County has a rather limited social services network. With only about three private agencies per 10,000 county residents, the community ranks third lowest out of the 12 for which we have data (2.25 is the lowest). Its per capita totals are less than one-half of the average across the 12 counties of 7.1 agencies per 10,000 inhabitants.

The other poor county, West Virginia, is also agency-poor, with 5.5 per 10,000 inhabitants. However, this figure is nearly double that of Texas County. Clearly income does not tell the entire story. West Virginia County, with less ethnic heterogeneity and a more even income distribution, has a greater concern for social needs and thus contributes more to meeting them.

While, as we will see in the next chapter, income is often related to the total size of the private agency network, this is not the case in our four case studies. Pennsylvania County, while relatively affluent, has only 2.8 agencies per 10,000 inhabitants. It appears that this predominantly blue-collar community simply gives less than others (its United Way giving is below average), but the large size of the agencies also is a factor. Midwest County, also blue collar in character and with a higher than average median income, has about five agencies per 10,000 inhabitants.

The proportion of the network that is devoted to meeting material needs is also not a constant. In both Texas and West Virginia counties, 23% of private agencies dispense some material assistance. These counties have the highest proportion of agencies dispensing material aid in the sample and almost twice the average proportion across the 12 counties. Perhaps this proportion somehow reflects the high level of need in the community: A larger proportion of agencies appears to deal with the poor in communities with a higher poverty rate and a more limited AFDC program. With less need, Pennsylvania County's proportion is a near average 15.2%. Midwest County has a material assistance program in only 8.2% of its private agencies. This figure is a bit misleading, however, because one agency represents a 90-member food bank. Adding these ninety programs triples the 8.2% figure.

The proportion of agencies that deal with material needs and the total number of private agencies per capita together dictate the per capita extensiveness of the material assistance network. The per capita effort, as measured by these two factors, is partly a function of resources, partly a function of need, and partly a function of the willingness of a community to support agencies. Thus, Texas County has few agencies, overall—owing, perhaps, to a low average income and thus few dollars for agencies, along with a low level of interest in providing social services. As a result, despite having a high proportion of its private-agency effort devoted to meeting material needs, it has only 0.6 such agencies per 10,000 inhabitants, the third lowest in the sample. West Virginia, also limited in its ability to support agencies, but with more interest in dealing with poverty, supports 1.3 agencies per 10,000 inhabitants, slightly above the 12-county average (1.1). Pennsylvania County, with few agencies and only an average proportion of the private effort devoted to meeting material needs, has 0.4 such agencies per 10,000 inhabitants, the lowest in the 12-county study. In Midwest County the figure per 10,000 inhabitants varies from 0.4 to about 1.3, depending upon how the 90 food banks are counted. In short, much about a community mediates the relation between need and resources.

Conclusion

The relation between needs and resources seems to be weak in the private sector. To be sure large problems such as transients, the homeless, AFDC recipients, and the unemployed receive some attention in communities where they are highly visible. But equally pressing needs, such as those of Hispanics in Texas County and the rural poor in Pennsylvania County, are virtually ignored. Community norms and structures may work against the provision of material aid to specific groups. Community members may have little desire or ability to fund agencies. Community resources and ideologies, views of funding agencies, religious interests in conversion and community, and secular interests in specific problems interact in providing aid that has little bearing on a community's social problems.

CHAPTER 5

Agencies That Dispense Material Aid: Statistical Relations

Agencies providing material aid are part of a community and private organizational network and must be discussed as such. In this context, how do they compete? Is the interplay between resources, needs, and the size of the material assistance effort that is implied in the case studies capable of more rigorous proof? Are the funding sources of agencies dispensing material assistance the same as or different from those of other agencies? How about their missions or auspices? What do the patterns tell us about their ability to meet needs?

There are statistical ways of answering these questions, and this chapter adopts a quantitative strategy. A reservation is in order, however. Owing to the lack of relevant data, this analysis cannot adequately measure the size of individual material assistance programs; it uses instead the number of such agencies in a community. Nevertheless, when combined with the estimates of the size of programs provided through case studies, the analysis still has much to offer. It can suggest why certain agencies dispense material assistance and others do not, as well as why some communities have more agencies devoted to this service than others.

Plan of Analysis

The research questions are addressed at three levels. At one level, the analysis looks at the community characteristics that result in a greater, or reduced, interest in dispensing material assistance. The capacity argument holds that agencies in communities with more resources, a greater degree of sophistication, and a past record of organizational successes are also likely to have more agencies to deliver material assistance. Is this argument substantiated? Or does need play the greatest role? It may be that communities with more poverty are more likely to set up agencies in order to serve the great number of individuals requiring aid. Or agencies may fill gaps in public programs so that when there are fewer public programs, private programs are more common. This relationship has been suggested by those who claim the New Deal public programs reduced private initiative and by those who believe that a new reduction in government programs would restore the private contribution. Of course, the notion of gap-filling implies that, when public benefits are low, there are indeed gaps in meeting needs. The existence of such gaps is well documented (Handler and Sosin, 1983).

At another level, dispensing material assistance may be unique to private agencies with certain types of internal orientation. In a noted article, Cloward and Epstein (1967) provide a detailed argument for this possibility. They note that family adjustment agencies (the outgrowths of the Charity Organization Societies) disengaged themselves from serving the poor between 1930 and 1960. Using the material assistance provided by family adjustment agencies as the indicator of services to the poor, Cloward and Epstein insist that the changes in missions of private agencies were as important as New Deal reforms (and increases in public programs) in causing the agencies to reduce their effort. According to these authors, many private agencies came to stress what can loosely be called problems in individual functioning, those relying on casework to help individuals and families adjust to their environment. This new focus was adopted because it promised to create more professional status for the agencies, to increase self-esteem of social workers, to ensure the support of the community, and to bring more middle-class clients into the agencies, further increasing status and support. The provision of material assistance was considered to be inconsistent with that image, and thus was avoided.

For present purposes, when the entire contemporary range of private agencies is at issue, Cloward and Epstein's argument raises a question: Do missions involving problems in individual functioning result in reduced emphasis on material assistance? If so, are other missions more consistent with this service?

A last level involves the modes of organization and patterns of funding, briefly overviewed in Chapter 3. The extent to which each type of organization and each funding source is consistent with the provision of material needs is considered. In general, to whom are agencies that dispense material aid beholden?

Community Forces

As the last chapter showed, the provision of material assistance by private agencies can be viewed as involving the community in two ways. First, the community helps dictate the number of private agencies in the local area. When there are more agencies, the *potential* to provide for material needs is higher. At the second level, a proportion of these agencies must decide to provide material aid. Understanding the role of the community thus requires two sets of analyses, studying how the community affects the range of private agencies as a whole, and how community forces affect the proportion of existing agencies that provide material assistance as opposed to other forms of aid.

THE NUMBER OF PRIVATE AGENCIES

The data from the 12-county study are too limited to provide a basis for a statistical analysis of the role of the community. Instead, the study of public emergency assistance programs described in Chapter 1 is used, although some of the measures, by relying on the views of officials, may be imperfect. In this study county public welfare executives were asked about their perceptions of whether a list of private agencies existed in the community. The list included agencies that often (but not always) provide material assistance: the Salvation Army, religious missions, and so forth.[1]

The number of such agencies that the executives claim are present in their communities is thus a rough indicator of the range of agencies that might potentially provide support, called the "extensiveness of the private sector" in this chapter. While it would be ideal to have a list of all private agencies in each community, this more limited list nevertheless can be related to variables representing the three causal arguments to

[1] The relevant agencies are church-related service agencies, the Salvation Army, a free-clothing center, sectarian social service agencies, nonsectarian social service agencies, and religious missions. The number of such agencies averages 4.1 in a community; the number providing at least "some" emergency aid averages 2.3.

One possible limitation of the dependent variables is that they rely on a measure of the type of each agency, rather than on the exact numbers of agencies that dispense emergency aid. This is not as important a problem as it may seem; the case-study data indicate that it is rare for communities—except very large ones—to have multiple agencies of each type that dispense emergency assistance. And, in this sample, there are few large communities. Nevertheless, it is possible that the use of the list reduces the correlation of population size with the extensiveness of the private emergency aid network.

help determine why some communities are more agency-rich than others.

Sets of independent variables test each of the three theories about community variation. Community variables for this analysis may be divided into three categories. First, there are those variables that represent the size of the public sector (and test gap-filling): total welfare expenditures, and the number of public agencies.[2] A second group of variables represents the capacity of the community as a whole: population size, urbanization, median income, and median educational level. A final group of variables represents the needs of the community: the percentage of the population in poverty, the percentage over 65, and the percentage under 18 (children and older people are more likely to require supportive services).

Table 5.1 presents a regression of these variables against the extensiveness of the private sector, reporting a final equation in which only statistically significant results are noted. It also presents simple correlations between the independent variables and the dependent variable, so that one can judge whether this mode of regression analysis loses any information that might be available from simple correlations.

Three variables are related to the extensiveness of private agencies to a statistically significant degree in this regression. There is a more extensive private network when there is a lower percentage of the population in poverty in the community, when urbanization is more complete, and when there is a more extensive public network.

One of the conclusions that statistical relations strongly imply is that the traditional gap-filling argument cannot be supported. There is no evidence that there are more agencies in communities in which the public sector is less active. There is no statistically significant relation between public welfare expenditures and the extensiveness of the private network, and thus no proof that private agencies are more *common* when public expenditures are low. In addition, there is a *more* extensive private network when there is a more extensive public network, and this flatly contradicts the gap-filling hypothesis. This piece of evidence is consistent with other facts about the private sector. The level of dona-

[2] The relevant public agencies on the list are a public housing agency, a public agency that dispenses housing subsidies, a public senior citizens' center, a public low-cost or free meal program, and local subsidized public transportation. While not all of these agencies are necessarily staffed by government employees, all are governmentally controlled in the sense that financial support stems mainly from the government and the very existence of the agency stems from a government initiative (Kramer, 1973). Thus, the list can be used as one partial measure of the extent of public services. The average number of such programs per community is 3.8.

TABLE 5.1
Determinants of the Extensiveness of the Private Welfare Network

Variable	Simple correlation coefficients (cases)	Final equation: standardized regression coefficient[a]
Public effort		
Extensiveness of public service	.44* (114)	.36*
Welfare expenditures	.13 (152)	
Capacity		
Population	.05 (181)	
Urbanization	.45* (181)	.19*
Median income	.35* (181)	
Median education	.12 (181)	
Need		
Percentage in poverty	−.27* (181)	−.26*
Percentage over 65	−.12 (181)	
Percentage under 18	−.11 (181)	
$R^2 = .35$		
$N = 114$		

[a] Given only for statistically significant results.
* $p < .05$.

tions to private programs has kept up with growth in the GNP over the last few decades (Grønbjerg, 1982), and the great growth of the United Way occurred after World War II and during the growth of the public sector (United Way of America, 1977).

Although other explanations are possible, the fact that the private network is more extensive in communities in which the public network is more extensive may suggest that the capacity argument is correct—that is, private agencies develop more frequently in communities that have an easier time in forming agencies in general. Perhaps in communities with larger public sectors, individuals learn skills that they can use to establish private agencies. Or public agencies may be "ground-breakers," setting up organizational forms and acquiring legitimacy that can be carried over to private agencies.

The fact that the private network is more extensive when urbanization is more complete provides additional support for the capacity theory. There may be more potential donors and clients when the population is dense. Or, in keeping with the traditional sociological perspective (Stinchcombe, 1965), the relation may indicate that urban communities are more differentiated and impersonal and thus promote the type of individual behavioral patterns that formal organizations require.

The fact that there are more private agencies when the percentage of the population in poverty is lower provides further, albeit indirect, support for the capacity theory. This relation, of course, is the opposite of the original prediction that agencies will be more common when needs are greater. Perhaps a lower poverty rate indicates that there are more individuals with incomes high enough to support private agencies. Indeed, as reported in the table, there is a large simple correlation between the median income of the community and the extensiveness of the private network. Median income does not enter the regression because it is so highly correlated with the percentage of the population in poverty ($r = -.72$), and the latter variable is found in the final equation. Both apparently measure the same thing: the ability to finance private agencies.

One capacity variable does not fit the pattern: the population size does not relate to the extensiveness of private services. Perhaps the size of the population (within the population range of surveyed counties) is irrelevant because only a small number of agencies are included in the list, and whether they exist in a given locale may be less related to the size of the population than is the number of agencies in general.

The table also makes it clear that there is no support for the needs-based hypothesis. The percentage of dependent individuals does not relate, in a statistically significant manner, to the extensiveness of the private network. Further, as has been mentioned, private services are more extensive when the poverty level is lower, rather than higher. Just as the results from West Virginia and Texas counties imply, the extensiveness of private services relates more to the availability of existing resources than to the level of need.

THE MATERIAL AID EFFORT

The survey of public welfare officials also provides some information about the role of community forces in the distribution of material assistance agencies. Public agency executives were asked whether each of the agencies on the list provided emergency assistance, using a four-point scale from "none" to "a great amount." The extensiveness of emergency assistance, developed from this list, serves as a proxy for the size of the private material aid effort in testing the three groups of hypotheses. In developing the measure in this analysis, it is best to divide each item on the scale into two categories—whether each agency provides "some" or

TABLE 5.2
Determinants of the Extensiveness of the Provision of Private Emergency Assistance

Variable	Simple correlation coefficient (cases)	Final equation: standardized regression coefficient
Public effort	−.14* (156)	−.18*
Capacity		
Population	.15* (182)	.15*
Urbanization	.14*	
Percentage of economy in manufacturing	−.02 (182)	
Median income	.11 (182)	
Need		
Percentage in poverty	−.09 (182)	
Percentage over 65	−.01 (182)	
Percentage under 18	−.16* (181)	
Number of private agencies	.39* (181)	.43*
$R^2 = .23$		
$N = 156$		

* $p < .05$.

"much" emergency aid, or whether it provides "little" or "none." This helps assure against biases caused by varying perceptions. The number providing at least some benefits in each community is thus the factor to be explained. In Table 5.2, this variable is related to the community factors that represent public effort, capacity, and need; consistent with Table 5.1, both simple correlations and a regression model including only statistically significant coefficients are provided.[3]

An additional variable is the number of private agencies that may potentially contribute emergency assistance (the dependent variable in Table 5.1). This variable is added to enable us to search for indirect effects. For example, it has already been determined that there are more

[3] Because this equation predicts the private emergency assistance effort, one measure of the public effort describes the number of public emergency programs—and thus helps test whether gap-filling occurs. The measure sums up the number of listed agencies (on the questionnaire) in the community. The list includes the use of Title XX service money to meet emergency needs, a food stamp emergency program, emergency General Assistance, the federally financed AFDC-Emergency Assistance program, a federally funded emergency program to meet fuel needs, a state fuel program, an emergency program for Supplemental Security Income clients, an AFDC-Special Needs program that meets such needs as medically required special diets, and any state or local program not accounted for otherwise. The average number of such agencies in a community is 5.5.

relevant agencies when the community has a low poverty rate and a larger rate of urbanization. If there are more emergency programs when there are more relevant agencies, an indirect relation is apparent: urbanization and high average income (e.g., a low poverty rate) lead to the existence of more agencies, which in turn leads to more agencies providing emergency assistance.

In Table 5.2, three variables have statistically significant relations with the provision of emergency assistance in a regression. The private emergency aid effort is larger when there are fewer public emergency programs, when the population is larger, and when there is a more extensive relevant private network.

These data offer some support for the gap-filling hypothesis, as the emergency aid network is more extensive when there are fewer public emergency programs. This picture is consistent with the case-study results.

Support for the other hypotheses is slight. Only one variable representing resources relates (to a statistically significant degree) to the dependent variable: the private emergency aid network is more extensive when the community has a larger population. Although this may be consistent with the claim that a larger population leads to a greater resource base, other measures of resources do not demonstrate statistically significant relations with the emergency aid effort.

The variables representing levels of needs do not enter the regression. It appears therefore that level of need in the community does not affect the extensiveness of the private emergency effort. Perhaps private agencies do not directly aim their services at emergency needs. Where community need is great, in general, all sorts of services are required, so agencies can freely select from among the social problems in a community.

Most important is the statistically significant relation between the extensiveness of private agencies and the extensiveness of the private provision of emergency aid. This relation is to be expected. Nevertheless, it is important to note that it is by far the strongest in the regression. Alone it explains 16% of the variance in the extensiveness of private assistance, while added together, the other two statistically significant variables explain only about 4%.

The implications of these statistical results are profound. They imply that the single most important community factor in the distribution of emergency aid is the number of relevant agencies a community has. And as Table 5.1 points out, the extensiveness of the relevant private network seems to relate to the level of income (represented by a low poverty rate) and urbanization in a community. It appears that communities with high average incomes and high degrees of urbanization have more relevant agencies, and thus more agencies that dispense emergency aid. Those with more resources to start with, end up with more resources for the poor.

In contrast, need apparently plays a small role. Although there are more agencies providing emergency aid when the population is large (and this may indicate greater need), the relation is only of moderate size. And, while there are a few more resources in the private sector when there are fewer public emergency programs, the extent of the relation is small.

Agency Mission and Community Variation

Much information about the nature of agencies that dispense material assistance can be gained from examining the 12-county data. Because information on each agency exists, it is possible to determine which characteristics of agencies, and their environments, relate to the dispensing of material aid. With 1024 private agencies, relationships involving agency characteristics can be assessed with particular confidence. Because there are only 12 communities, data about community differences are less reliable.

This data set is used to test hypotheses concerning the role of missions, the role of community needs (including the gap-filling argument), and the role of the capacity of the community in determining the size of the material aid effort. A large number of variables are available to test each hypothesis, and the list will be explicated along with the analysis of the data, reported below.

One way of analyzing the data from the 12-county study is to compare the traits of agencies dispensing material aid to the traits of those that do not, to determine if there are differences that might explain why some agencies dispense this tangible assistance while most fail to do so. In our analysis, *t*-tests compare these agencies, as is appropriate for analyzing such two-variable relations (Huntsberger, 1967). Because chi-squared is the more common statistical technique, chi-squared tests were also calculated; results were identical to those obtained from the *t*-tests, and are not reported in the text.

To deal with this large number of relations, it is helpful to develop a multivariate analysis. Accordingly, this analysis uses a discriminant analysis, starting with variables that have a statistically significant bivariate relation to the availability of material assistance programs. This technique indicates the extent to which each variable predicts whether (in this case) an agency has a material assistance program or does not have one. Statistical significance can be tested with an *F*-test and the Wilks lambda ratio (Cooley and Lohnes, 1971).

One possible analytic technique would be to include all of the relevant variables representing mission and community factors in the discriminant equation. This procedure is not adopted. Many independent variables are closely correlated to one another, so that the results of such a procedure could be quite misleading. If two closely related independent variables are in the same equation, neither may demonstrate a statistically significant relation with the dependent variable, even though each, if in the equation alone, would demonstrate a significant relation.

A stepwise discriminant analysis was used to find the extent to which each variable predicts whether an agency has a material aid program. First, a causal ordering among the categories of variables was postulated. Presumably, the variables involving agency mission are most proximate to the dependent variables. The community-need variables and the public welfare measures might operate partly through mission variables, and variables representing community capacity might have the most indirect relations. In the stepwise procedure, these variables were entered in the equation in their presumed causal order. The mission variable with the strongest relation is entered first, the mission variable with the strongest relation controlling for the first variable is added next, and so on until all mission variables with statistically significant relations (at the .05 level) have been entered into the equation. The next step is successively to add each variable representing community need or public welfare benefits, if it retains statistical significance. Statistically significant variables indicating community resources are entered last.

A potential problem with the stepwise procedure is that it excludes from the final equation variables that have a strong relation with the dependent variable but are also closely correlated with another variable that has already entered the equation. A careful analysis has therefore been made of the way in which variables that enter the equation affect the contribution of other variables with bivariate relations. Any potential problems with the procedure are reported, and the possible implications of the problems are discussed.

Table 5.3 reports the bivariate relations, and Tables 5.4 and 5.5 report the discriminant analysis results. The procedure appears quite successful in predicting the availability of material aid programs. Six variables are included in the final discriminant equation in Table 5.4. Together they correctly categorize almost 80% of the agencies, as shown in Table 5.5. This occurs using a type of discriminant analysis that does not assume anything about the percentage of cases in each cell in advance.

TABLE 5.3
Bivariate Relations Involving the Availability of Material Aid through Private Agencies

Variable	Frequency or mean		
	Agencies dispensing material aid (N = 138)	Agencies not dispensing material aid (N = 887)	All agencies (N = 1025)
Mission of agency			
Mental health problems	1.5%	9.7%	8.6%*
Individual and family problems	21.7	29.2	28.0
Problems of the handicapped	5.8	10.8	10.2
Problems of the developmentally disabled	2.2	8.5	7.6*
Age specialization	14.0	61.6	55.0*
Drug problems	1.5	3.3	3.0
Alcoholism	9.4	7.4	7.7
Unemployment	15.2	9.4	10.2*
Aging	10.1	8.8	9.0
Criminal justice	2.9	3.4	3.2
Religious auspices	34.8	5.3	15.3
Level of need in community			
AFDC per capita	$22.24	$26.07	$25.56*
General Assistance per capita	$0.41	$1.01	$0.99
Total public welfare per capita	$20.37	$17.91	$18.23
Public emergency programs (number)	4.3	4.5	4.5
Poverty rate in county	11.7%	10.0%	10.2%*
Unemployment rate	4.6%	4.6%	4.6%
Community capacity			
Population	279,174	241,172	246,236*
United Way index[a]	94.2	87.0	88.0*
Average income per capita	$4451.04	$4543.96	$4531.45*
Urbanization of county	74.4%	66.1%	67.2%*
Average educational level	12.0	12.2	12.2*

[a] Index developed by United Way (1980). Higher scores indicate higher donations compared to resources.

* $p < .05$.

TABLE 5.4
Discriminant Analysis: Provision of Material Aid by Private Agencies

Variable	Standardized coefficient	Wilks lambda ratio to enter equation	Level of statistical significance
Mission			
Age specialization	−.696	.889	.001
Religious auspices	.494	.846	.001
Mental health problems	−.304	.829	.001
Problems of the developmentally disabled	−.179	.818	.001
Unemployment	.142	.811	.001
Community need level			
AFDC payment per capita	−.265	.807	.001

Thus knowing only the scores on the six variables of each agency, the discriminant coefficients, and the score that indicates when an agency should fall in one of the two categories (having emergency program or not having emergency program), one would be able to predict whether or not an agency has a material assistance program about 80% of the time.

MISSION

Cloward and Epstein's prime point, that the propensity to dispense financial aid is reduced when the agency concentrates on problems in

TABLE 5.5
Results of Final Discriminant Equation

Actual classification of agency	Predicted classification by discriminant analysis: No material aid program	Material aid program
No material aid program ($N = 887$)	81.6%	18.4%
Material aid program ($N = 138$)	24.5	75.5

Note: Final equation uses coefficients of the variables in Table 5.4 to predict whether an agency will have a material aid program. Rows total 100%.

individual and family functioning, is supported by the analysis. Four variables in Table 5.3 represent such missions: the focus on mental health problems, individual and family problems, problems of the handicapped, and problems of the developmentally disabled.

The *t*-tests tend to support the idea that these missions play a role in inhibiting the formation of a material assistance program. To a statistically significant degree, agencies that dispense material assistance are less likely to focus on mental health problems and problems of the developmentally disabled. The differences between agencies dispensing material assistance and those that do not are large; the percentage of agencies dealing with these problems is four to six times as high among agencies that do not dispense material aid. For the other two variables, the relations are in the same direction, and are slightly too small to be statistically significant. Both are statistically significant at the .10 level.

Age specialization, which (as has been mentioned) seems to be closely tied with the mission of serving a specialized problem, is also inconsistent with the provision of material assistance. Only 13% of agencies that dispense material assistance specialize in an age group, while 62% of other agencies specialize. Again, there is strong evidence that a professional mission is inconsistent with the provision of material aid.

Since Cloward and Epstein (1967) presented their theory, many private agencies have expanded their interest in the poor and underprivileged. It seems possible that missions which include services to these groups are more consistent with the provision of material aid, which is also directed toward the poor and underprivileged. Thus, *t*-tests on Table 5.3 also explore whether agencies that deal with drug problems, alcoholism, unemployment, aging, or criminal justice are likely to dispense material aid. Few significant relations were found. Perhaps the use of professional counseling methods, on which many of these agencies rely, is inimical to the provision of material aid. There is one exception to this pattern: agencies that dispense material aid are more likely to also deal with the unemployed than are other private agencies. In this case, it appears that agency missions involving one type of poverty-related problem, unemployment, are consistent with the focus on a second such problem, material needs.

A final mission-related variable is whether the agency is under religious auspices. As Table 5.3 reveals, agencies that dispense material assistance are unusually likely to have a religious affiliation. In fact, material assistance agencies are nearly four times more likely to be religiously oriented than other agencies, and nearly half of all agencies that dispense material assistance have a religious connection. Based on the historical portrait of agencies painted in Chapter 2, this is what we would expect.

Historical philosophies apparently still play a great role in the material assistance network. In the discriminant analysis in Table 5.4, five of the six variables in the final equation represent the mission of the agency. All of the variables with statistically significant bivariate relations are included.

From all of these results, one must conclude that the propensity to maintain a material assistance program among existing agencies is closely tied to the other aspects of the agencies. Those agencies that provide professional services to deal with problems involving individual functioning and family issues are less likely to maintain material aid programs. The standard coefficients in Table 5.4 show that the largest relation involves age specialization. Adding together the focus on mental health and developmental disabilities, the tendencies for agencies that focus on these two areas to avoid material assistance programs is also great. Another large relation involves religious affiliation. Once again, there is strong support for the notion that agencies under religious auspices are much more likely to provide for material needs. Agencies that deal with the unemployed are more likely to maintain a material aid program. This is not a very important predictor; the coefficient, .14, is comparatively small.

PUBLIC WELFARE PROGRAMS

Four variables on Table 5.3 represent the extensiveness of the public welfare network: the dollar value of AFDC per capita, General Assistance benefits per capita, total public welfare expenditures per capita, and the number of public emergency programs. These variables assess the extent to which private agencies are more likely to provide material aid when the public welfare program is less sufficient. Evidence for gap-filling exists in the relationship between AFDC benefits and the provision of material aid by private agencies. In communities with lower AFDC benefits per capita, private agencies are more likely to dispense material assistance.

This relation is similar to the one found in the data set involving the larger sample of communities. In both cases, there is some evidence that private agencies are indeed more likely to meet material needs when the public network is less sufficient. However, in the 12-county study AFDC benefits demonstrate this relation, while emergency assistance programs are key in the larger data set. The relation is small in any case, and differences in the data set can clearly cause this variation; we need not be too concerned about this difference.

Other variables in this group do not demonstrate statistically significant relations. It seems that total public welfare expenditures and General Assistance expenditures are poor predictors of the propensity of an agency to provide for material needs. Perhaps agencies only respond to the size of AFDC benefits because of their focus on families. The discriminant analysis is completely consistent with the bivariate results. Agencies provide for material needs more frequently when AFDC benefits are lower. But the coefficient is relatively small.

LEVEL OF COMMUNITY NEED

Two variables representing community need may affect the propensity of agencies to dispense material assistance: the poverty rate in the county and the unemployment rate. These were included to determine the extent to which agencies show sensitivity to the level of need by providing more programs when need is greater. Although the unemployment rate bears no relation to the dependent variable, it appears that agencies are slightly more likely to dispense material assistance in communities with a larger percentage of the population in poverty.

While at first this relation appears to contradict results from the larger county sample, a statistical artifact may be involved. When variables are controlled in the multivariate analysis, this relation loses statistical significance. Looking at the stepwise procedure, one sees that the poverty variable loses its statistical significance when the variable measuring AFDC benefits is added. Communities with higher poverty populations and more unemployment have lower AFDC benefits—and this relation remained in the final equation.

EXTENT OF COMMUNITY RESOURCES

Certain measures of community resources are also included in Table 5.3: the size of the population, the level of United Way contributions, average per capita income, percentage urban, and average educational level. Do communities with greater resources support more material assistance programs? The analysis seems to be contradictory. On the one hand, agencies in communities with a larger population, larger donations to the United Way, and a larger percentage of the community in urban areas have a higher propensity to have a material assistance program. On the other hand, a smaller average income and lower educational level are also related to the propensity to provide material assistance. But all of the relations disappear in the multivariate analysis.

Education and income levels in this sample are lower in counties in which public AFDC benefits per capita are smaller. (The relations are statistically significant.) As was the case with the poverty rate, these variables lose statistical significance when the measure of AFDC enters the discriminant analysis.

Statistically speaking, the AFDC per capita variable is also responsible for the reduction in the effect of urbanization, population size, and United Way effort, all of which lose their statistical significance when the AFDC level is entered in the equation. Indeed, the five community-resource variables, when placed in a regression (not in a table), explain 94% of the variance in the measure of AFDC. When a community has a larger population, higher level of urbanization, larger United Way benefits, lower average income, and lower educational levels, than AFDC benefits are lower. Perhaps this combination of traits defines a high level of need that is reflected in AFDC benefits. These indirect relationships thus tend to support the conclusion that private agencies are slightly more likely to have material assistance programs when there is more need in the community. Needless to say, the hypothesized role of community resources in increasing material aid is completely contradicted.

A second set of indirect relations also exists. The rate of urbanization of a community is higher (to a statistically significant degree) when agencies have religious auspices (a mean of 71.5% as opposed to 66.5%, otherwise) and avoid specializing in an age group (a mean of 69.9% compared to 65.4%, otherwise). Perhaps urban communities have more religious diversity, and thus more religiously affiliated agencies. Urban communities may also have stronger community-wide demands for service, thus leading to a commitment to meeting needs of all age groups. Because religious auspices and less age specialization are consistent with a higher propensity to maintain a program, apparently urbanization indirectly contributes to the availability of material aid programs. But the relation between urbanization and these two measures is indeed small. The role of resource-related variables is thus limited. According to the data, therefore, missions have the primary role in determining whether agencies supply material assistance. Gap-filling in the face of inadequate public programs has a small role. The level of need in the community and the capacity of the community to supply aid have almost no impact.[4]

[4] Because some agencies focus only on material aid, it may be objected that results from the multivariate analysis involving age specialization, programs for the handicapped, and religious auspices, in particular, simply describe these specialists. Indeed, 37% of all agencies providing material aid carry out no other service activity. However, an attempt was made to control for these agencies by entering a variable—specialization in material

Organization and Funding Sources for Material Assistance

Because reliable information exists for only 6 of the 12 counties, data concerning the organization and funding patterns cannot be added to the equation developed above. Nevertheless, as Table 5.6 demonstrates, these patterns are quite important in understanding the framework within which material assistance is dispensed. The table presents non-parametric correlations involving the relation between organization and funding source and the likelihood that an agency dispenses material aid. To help understand the patterns more fully, the table also reports the relation between the organizational context and a small number of problems that seem to involve material assistance. One caveat is needed: correlations are at the agency level, not the program level. Thus, for example, government funds may support child welfare services in an agency that also provides material aid; all we know from the data is that the agency receiving government funds dispenses material assistance.

ORGANIZATION

National organizations focus largely on broad problems involving health or individual and family life (see Chapter 3). Yet, according to Table 5.6, these agencies do not ignore material assistance. Compared to other private agencies, those receiving support from national organizations are somewhat more likely to provide material assistance (the relation is statistically significant). Looking at the specific problems for which material aid is provided, it is apparent that nationally affiliated organizations are more likely (to a statistically significant degree) to be involved in meeting emergency needs and to some extent providing disaster assistance. These are somewhat unexpected results. Most observers believe that material needs are not frequently met by national organizations.

The explanations for the relationship are manifold. Historical continuity is one. National organizations that developed before the turn of the century have continued to dispense material assistance. The Salvation Army is a prime example. A second is that, while the trend is away from

---

matters—into the discriminant equation before entering the other variables. After it was entered all of the original relations remain, although they are slightly attenuated. The results thus cannot be explained solely by the attributes of agencies that specialize. They have a more general applicability.

TABLE 5.6
Material Aid Programs and Organization Patterns ($N = 570$)

	Correlation			
Pattern	Material assistance overall	Homelessness	Emergency assistance	Disasters
National organization	.07	.08	.08*	.11*
Federal funding	−.04	.00	−.05	−.06
State funding	−.11*	.02	−.11*	.02
County funding	−.06	−.07	−.08*	−.04
United Way funding	.11*	.02	.10*	.19*
Religious funding	.18*	.14*	.19*	−.03
Donations	.19*	.05	.16*	.05

* $p < .05$.

it, national health organizations may spend small amounts for financial assistance or to meet material needs in other ways, to deflect criticism and gain legitimacy. The March of Dimes, for example, which is most interested in research and large equipment, often dispenses small grants for special needs to families whose children meet the health-related criteria. Local boards help divide up the funds and gain a commitment from the March of Dimes in the process.

PRIVATE FINANCIAL SUPPORT

As the discriminant analysis made clear, organizations under religious auspices are very likely to dispense material assistance. Table 5.6 demonstrates that such organizations are more likely to dispense material assistance in general and are also more likely to furnish shelter and emergency financial aid. Disaster assistance, the province of the nonsectarian Red Cross, is the only service that religiously funded agencies are not more likely to provide.

The correlations are a result of the activities of a number of agencies. Most shelters are under religious auspices and receive some religious funding. Emergency financial aid is largely viewed as a duty by Western religions.

Private agencies that dispense material assistance are also more likely to rely on direct donations and funding from the United Way. Direct donations are, of course, common among religiously affiliated agencies.

The United Way, while often claimed to be uninterested in material needs, appears to provide assistance to agencies that dispense emergency aid and to those that provide disaster aid. Why is this so? Most of the explanation is historical. The Red Cross and Salvation Army had sufficient support to raise money on their own. When they joined the United Way, they agreed to reduce their own fund raising in exchange for support. Thus, the United Way is committed to support these agencies, both of which have material assistance programs. But it is possible that the United Way most heavily supports the other, nonmaterial services that agencies dispensing material aid provide (such as Salvation Army counseling programs). As Chapter 4 indicated, the United Way is certainly no major provider of material aid.

Many other organization patterns (not represented in the table) are neither more nor less common in agencies that dispense material assistance. These organizations are neither more nor less likely than others to receive corporate contributions, membership fees, support from foundations, and so forth. As might be expected, however, agencies that provide material aid seldom accept fees from clients. This very important source of support is naturally unavailable when clients are destitute, but it is interesting that these agencies also are less likely to have fees for all their services ($r = -.25$, $p < .05$). This though, is consistent with other relations. Agencies charging fees often deal with professional problems that are uncommon in agencies providing for material needs.

GOVERNMENTAL SUPPORT

The relations are not great, but the agencies that dispense tangible assistance are less likely to receive aid from government than are other agencies. The negative relation involving aid from federal sources is not statistically significant, but this is somewhat misleading. At present, federal funds do not go directly to providing tangible aid, but they may go to agencies that use other sources of funds to meet tangible needs. Community Action agencies, for example, may receive federal funds for employment programs and rely on community donations to run a food pantry.

To a statistically significant degree, county funding is less likely to support emergency assistance. It also tends not to support services to the homeless, even though homelessness is a major problem in many localities. (Cities, likewise, provide so little support for material aid programs that it is not reported in the table.) The public sector must assume that public welfare meets all needs, or that any extra money should be dispensed on General Assistance and not given to private agencies that serve the poor.

Conclusion

These gross statistics suggest some of the difficulties inherent in any attempt to provide tangible assistance. At the community level, statistical analyses suggest that the most important factor in the provision of material aid is the availability of a resource base. Indirectly, resources permit the relevant agencies to exist, and thus to provide material benefits. However, when these resources are greater, levels of need tend to be lower. So, the communities with the greatest ability to meet material needs have the smallest poverty-related problems.

Some direct relations suggest that existing private agencies tend to mobilize more resources to meet material needs when the public sector is less sufficient and when the population is large. But, statistically, these relations are limited. One must conclude that agencies only compensate to a small extent for inadequate public resources or widespread poverty.

The statistical analysis also suggests that many traditional values are of paramount importance. A very large proportion of agencies that provide material aid are under religious auspices. Apparently, a host of values—the interest in good works, the desire to promote a Christian community, the desire to maintain religious solidarity, and the desire to use material aid to convert the down-and-out—retain the importance that was apparent before the New Deal (see Chapter 2). In addition, because agencies that dispense material aid do not specialize in an age group, there is some evidence that material aid tends to be provided more frequently when agencies put less emphasis on professional, age-specific services. The only nontraditional factor consistent with provision of material aid is the unemployment rate.

The same message can be obtained from an examination of the types of agencies that are less likely to maintain material assistance programs, because the statistical analysis reveals that the emphasis on problems in individual and family functioning is common in these agencies. This is the essence of the professional orientation to social services that has become dominant since the New Deal, as Cloward and Epstein (1967) point out. Apparently a desire to maintain a professional status and professional services for the middle class is inimical to the provision of material aid.

The service of dispensing material aid may be a difficult one to expand. Religiously affiliated agencies—those most likely to dispense such aid—are a small fraction of private agencies: 15.4% (see Table 3.5). The religious values that give rise to the relevant agencies are no longer dominant in the organization of the private sector. Employment agencies, also more likely to dispense material aid, are similarly uncommon in the private sector, representing 10.2% of all agencies. Only the lack of age specialization, common in agencies providing material assistance, is also typical of many private agencies. But this does not necessarily indicate a potential for providing material aid, since many agencies that do not specialize in an age group do not provide material assistance (e.g., mental health or individual and family life agencies). More telling, agencies that deal with professional-type problems are among the most popular private agencies. Individual and family life problems are dealt with by 28.2% of all agencies, mental health by 8.6%, and services to the developmentally disabled by 7.6% (see Table 3.4). In general, there are more agencies whose mission appears to be inimical to providing material aid than agencies whose mission is consistent with its provision.

Agencies that provide material benefits rarely rely on fees for service, and only a few of them obtain funds from the United Way. Public funds are not a particularly noteworthy source, and statistical relations indicate that, in some instances, agencies dispensing material aid are less likely to obtain public funds. Consistent with the results in the discriminant analysis, it seems that religious funding and direct donations are the most common ways of supporting a material assistance effort. Again, it is the traditional approaches—religion and direct donations—rather than the more contemporary, larger-scale sources of funds on which the material assistance effort is most fully based.

One must conclude from these data that the struggle to provide for material needs is an uphill battle. The majority of the private sector involves professional, nonsectarian services, whereas material assistance is more likely to be provided by nonprofessional religious agencies. Material aid is also provided less often by agencies relying on some major funding sources. Furthermore, communities that provide the least aid to the poor have larger numbers of poor to aid. Material aid runs counter to the dominant spirit of private agencies and to the nature of community support.

CHAPTER 6

Rationing Material Assistance

Agencies providing material aid find themselves dealing with a problem in which relatively few have an interest and serving a subgroup of the population often thought to be little deserving of support. Nevertheless, community pressures exist to meet needs—whether to get transients out of town or shelter the homeless—and private agencies attempt to meet them with whatever resources they have.

To balance pressure to meet needs with budgetary limits, agencies ration aid. They decide which clients to serve and which to reject, and they limit the type of aid that is dispensed—cash, food, shelter, and so forth. The missions of agencies as well as shortages of funds may play a role in the rationing decisions.

The need to ration services is not unique to agencies providing material aid. Thompson (1967) pointed out, for example, that when resource constraints become great, an organization first seeks alternative sources of support. When alternatives cannot be found, rationing occurs.

Just how rationing is accomplished is a matter of controversy. Thompson believes that it is common to ration by setting financial limits for each department of an organization, but this tells us little about the patterns in the less complex private agencies providing material aid. Lipsky (1980) argues that the need to ration aid leads many human service organizations to give line workers the discretion to decide which clients to serve. On the other hand, in the case of the basic AFDC grant, evidence suggests that the rationing strategy consists of reduced discretion, with aid dispensed on the basis of a simple, relatively inflexible set of criteria (Handler and Sosin, 1983). Applicability of these patterns to private social welfare agencies is not clear.

As the perspective offered in this book suggests, rationing techniques of agencies dispensing material assistance may vary because they reflect a range of organizational pressures—from demands from the broader environment to the missions of the agencies. One must focus therefore on the manner in which the basic constraints facing the agencies contribute to choices determining who is served and how the service is provided.

One useful way of focusing the discussion is to compare the rationing techniques of private agencies that deliver material assistance to the techniques used in the corresponding public sector programs—emergency assistance and special needs programs. The comparison provides a yardstick against which the behavior of the private sector can be measured. It also helps further the examination of what (if anything) is unique about the private sector, and thus what its special contribution to providing for the needy may be.

A detailed survey of public agencies dealing with emergency and special needs describes the general patterns of rationing (Handler and Sosin, 1983). According to the survey, one way of limiting aid is by forcing individuals to exhaust other resources first. In about one-third of the programs clients must exhaust resources from the private sector before public benefits are offered; in roughly half of the programs emergency assistance is only offered after public benefits from other sources are exhausted.

There are few attempts to ration aid by setting up complicated verification procedures. Most public programs verify income, assets, and the existence of the emergency. Less than half verify attempts to obtain other public assistance; and about 30% verify attempts to use private agencies.

The most significant rationing devices used by public agencies are limitations on eligibility and coverage. Generally, programs serve some but not all groups of clients: the vast majority of programs include AFDC recipients, over half include migrants, transients, and food stamp recipients, while about a third include recipients of Supplemental Security Income, General Assistance recipients, or intact families. Moreover, about three-fourths of the programs specialize in one category of aid. It is common for a program to focus on special winter needs, lost or stolen welfare checks, disaster aid, or chore service. Needs for basic goods such as clothing, food, or aid in paying utility bills are seldom the principal focus of programs; however, roughly half of the programs occasionally provide for each of these needs.

Benefits are supposed to take the form of vouchers or direct payments to vendors about half of the time in state programs. Counties, however, actually rely on them 80% of the time. A voucher, which specifies exactly what can be purchased, is an effective form of rationing.

Finally, a small minority of public programs impose a special condition, such as a protective payee (the payment goes to someone other than the client) or a work requirement. These generally affect only about

5% of recipients when implemented. In about half of the programs, however, repeated requests for aid are either rejected, or the recipient is required to accept budget counseling or another special condition.

The study concludes that the patterns reflect a few of the basic views about emergency aid inherent in the public system, along with the reactions of the bureaucracy to outside pressures. It is widely recognized that short-term aid is necessary and that the public sector has a responsibility to meet crisis needs. But there are also pressures to treat all clients alike (horizontal equity) and to keep costs low. Officials want to keep the programs simple and abide by standard rules. There is also a desire to avoid making too many rules, or rules that require a large amount of interpretation and administrative stress. Finally, there are fears of serving those who abuse the system—notably individuals who shouldn't need help (such as the able-bodied) or who need goods (food, clothing, or housing) that are in theory covered by basic public welfare grants.

The private sector appears to have somewhat different motives. Unlike public organizations, most private agencies have commitments toward the goals of conversion, good works, serving the community, or serving a special population group. Yet, like the public agencies, they fear abuse, divide clients into deserving-undeserving categories, and have some interest in equity—or at least are fearful of complaints if they demonstrate favoritism. Also, like public agencies, they have a clear desire to control costs—an obvious necessity given their limited budgets.

One might suspect that, given these similarities and differences, private agencies ration in ways that are similar to the patterns in public agencies but not identical. This chapter examines these patterns of rationing and the missions and pressures they reflect. Because case studies represent the best source of data, they are the focus of this chapter. The discussion is divided by groups of programs—shelter and meal programs, food pantries, general material assistance agencies, special-purpose agencies, and "side" programs of agencies with other types of missions.

Shelter and Meals

> The interview took place in the church center attached to the Catholic Meal Program hall. This room also serves to hold meetings, parties, weddings, and the like. . . . For the purposes of this study, this room is also used to serve evening meals to upwards of 450 clients a night, six nights a week. The meals are brought to the center in private containers and cars by parishioners from other churches in the city . . . the types of people I observed to be using the program were: primarily white (per-

> haps 10% were black or members of other minorities), about 95% male, and I would say the predominant age range was approximately 80% in their forties and fifties, with 10% younger and an equal percentage older. (Project Field Notes)

> Mike was dissatisfied with the Rescue Mission because the agency required attending a church service before receiving a meal. Mike felt the Rescue Mission had no right to force religion on him. Nevertheless, he said that he supposed they could do whatever they wanted and that he was grateful to be able to get a free meal. (Project Interviews, see Chapter 7)

When people need shelter or meals, they generally are at the end of the line. Food and shelter are the basic needs in any society. Those in need of shelter would be homeless without aid, and meals served by agencies tend to go to people whose living accommodations are such that no food can be prepared at home.

Often those in need of such life-sustaining aid are not eligible for any program from government: single individuals cannot obtain AFDC; transients are not eligible for benefits from government because they have no address, and those receiving inadequate public welfare grants are not entitled to more. Food stamps may be available for some, but one cannot sleep in stamps or prepare hot food with no shelter. Victims of natural disasters may also need emergency food or shelter, and do not always have recourse to public programs.

Although there are a few public shelters in the nation—in New York City, for example—normally shelter and meal programs are private, peculiar, and distinct. They are likely to require religious services, limit eligibility to a number of days, and serve exclusively on the basis of sex. Most seldom bother to verify need, on the assumption that no one less than desperate would choose to ask for their help, although other forms of selectivity may occur.

The Midwest Rescue Mission is a clear example of a traditional, religiously oriented shelter facility for men. It is comparatively large, having two hundred beds in two large rooms and providing three meals a day. Supported primarily by private donations, the Rescue Mission places religion before anything else. Thus, while residents pay nothing for food or lodging, they are required to attend nondenominational Christian services before breakfast, lunch, and dinner, and again in the evening if they plan to spend the night.

There is no formal verification procedure, merely an interview between a pastor and the applicant. Although aid may be denied if the individual seems to be abusing the system, this rarely occurs. The interview, which is likely to end up in a Bible-reading session, is more concerned with conversion than anything else. Agency officials claim that just about anyone who is polite when the conversion attempt takes place will be allowed to stay. Men are turned away only when the facility is full.

One of the unique aspects of this mission is that repeaters are admitted. As long as a guest follows the rules, he may stay. Lengthy stays increase the opportunity for conversion. However, there seems to be a tendency to refuse shelter "mission stiffs" who "hang around as long as we feed them," although the policy is informal and difficult to quantify. Some outsiders believe that those who do not speak English and thus cannot be converted are also refused aid.

According to our interviewee, the primary problem that the Rescue Mission addresses is "S-I-N." Food and shelter are provided as a means to attract a captive audience for conversion. Thus the constant religious services are virtually the only services offered. The agency has discontinued an earlier practice of allowing recruitment for day labor to take place on the premises, because when there wasn't enough work to go around, fights took place. There are also strict behavioral rules: anyone who swears will be banished from the shelter for a few days, and three swearing incidents will result in a permanent expulsion.

Clearly, the Rescue Mission's minimal eligibility criteria are partly a function of its focus on shelter as an opportunity for conversion. Indeed, there are more strict criteria for its small free-clothes program. While our interview was taking place, a man requested a pair of shoes. He had injured a foot, and the shoes he was wearing were too small. He was offered another pair, but only if he relinquished the shoes he already had. He refused and was denied aid. We were told that the agency is careful because individuals who receive clothes they do not need may simply sell them for wine.

With some variation, many of the religious missions are similar to the Rescue Mission. For example, the Religious Help Mission in Texas (see Chapter 4) also allows people to stay for long periods of time, has a religious service, and focuses primarily on men. But this mission, with a commitment to good works as well as conversion, tends to provide more in the way of an employment program, and it also houses some women. Both the West Virginia mission (the City Mission) and Pennsylvania Rescue Mission (see Chapter 4) require a religious service, and have few formal verification procedures, though they differ in their limit on length of stays—2 days in a 30-day period in Pennsylvania and 2 months a year in West Virginia.

Some shelters are run by the Salvation Army, an organization that has shed some of its conversion-oriented approach in exchange for entry into the United Way and legitimacy in the community. Salvation Army shelters now tend not to require religious services. In exchange, however, they may have somewhat greater verification requirements for residents. For example, the shelter in Texas (see Chapter 4) makes an effort to distinguish the deserving from the undeserving. Believing that younger people "should be settled down and working," the agency gives priority to those who are over 50 years old. It also refuses to help some individuals who are eligible for public aid, sending them instead to the appropriate agencies. Although there are no formal rules, the agency also rejects persistent repeaters or those who appear to abuse the system.

Like many others, the shelter program of the Salvation Army is a limited one: meals are dispensed and lodging is provided, but there are few other services. Between meals residents stay out on the street. The agency may, however, refer some individuals to jobs and deny aid to those who do not appear to be serious about working.

Other good-works shelters may be somewhat less selective. It thus appears that the Salvation Army in Pennsylvania County and Catholic Workers' House in Midwest County tend to provide housing, albeit for a limited time, with fewer conditions and less concern about abuse. The Catholic Meal Program (see Chapter 4), like most meal programs not attached to shelters, demonstrates almost no selectivity.

Very occasionally, a program has no religious overtones at all. "Friends House" in Midwest City is one of these. It is a shelter for women and children, funded largely by an endowment dating back to 1865. At that time, it provided a place for women to stay who were awaiting the return of their husbands from the Civil War. The service, delivered mostly by volunteers, has remained relatively stable. Only the client population has changed.

The clients of Friends House are now often battered women, those evicted from apartments, victims of fires, or the chronically mentally ill, who often live on the streets. Those in need are generally served; few are turned away; and there is no formal verification procedure. However, volunteers can turn down clients if they desire, and the most threatening chronically mentally ill may often be refused.

In general, the maximum length of stay is 2 weeks, although the rule is unwritten and flexible, especially for the chronically mentally ill. Repeaters are allowed, but only after a 6-month break. In addition, once in the facility, clients can be asked to leave if virtually anyone on the staff—from the volunteers to the cook—believes they are disruptive.

The facility has no special conditions. Residents are expected to follow simple rules, such as making their own beds and turning off the lights by 10 P.M. Many remain in their rooms for most of the day.

Looking at the nine shelter programs in the case studies (some not summarized), certain patterns are quite common. In general, facilities have very little formal selectivity except on the basis of age or sex, although three weed out particularly unworthy clients. All assume need and do not verify it formally. In general, only a small percentage are turned away, but some selectivity occurs on "moral" grounds, and there is a tendency to evict the disruptive.

One prime difference involves length of stay. Two of the religious, conversion-oriented missions allow individuals to stay for an indefinite length of time and to return frequently. One of these assumes that a long stay improves the chances for conversion, while the other looks at the shelter as a place where individuals can readjust and find new jobs. In six other cases the length of stay is shorter and repeaters are discouraged or formally forbidden. A mixed case is the Pennsylvania Rescue Mission, which provides shelter indiscriminately for 2 days but allows only those who wish to be rehabilitated to stay longer. Basically, then, extended stays are the product of a philosophy of seeking to change the individual.

The second major difference between shelters involves conditions. All four conversion-oriented shelters demand that individuals attend prayer meetings in exchange for lodging and food. The other missions tend not to have such a requirement. Indeed, in most instances very little at all is required of residents.

It appears that two factors determine the style of shelter and meal programs—the desperate situation of those who require lodging and meals, and the extent of a conversion orientation. Given the loss of autonomy, the sense of crisis, and the indignity inherent in asking for food or shelter, very little in the way of verification is required, and abuse and fraud are not issues. Selectivity (time limits and repeater limits) often appears to be designed to ration services fairly. And moral issues and unruly clients elicit some concern.

Food Pantries and Clothing Dispensaries

> Christian Food Bank was located in the basement of a church. It could only be reached from a relatively hard-to-locate side door of the church. Entry is into a very large room. Straight ahead are about three large rows of clothes, on hangers. To the left, about twenty feet away, a man sits behind a cardtable. He has a small stack of 3 by 5 cards on his desk. A client receiving aid would first talk to this man, and would then be taken to the food pantry, which is behind him, through a door. The pantry takes up three rooms, two full of staples such as bread, and one with a refrigerator that holds perishables. The facility, while not new, is well kept up and quite comfortable. (Project Field Notes)

Food pantries serve those who have completely run out of food and require at least a few days' supply simply to survive. Since most food pantries also dispense clothing, the two are treated together here. Many agencies with pantries also dispense other goods. These are covered in this chapter under "general material assistance agencies."

To some extent food pantries overlap with public programs. The Expedited Food Stamp program is meant to deal with food crises. This program will dispense 5 days' worth of stamps to an applicant for food stamps who has no income. But these food stamps may actually take a day or two to obtain, and in the meantime a food pantry is needed. Moreover, emergency food stamps are given only to applicants for the program, and no additional stamps are dispensed to those who are already receiving benefits but have run out of food. Those who are not eligible for stamps but who face a sudden crisis, such as victims of a fire or burglary, also require aid from a private source.

There is also a small amount of overlap between public programs for emergency needs and food pantries, since nearly half of all emergency programs dispense some vouchers for food. But state regulations may limit the public programs. For example, in Pennsylvania and Midwest County, food is only dispensed to those facing an emergency from a natural disaster or similar major crisis; Texas County gives little aid to transients and only a one-in-a-lifetime grant to current welfare recipients; and even in West Virginia, a "true emergency" must exist: to be short of cash is not sufficient.

Many such programs are carried out by churches, often in a combined effort. These programs continue the historical function of churches in meeting material needs of parishioners and others. For example, the Inner-City Churches Coalition in Midwest County represents a loose amalgamation of 10 inner-city, Midwest churches, most of which are struggling to survive. As conditions in the central city deteriorated, the churches were forced to become more involved in meeting economic needs. Most, the director of the agency believed, did so reluctantly. They felt they were unable to refuse, given their mission of serving their communities.

Each of the churches has its own stock of food, clothing, and a few other necessities. One of the points of the coalition is to ensure that one facility is open at all times. In addition, there is a central registry, which prevents clients from going from church to church to maximize their benefits. Most of the church programs dispense enough food for three to five days. Generally, requirements are lax, and anyone who faces an emergency will be served. Churches find it hard to turn anyone away even if they wish to; it simply goes against the prevailing ideology of Christianity.

Repeaters are sent to the central agency, where a sort of rationing is in force. Applicants at the central agency must seek public welfare before being served. Further, while there is no formal policy regarding repeaters, the director feels that "churches don't have to be suckers" and should not "become a second welfare system." Nevertheless, rather than turn someone down, she is more likely to informally persuade the person not to return. She may mandate budget counseling for those who return frequently—an individual will be told that food vouchers will be provided after the counseling session.

West Virginia County has a similar organization, Christian Food Bank, which dispenses food and clothing for the county's entire church community. The agency was established because the churches felt the time spent on material assistance prevented them from meeting spiritual needs. A central agency was a compromise between the religious mission of serving the poor and that of tending to the spiritual needs of the congregation.

Christian Food Bank seems to have a cycle of policies that determines its size. In 1970, when the agency opened, 104 families came in each month. This number increased to about 1000 families by 1974, decreased slightly after that, and increased to over 1100 in 1981. In the current year, the number has been cut in half.

The cycle has much to do with the use of Information and Referral, the county's central intake unit. In the mid-1960s, the Food Bank became concerned over abuse of the system. Many people used the service "over and over," and the job of determining eligibility was "too much of a load." Like most church organizations, the agency tended to turn no one down; but when Information and Referral took over, there was a decrease of about 200 families a month.

Within a few years the caseload was back to its former level. As a result, the policy was changed again. Currently, clients will only be seen if there is a "true emergency," that is, if a specific event has triggered need. Again, it is up to Information and Referral to make the decision, and the agency serves all who are approved. It seems that by itself Christian Food Bank would have been unable to make such rules.

The agency will serve repeaters and tends to serve many current AFDC recipients as well as those receiving food stamps or child support. Transients comprise less than 5% of the caseload. Services have been "amazingly constant" since 1970. Five days' supply of goods—worth perhaps $30—are dispensed from a rather large food pantry. The food consists primarily of such staples as bread, milk, and canned foods.

Some clothes are available, for which an individual or family has merely to ask.

Perhaps the least restrictive coalition is "South Midwest Coalition," the only private emergency material assistance agency in the south Midwest area. This is another church-related organization that obtains supplies from many of the local churches. Those who enter the office to request food and clothing are asked a few questions, the answers to which are recorded on an index card. There are no other records or obvious rules; the worker on duty on any day (a volunteer) has complete authority to grant or refuse assistance. Refusals are quite rare (and can be appealed to the board of directors). During the interview one woman entered and stated that she "just couldn't make ends meet this week." She was directed to another volunteer in the next room, who selected groceries for her, and no further investigation was attempted. Repeat requests are common, and the agency says it attempts to "meet the need as long as it exists." All area residents are welcome. Most who come, however, tend to be recipients of one form or another of public assistance. On the average, a family is given enough food for 1 week, mostly in the form of canned and boxed foodstuffs donated to the program.

Except in Texas County, similar church-related food pantries existed in many neighborhoods in all counties, and one outlying region of Texas County had a similar program. A simple application procedure, vague rules for repeaters (often ignored), and limitations on the amount of food are common, along with informal attempts to get people to use public welfare or budget counseling.

The only other group of pantries in our sample seemed to be community-oriented, conducted by local Community Action projects, or occasionally by governmentally funded ethnic self-help agencies. One food pantry is conducted by a Community Action project in Midwest County. The project as a whole is an effort to involve senior citizens in the local community. Thus, the project employs 91 senior-citizen workers, each of whom is at least 55 years old. All are paid and are former clients of the program.

The food pantry, located in four separate offices, serves about 100 individuals per month. Decisions to provide aid, made by the senior worker in each site, are largely subjective in nature. Although no one is forced to accept services, an attempt is made to interest recipients in budget counseling or the broader program of the agency. Basically, dispensing enough food for a few days is almost routine, and few are turned away. Applicants under 55 years old are served, although an effort is made to "discourage" the use of pantries by the nonelderly.

A similar system is at work in the Community Action project in Pennsylvania County (Chapter 4) and the "Peace Project," a black organization in Midwest County. In both instances, goods are dispensed rather freely, rules dealing with repeat requests are either generous or nonexistent, and few are turned away. The major limit is that the programs appeal to one community rather than to the county at large.

A host of similarities appear among the eight pantries and clothing programs in the sample. Most dispense material aid as part of a responsibility to the community. This responsibility may arise from a religious orientation, as in the case of four church programs, or from solidarity with the neighborhood, which motivates the Community Action programs. The pantries limit aid primarily by dispensing a small amount of food, enough to last for three to seven days. And while repeat requests may be discouraged in some locations, they often are tolerated, even if it goes against the judgment of the workers, who find it difficult to turn someone down who claims to have nothing to eat.

If there are any differences between programs, they appear to involve a trade-off. Most of the Community Action programs appeal only to a neighborhood or age group, and this forms the major limitation on the program. Within this limit, goods are given relatively freely. Church programs tend to attract a wider range of clients and are somewhat more likely to be selective. Thus, in West Virginia County a "true emergency" is necessary, and the Inner-City Coalition might either tell people that they should not return or mandate budget counseling.

It is possible that the number of applicants is also a prime variable in influencing selectivity—the south Midwest organization serves less than 50 a month—but the effect of this variable is based on its relation to willingness and ability to provide benefits. Perhaps the difference can also be traced to the ability of larger programs to create buffers that can more easily reject applicants—such as Information and Referral or the central office of Inner-City Churches Coalition. Religious organizations do not like to refuse the needy. They ward off pressure by allowing others to refuse for them.

General-Purpose Agencies

> The interviews took place at the Salvation Army. . . . The center provides a variety of services, including day care for children, grocery distribution, emergency accommodations, and referrals to other agencies and food pantries. . . . The building itself is spacious, having once been a grade school, and includes a large recreation area, the day care center, a chapel, a spacious kitchen and dining room, some accommodations and offices upstairs, reception and interview rooms, and offices downstairs. The front door opens into a foyer which is decorated and used as a

> waiting room. There are about six colored foam chairs, both comfortable and movable, a notice board, and pictures on the walls. Off this room is the main interviewing room, which is also decorated in a warm, comfortable manner. There are usually two interviewing staff present, including the receptionist, who is a psychology graduate. The staff's attitude seems to be nonjudgmental, and one of concern for clients. (Project Field Notes, see Chapter 7)

General-purpose agencies provide a broad range of services for selected clients in specific situations. Goods furnished range from food and clothing to rent deposits and aid for transportation. The situations vary from natural disasters to a shortage of cash.

These agencies overlap, at least in part, with public programs. They meet some of the same needs. For example, each community has a Red Cross to deal with natural disasters, yet in three out of the four communities in the case study, the AFDC-Emergency Assistance program is at least in part designed to deal with fires, floods, and similar emergencies. As Chapter 4 demonstrated, there is no automatic tendency for the public and private agencies to specialize and complement each other. But, as we will see, some level of after-the-fact coordination does occur.

The general-purpose agencies have organizational similarities to public programs as well. There are similar rules for repeated requests for aid, limits on circumstances covered, verification procedures, and required conditions. Except for some slight differences in the clients served and the needs covered, along with obvious differences in the extent of resources available, the public and private programs are very much alike.

As might be expected, the range of problems stressed in general-purpose agencies is large. The Red Cross stands at one end of the continuum—a secular program concentrating on a small set of issues: disaster needs and the needs of military personnel. At the other end are religiously based organizations, such as the Salvation Army or Catholic Charities, that cover a larger set of material problems.

The material assistance effort of the Red Cross, though it varies in generosity, is fairly constant in form across the nation. It consists of two components: a small program to aid veterans and current members of the armed forces, and a program to deal with natural disasters. In Midwest City, the military program is relatively small. The director claims that the program was not publicized—thus limiting access—partly in response to a fear of public criticism about a military program during the Vietnam War. Among the services of the program is locating soldiers who have lost contact with their homes. When the Red Cross receives a request from a member of a soldier's family, it traces the solider through the base.

Cash assistance of up to $50 is dispensed to veterans or present members of the military. The major contingency is that the problem must be "directly connected to the military experience"—for example, a veteran might have drug problems stemming from time spent in the army, or may have a delayed military pension check. The verification procedure is relatively tight. A formal application is used, military bases are contacted to verify the information, and a set of rules governs eligibility. Assistance may be withheld from "chronic" repeaters or those facing continuing rather than emergency problems.

The disaster program is partly designed to deal with large-scale acts of God, but more frequently in Midwest County it provides assistance to victims of fires. The fire department notifies the Red Cross about a major fire, and a Red Cross volunteer comes to the scene to dispense emergency aid. Volunteers are authorized to issue food and clothing vouchers as well as vouchers for emergency lodging, all according to strict guidelines.

The following day, when a victim and a Red Cross worker make a long-term plan, additional aid may be offered. The intention of the aid is not to replace all goods that are lost; rather, the Red Cross desires to give people a start in rebuilding their lives. For example, a repairman's tools will be replaced if they are lost, so that he can work; if anyone else loses tools they will not be replaced. There are firm national guidelines on such issues, and also a national rule that aid be limited to a 30-day supply of goods, barring unusual events. Food assistance is provided for a maximum of 2 weeks. Only two changes of clothing are furnished. Rent is typically paid only for the remainder of the month during which the disaster occurred. Most aid is in the form of vouchers.

The Red Cross appears to be much like a typical public agency in the manner in which emergency aid is rationed. The agency limits aid in a number of ways. It avoids publicizing one program (for veterans); it limits eligible groups (veterans or military persons in one program) or covers restricted circumstances (disasters in the second program). Verification is standard, and rules determine the amount of aid to be dispensed. Long-term aid and repeaters cause concern. And there are maximum benefits.

This pattern of selectivity is a common one, particularly for secular agencies. A newspaper in West Virginia County runs "The Special Fund," a material assistance program funded by the publisher, which carries selectivity to an extreme. The agency dispenses rather large grants to cover many needs, from furniture to rent to utilities. But aid is only given to particularly deserving cases—especially to those caught up in heart-rending situations. (Private agencies take particular satisfaction in funding this condition.) Fully 75% of applicants are turned down. About three-fourths of the aid goes to needy families, defined by the program as more legitimate than individuals. In every case, a verification process is undertaken that includes telephone calls to selected individuals. Aid is normally in the form of vouchers or vendor payments, not cash. This aid is a once-in-a-lifetime proposition.

Many such programs seem to have a strong bias to serve the "deserving." Though aid is hard to come by in Texas County, an extensive program functions for soldiers in the local military base. The military agency dispenses about $300,000 a year in direct assistance and covers a number of different needs. Individuals have received grants that average $200 and that can be as high as $750 without special approval. About half of the aid is in the form of loans. Members of the military and veterans can receive such aid whether they are the victims of unforeseen emergencies, have mismanaged money, or have failed to receive a check. All are treated equally, though chronic repeaters are more likely to get loans than grants.

Some material assistance programs are less selective in the clients they serve, rationing instead the amount of aid and separating clients into those who should receive more or less assistance. Catholic Charities uses this technique (see Chapter 4). It dispenses a wide range of supplies from food vouchers to furniture. It serves transients, local families, and the elderly: virtually anyone who may have a need for short-term material assistance. But all aid is in the form of vouchers. This both assures that the assistance is used for the determined need and saves money, because the agency gets discounts from Greyhound, a local gasoline station, and a local supermarket. In addition, single male transients who appear to be drifters are limited to a small food basket and perhaps enough gasoline to move on. Local families who have run out of cash are treated more generously.

To assess needs, workers carry out a verification procedure based upon a written application. There are also a number of rules concerning who may be aided and how much aid should be dispensed. Workers may dispense aid on their own authority up to about $50; beyond that amount, higher-level approval is necessary.

Very rarely will an agency dispense goods without selectivity or verification. Generally such agencies ration goods by dispensing very limited amounts. One example is the "Christian Ministry" in Texas County. This agency is located in a distant, resort suburb within the county. It is partly a church and partly a service program run for the many low-income people on fixed incomes in the community. Among its services is a craft program for the elderly.

Nevertheless, about two or three persons request material assistance each day—up from two or three a week the year before. Most are either elderly or transients looking for jobs. Aid is given to all who ask; as the director told us, "It always bothers me that there are people in some agencies who believe they can tell who needs help and who doesn't. I can't tell, just like I can't tell who needs to be saved and who doesn't."

The ability of the agency to dispense aid so freely is partly a function of the fact that financial support comes from a church in a distant city, where the obviously charismatic director had once worked. Nevertheless, money is tight and aid is limited. Cash awards of $10 or $15 are generally given—down from the $25 awards that were common two years ago, when applicants were fewer. The director at one time also referred those in need to jobs, but now few jobs are available.

The pattern so far appears to be that religiously oriented agencies tend to be less selective. This is often but not always the case. For example, as Chapter 4 pointed out, the St. Vincent De Paul Society in Midwest County was quite selective, and in fact appears to be very similar to The Special Fund in West Virginia County. The major difference is a firmer desire to offer counseling in the religious agency.

In general it can be said that there is some differentiation among the fifteen agencies in this group. Secular agencies often have a mission that is legitimated on the basis of serving a particularly worthy client group. As a result, aid is limited to that group. The focus may be on veterans, disaster victims, current members of the armed forces, or those who are experiencing unusual, morally acceptable problems. Five agencies in the case study have this pattern. Another form of selectivity is by neighborhood or ethnic group—the four Community Action and ethnic programs and the settlement house in West Virginia County (described in Chapter 4) have such a focus.

Of the six religiously oriented agencies, all but St. Vincent De Paul tend to have fewer formal requirements for eligibility. Nevertheless, some internal selectivity between the deserving and undeserving may occur. Families are aided more often than single people, and those who desire to work also tend to receive more aid. Alternately, aid may be rationed by limiting the size of individual benefits. In general, the good-works ideology appears to result in fewer formal selection criteria, but it does not rule out internal attempts to make choices in the amount of aid offered.

Nevertheless, there are many continuities across agencies. As with public agencies, few attempts are made to publicize most programs. Formal application forms plus some amount of verification are also quite common. In addition, aid is generally dispensed in the form of vouchers or vendor payments, not cash. Also, in perhaps half of the programs, repeat requests tend to be denied or at least discouraged. Another continuity is that very few programs condition aid on budget counseling, and none requires any type of religious service.

The general-purpose agencies appear to be most interested in meeting an immediate need fairly, within a definition of who is deserving of aid. All the basic ideologies involve service, not conversion, and the programs are thus unlikely to demand much of those who receive an award. Rationing is quite similar to the pattern in public agencies. In both sectors the point of the program is to meet certain needs, and little else. The rough consistency of ideology results in a rough consistency of practices.

Special-Purpose Programs

Some material assistance programs are established for a special purpose—that is, to meet one kind of need only. To be sure, emergency shelter fits this category, but there are other programs that do not include housing, and they tend to be similar to one another. Generally special-purpose programs are established by a special funding source that has its own priorities; the agency merely carries out the wishes of others. In our sample, most of the special programs are emergency energy programs, funded by the federal government but administered by Community Action agencies, though this is not the only possible pattern for dispensing energy assistance. An energy program in Pennsylvania is a special agency set up by a benefactor. While unusual, special programs also exist in the private sector. In one of the twelve counties not visited, a special program dispensed shoes to the needy, the program having been established by a benefactor who, as a child, did not have shoes.

Those programs established by a benefactor may overlap with a government program, but this is not critical to their operation; they may be established through a very old foundation that does not at all relate to recent public programs. In the case of the energy programs, the material assistance awards are dictated by the federal government.

Most such programs have fairly rigid rationing rules, established by those who offer the funds. The programs may dispense aid to many in need of the particular good or service, but only if very specific eligibility criteria are met. Often the programs appear to have little leeway, although there is always some discretion to deal with repeat requests and to determine how often the private program will be utilized.

The emergency energy program offered by the Midwest Community Action Agency seems to exemplify many of the patterns. It has five offices in Midwest County and uses a media campaign to alert the community of its benefits. A means test restricts access. The workers establish why heat has been (or will be) disconnected and what is needed to reestablish heat. Supervisors in a central location make the final decision.

This program supplements a standard grant dispensed to those who meet the basic criteria for eligibility. Thus, in theory it is highly discretionary. However, the agency does not use all of its discretion. There are predetermined amounts of aid for each request, dependent on family size and other criteria. Repeat requests receive half of the amount granted previously. When third requests are made in a single winter, the agency will provide aid, but will notify the welfare department. The head of the program noted that the agency fears that clients decide to use their cash for other purposes because they know that a grant exists to pay for energy emergencies. But the agency seldom turns anyone down. The rules developed concerning repeaters all continue aid, for if aid were refused and someone froze to death as a result, the public response would be sensational.

Thus special-purpose programs (four are in the sample) are relatively straightforward and similar. They meet one set of needs. They are limited by this constraint, by verification rules, and by norms favoring dispensing equal grants. Little other selectivity is possible given the conditions under which all special-purpose programs in our sample were established.

Material Aid Programs as Side Programs

There are also a small number of programs that are less central to the agencies in which they reside, almost afterthoughts. These programs meet important needs that arise in the context of the more general mission of the agency. The material assistance program appears to be provided because it is a logical extension of another, more central service, not because it is highly valued in itself.

These side programs have very little overlap with government because they tend to address needs that are not public priorities. In general, side programs are conducted by national organizations that furnish services not covered by public agencies.

The side programs are small and highly discretionary. As mentioned earlier, the March of Dimes, while normally dispensing funds to doctors and hospitals for research and equipment, does devote a very small proportion of its budget to the emergency needs of families whose children have birth defects. In West Virginia County the March of Dimes dispenses $4000 to $5000 a year in aid, largely because community sentiment strongly favors direct assistance. Referrals must come from a hospital, a doctor, or a social worker. Grants, which may run up to $1000, can be used to help a family defray bills after an infant dies, or may cover specific medical needs that other programs do not cover, such as hearing aids. The program receives only about ten to twenty requests a year. Few are turned down. However, checks are generally sent to the hospital or vendor rather than to the client, and access is limited by keeping publicity to a minimum.

Such programs are common in other health settings. The American Cancer Society often provides nursing help for families of cancer victims, and organizations that serve the handicapped may provide aid to purchase crutches or other equipment. In all of these medically related cases, referrals tend to come from professionals, and aid is limited to health care needs. Within these limits aid is frequent—there are few moral concerns when dealing with health.

One side program is somewhat atypical. Jewish Community Council of Texas County has an emergency aid program that is only for Jews. The program is supported by the national United Jewish Appeal. In Texas County there are only about 1500 Jews, so that the universe of individuals who are served is small. In fact, the agency's other service programs are open to the general public (they primarily involve recreational activities and other community services).

The director of the agency sees each person who desires aid—about five or six a month. Nearly all are transients who have come to Texas to avoid the winter. The director ascertains that they are Jewish and dispenses cash for food, clothing, or shelter. But the budget is small and aid is generally limited to about $15. The director will only dispense larger sums with the approval of the board of directors.

Though this is a very tiny program, it should be noted that it is taken seriously. Often the director refers people to other agencies. He may even spend part of his day transporting his client. The director of the agency was more aware of other resources than any other person we talked to in town. The agency also has other tangible programs not limited to Jews. These include lending equipment for medical use, and helping the elderly obtain appropriate nursing care. Basically, the agency has a philosophy of serving the needs of the community. It dispenses emergency aid as part of that philosophy.

In sum, side programs tend to be conducted by national organizations concerned with some broader—though related—issue. Owing to the small size of the eligible population, the programs tend to be informal and have few discretionary aspects. A limited amount or type of aid is given freely to those perceived as deserving within the limits of the program.

Conclusion

Private agencies that dispense material aid, severely limited by the resources available to them, resort to rationing. The rationing decisions agencies make demonstrate some amount of sensitivity to the most crucial unmet needs. One of the major ways of dealing with scarcity is to limit the type of circumstances to which an agency responds.

Private agencies focus on shelter, food, and clothing to a very large degree—areas that may be overlooked by public agencies. In many agencies, aid is dispensed to deal with severe, immediate, life-threatening problems.

This aid, however, is often of limited duration. Private agencies keep expenses down by limiting shelter stays, dispensing enough groceries for only several days, and discouraging repeat requests within specified lengths of time. This form of rationing, of course, is common to the public sector as well; the major difference is that private agencies dispense less aid to each individual because they have less to offer.

The private sector also tends to mirror the public in its selectivity concerning client groups. The majority of shelters, meal programs, food pantries, general agencies, and specialized agencies tend to serve almost all who need a given good, the major exceptions being shelter programs that serve only men or only women and military programs. More frequently, there is some selectivity on an informal basis. Agencies may refuse aid to those who appear to abuse the system, or (in the case of religious missions) who are poor candidates for reform. The able-bodied might receive less aid than families with children, owing to a perception that the former can work, or at least that their needs are not as important as those of children.

If anything, the verification requirements of private agencies tend to be less strict than those of the public sector. Dealing with those who are in crisis, agencies tend to take a client's word. General agencies and those with a single good to offer are more likely to verify needs and to have more rules and procedures than other private agencies, but in general, rules seem to be less strict in private agencies than in public ones. The use of vouchers is one area in which private agencies are a bit more restrictive.

Again looking only at general patterns, in many cases private agencies are even less likely than public agencies to impose conditions. Most do not require a religious service, budget counseling, and so forth. Time constraints and the philosophy of most agencies limit these practices. But there are some differences between the sectors. One is that private agencies may demand that clients exhaust public benefits first (public agencies can do the opposite). The reason is resource-related—such coordination seems to have increased as monetary resources have become more limited.

One should not paint a picture of the private sector that ignores its variability and selectively. Particularly in housing, aid may be combined with moral or religious sentiments that limit eligibility and make demands on clients. Church services are required in religiously oriented shelters, and often those who wish to stay in the facility for a long time must express a willingness to convert. These and other agencies may weed out those who appear to be particularly undeserving. Private agencies are under no legal obligation to aid anyone.

The patterns of rationing can be explained by the missions agencies develop, either on their own or owing to external pressure. The food pantries offered by churches reveal the strong role of the expectations of others: Churches are expected to feed the hungry, even though they may be reluctant to spend time dealing with material, rather than spiritual, needs. Some side programs also exist as a logical extension of a mission that reflects long-standing expectations. Some officials told us that the March of Dimes prefers to make major purchases of equipment or provide training programs, rather than dispensing material aid. But communities continue to expect the agency to deliver some material assistance. Such assistance, dispensed to individuals or families with needs that fit within the general missions of agencies, tends to be dispensed with a minimal amount of selectivity or requirements.

Good-works philosophies, on the other hand, may make agencies somewhat more autonomous. Catholic Charities meets needs that reflect a religious tradition not demanded by parishioners. Such agencies are often less selective than others; they spread aid equally among needy individuals they cannot choose between. But many refuse aid to single persons in order to aid families, and they ration resources by setting limits on repeat requests.

Like good-works agencies, Community Action agencies and ethnic self-help agencies consider aid to individuals as an end in itself. These agencies appear to owe particular allegiance to a community or group and tend to view members of the group as deserving. Thus, though these small programs ration aid by giving each applicant a limited amount, selectivity and verification appear to be minimal.

The extreme internal mission is that of religious conversion. The conversion orientation appears to be most distinct from the mission of public agencies, and the services are also most distinct. A desire to change behavior dominates the rationing procedure of such agencies.

It must be concluded that although private agencies meet very important needs, there is a clear relation between mission, external pressures, and forms of rationing. Because missions and pressures reflect a wide variety of ideologies, the resulting rationing strategies are not necessarily tied to analyses of the level of need. The fact that rationing patterns reflect missions means that there is no guarantee that all needs are met or that the most needy are always aided. Rather, many agencies deal with only part of the problems for which assistance is required, that part that reflects their values or the values of the communities in which they are located.

CHAPTER 7

Clients and Agencies

Private agencies must inevitably be judged by their effectiveness in meeting the needs of clients: by filling gaps in the public system, adapting to local conditions, and responding with sensitivity to those they serve. We have seen in previous chapters some of the difficulties private agencies face in reaching these goals. Many are not oriented toward meeting all needs, since there are limits to community generosity. Another part of the issue, not yet examined, is the extent to which the specific demands of clients correspond to the services agencies offer. This chapter focuses on the demand. What are client needs and how successfully are these needs met?

Housing Needs: Surveys of Clients

No need is more sensitive than that for housing; a place to stay at night is a grave necessity, especially during cold winters in the North. Probably due more to its cost than its availability, housing is a growing problem. Recent estimates by a national coalition indicate that there may be 2 million homeless individuals (Hombs and Synder, 1982). A federal report estimates that between 250,000 and 600,000 individuals are homeless each night (U.S. Department of Housing and Urban Development [HUD], 1984). Some of the homeless find emergency housing, but the majority (according to both reports listed above) live in tent cities or over heat vents on city streets on any given night.

Who are the homeless? This is not an easy question to answer. Many such individuals try to stay "invisible," and others move in circles that interviewers cannot approach. One way of understanding this group is to look at those with a potential to be homeless, those living in boarding houses or cheap hotels. In fact, the reduction in the number of such facilities may be partly to blame for recent increases in homelessness (Kasinitz, 1984).

LOCAL SURVEYS

A survey of 194 residents in 43 such facilities was completed in Milwaukee County in 1978 (Goodrick and Howden, 1978). The facilities included rooming houses, in which rooms are rented to unrelated people who share common areas, boarding houses, and "second-class dwellings"—apartments with shared baths.

The survey reveals that about one-half of the residents are much like the common view of transients, in that they are able-bodied and unemployed. They are middle-aged (65% of all in the sample are over 40) Caucasians (85%). The vast majority are male. The other half of the residents receive social security benefits or SSI, and many of these are elderly or partly disabled. Both groups have very limited incomes. Of those receiving social security or SSI benefits, 82% receive $300 a month or less; 20% of all respondents have a monthly income that is less than or equal to the cost of room and board.

Not only are the respondents poor, but they also have many problems. In the judgment of either the respondent or interviewer, one-fourth of them had an alcohol problem. Twenty-eight percent of the total population in the survey have had a previous admission to a mental hospital, nursing home, or similar facility; this represents a majority of the SSI recipients under age 65.

Some of those receiving disability payments from social security appear to be part of a group that has come to be known as the CMIs, the chronically mentally ill. Until the mid- or late 1970s, many such individuals frequently checked in and out of state mental hospitals. But deinstitutionalization reduced the use of this option; the number of available beds has been cut by two-thirds nationwide. Ideally, communities have an outpatient treatment program for the CMIs, but in practice this is the case in a small number of cities. More often, the CMIs must fend for themselves, without jobs and often without the capacity for complex social interactions.

Another set of data comes from those applying for shelter. During 1981 Milwaukee County adopted a central intake unit for most of its facilities to demonstrate the range of the needy (Wisconsin Information Service, 1982). The unit completed a survey of those asking for shelter. According to the survey, of those requesting shelter, 34% were single men, 30% single women, and 36% were in families. This high proportion of women and families occurs in part because the men-only rescue missions are not included in the survey. (Unlike mission residents, 68% in this survey were between ages 20 and 39.)

Nevertheless, the large percentage of families may also have to do with the state of the economy. Thus direct economic problems were given as the most important reason for seeking emergency shelter for about half of the cases. Twenty-six percent of the applicants simply said they had no income, about 18% were evicted owing to nonpayment of rent, and 5.4% were forced out of overcrowded dwellings. In addition, roughly 20% recently suffered a family conflict that led to homelessness, and 4.6% had been discharged from an institution. Only 4.2% were labeled "chronic street people."

Both of the above surveys grossly underestimate need. Individuals who do not ask for help, either because they have been turned down before, or do not desire housing, or do not know about its availability, cannot easily be surveyed. Nevertheless, it is clear that there is a good deal of homelessness and a large proportion of individuals who do not ever stay in shelters. For example, the Milwaukee survey notes that 15.4% of those who asked for housing stayed on the street the night before. Another 3.7% were in transit.

Further, large proportions of those applying to the Information Service were turned away—56% of all requests. In the overwhelming majority of cases there were no available beds; for small percentages, eligibility requirements or behavioral problems led to refusal. Roughly 40% of families are turned down, as are the vast majority of those who are single.

According to the survey, those with economic problems are most likely to be turned away, while runaway youth make up a much larger proportion of those served than of all requesting shelter. The chronically mentally ill are also accepted in facilities more than the average. In fact, it is possible that this discrepancy accounts for some controversy about the homeless. For example, a survey of New York's homeless (Crystal et al., 1983) found 34% of the clients suffering "only" a psychiatric problem, while 19% had a purely economic problem. But the survey included long-term shelter at the type of facilities that, as we will argue later, are the least desirable to the needy and most likely to serve CMIs. The study thus overrepresents those with chronic problems as compared to the Milwaukee study, as may other studies that imply that one-half of the homeless are mentally ill (Hombs and Snyder 1982; Arce et al., 1983; Lamb, 1984).

When people are turned away, where do they go? We know that many live on the streets, stay in bus terminals, or simply wander. Others find temporary lodgings with friends or relatives (roughly half of those who called the Milwaukee Service had stayed with relatives or friends the night before). But the numbers who use each alternative are in question. We do know, however, that there is a great need. Public defenders of Milwaukee County believe that one-fourth of the commitments to mental hospitals occur because there are no other beds available (Zandar, 1980).

Even when temporary shelter is available, it may not solve the entire problem. A survey in Madison, Wisconsin, found "cycles" of need. Those who need emergency housing for long periods are especially vulnerable (City of Madison, 1982):

> Observers commented that the greater the length of the homelessness situation, the greater the difficulties associated with obtaining satisfactory long-term housing arrangements. Thus, homeless individuals tend to become entrapped in a cycle of diminishing resources which contribute to physical and psychological concerns of increasing magnitude. (p. 3)

A study in Boston suggests that the lack of permanent housing, continuing low incomes, chronic mental health or alcohol problems, and (for battered women) a need for security mean that temporary shelter is only a first step (McGerigle et al., 1979). How people solve their long-term problems is unclear. Agency directors believe that some individuals are continually homeless and survive by moving from place to place, staying in shelters or on the street, without the resources that are needed to find a permanent residence. Often one needs a permanent address to receive welfare benefits, but without benefits, rent cannot be paid. Similarly, if a homeless person finds a job, he or she may not be able to wait three weeks for the first check and pay a security deposit, and thus shelter cannot be purchased until the first paycheck arrives.

For those who remain homeless, life is grim. It is characterized by a constant search for food, shelter, and safety. Day-to-day problems include attempting to "blend in" with others on buses and in parks, in order to avoid being forced to leave; looking for restrooms and timing intake of food and drink to take advantage of the hours in which such facilities are available; and trying to avoid the winter cold. A low estimate of deaths from exposure during the winter of 1981 in 13 cities was 539 (Hombs and Snyder, 1982).

For the chronic homeless, assault and brutalization may be common. One reporter who lived on the streets reported this incident:

> Norton, Blair's security guard, came outside with his nightstick to look for fun. . . . He swaggered outside and declared, "All right, single up, single up. Whoever ain't in line don't sleep here tonight. . . ." Most of the men scrambled back against the base of the four-story brick school house. . . .
>
> "Didn't I tell you to move, man?" Norton hollered at one scarlet-eyed old drunk who appeared too wasted to budge. . . . The old man stood his ground, peering at Norton with perplexed eyes. . . .
>
> When Norton grabbed him by the collar and prepared to rap him with the stick, another bum zig-zagged his way down the line to get a closer look. Norton, still

holding the other man, said to this bum, "Did I invite you, nigger? Get back in your own damn category."

So this onlooker was drawn into the ring and began talking his own brand of dignity. Norton grabbed him first and leveled his nightstick twice. . . . Norton dragged him by the back of the collar out in the middle of I Street and told him to find somewhere else to sleep that night. Then Norton came back and told the other old drunk to leave unless he, too, wanted the stick. The drunk mumbled and turned his back and slowly walked toward the street, but Norton hit him twice more for good measure across the top of his hunched back and the bum fell into the street cursing and shaking his fist. . . . (Hombs and Snyder, 1982, pp. 112, 113)

A NATIONAL STUDY

The advantage of much of the above material is that it includes a rather intensive examination of the homeless. The Milwaukee studies are particularly noteworthy in their apparently near-universal coverage of those who ask for shelter, along with their reliance on detailed surveys of individuals. However, these surveys provide data on only one locality.

In an attempt to develop national data, the U.S. Department of Housing and Urban Development (1984) carried out a national survey. Existing reports, estimates from those who run shelters, the perceptions of public officials, and the perceptions of other knowledgeable people were used to estimate the number of homeless in randomly selected cities. An independent estimate of the number living on the street was conducted in three cities.

The estimate from existing reports suggests that there are 586,000 homeless individuals each night. The authors claim, however, that the estimate uses the highest figures available in the reports, which may bias figures upwards. It also assumes that a few homeless are to be found in suburbs (those were not surveyed), and thus the figures are biased downwards. Nevertheless, this is the highest estimate in the government report.

Other sections of the report rely more on estimates from those who operate shelters, bolstered by the few examinations of those living on the streets. Using such methodologies, the report suggests that there may be between 250,000 and 350,000 homeless on a given night.

This figure is of course far below the estimate of an advocate group that there are between 2 and 3 million homeless (Hombs and Snyder, 1982). The differences largely reflect modes of counting those who live on the streets, with the advocates claiming that there are much larger numbers than are generally counted. Most counts of people on the street tend to underestimate the homeless, owing to the difficulty of locating those living in automobiles, abandoned buildings, or other illegal shelters. Some advocates have even suggested that the HUD study ignores small shelters and asked shelter operators for numbers in ways that resulted in underestimates. For now it can only be said that the estimates differ widely.

Interestingly, the national study admits that there are only 110,000 beds for the homeless in the nation, suggesting a ratio of 178 individuals living on the street to 100 living in shelters. Need is greater than resources according to all studies.

Needs for Material Assistance

MINNEAPOLIS SURVEY

Evidence about need is often confined to agency data, which will be summarized in the next section. Fortunately, there has been one comprehensive examination of individuals in need. This was completed in Hennepin County (Minneapolis is the central city) in May 1982 (Urban Coalition of Minneapolis, 1982). This very complete survey includes interviews with 1097 individuals applying for emergency aid in 17 agencies. It should be noted that one surveyed agency was the public Department of Welfare; thus the study is not solely of those using private resources.

The range of individuals in some financial need seems even more diverse than the range in housing. These individuals were of all ages: 49% were between ages 26 and 40; 21% were older; while 30% were younger. Three-fourths of all applicants had children but only 11% were currently living with spouses. Unlike housing residents and applicants, only 12% lived alone. Even in Minneapolis, the majority of applicants were nonwhite. Women made up 62% of the sample, perhaps representing the feminization of poverty along with the fact that women tend to have custody of children and be less transient and thus more likely to use emergency services unrelated to housing.

Needless to say, the respondents tended to be quite poor: 16% had no income at all and 56% reported a family income under $500 a month. Roughly one-half of those reporting income received AFDC; food stamp recipients were similarly distributed. Others—less than 10%—received social security, General Assistance, SSI, or unemployment compensation. Only 14% reported steady jobs, and 12% received income from day labor. About 40% of the recipients did not receive public welfare benefits of any sort. The population included those who are less likely than average to be able to obtain a job. About half did not complete high school, for example.

While the survey did not ask about general life circumstances or crises that led to coming to the agency, it provided rich detail about the general economic situation of the recipients. Most, obviously, relied on private agencies because they were short of cash. At times this shortage was exacerbated by the activities of the public sector. Very large percentages had problems in maintaining their public welfare benefits. Twenty-one percent had been removed from the welfare rolls; another 18% reported reductions during the last year. Only 31% of these were able to make up the reduction by working; 26% had made no adjustment; 18% began to delay bills longer or otherwise reduce their life-style, such as by eating less. Some obtained cash by selling blood or begging (10–15% relied on each).

The respondents' hard times are also apparent in their housing arrangements. Although nearly 80% lived in somewhat permanent housing, frequent displacement was common. During the previous year, 45% had been forced to move, mostly owing to the high cost of housing. Another problem was utility bills: 30% had a utility shut-off notice during the last year.

The ex-institutionalized were also highly represented in this sample. Thirty percent of the sample had been in an institution during the last year. Most of these had been in drug or alcohol programs, and about one-fourth had been in jail. Only 4.8% of all respondents had previously been in mental institutions—the previously institutionalized chronically mentally ill were a small proportion of all in need.

What needs did these individuals have, and how well were they met? The majority needed the basics: food or clothing. This need indicates total destitution. Other needs varied greatly, except for the need for housing, required in about one-seventh of the cases.

The questionnaire did not ask about the adequacy of the services received, but did ask about past services. As Table 7.1 demonstrates, there were some unmet needs in each category. Roughly one-third did not receive the food they needed, and larger amounts did not have housing or clothing needs met.

The unanswered question is what individuals do when these very basic needs are not met. In the short run, some seem to go from agency to agency. Thus, only 23% of the sample said they were using an agency for the first time. The use, however, is not very frequent: 50% relied on a facility once a month or less often. Indeed, chronic users were rare, as

TABLE 7.1
Success in Obtaining Emergency Services Other Than Those Received at the Agency Where the Coalition's Survey Was Completed

	No. reporting "service needed"	No. reporting "found agency to meet the need"	Reported needs met (%)
Health care	122	92	75.4%
Meal	166	133	80.1
Food shelf	589	392	66.6
Housing	423	259	61.2
Clothing	222	139	62.6
Personal	287	176	61.3
Emergency	67	37	55.2
Transportation	108	56	51.8
Work	116	38	32.7

Source: Urban Coalition of Minneapolis, 1982, p. 8.

only 16% reported using an agency for three years or longer. The majority seem to have used an agency a small number of times during the past two years; only 32% had been using agencies less than a month.

When clients were asked where they would go first to handle a financial problem, 30% said they would rely on friends, 38% on their family, 11% on the church, 11% on a public agency, and less than 1%—eight responses out of the entire sample—said they would go to a private agency first. Thus, by the time these people are turned down by private agencies, they are at the end of the line—with no place else to go.

BALTIMORE SURVEY

As with the homeless, the perceived nature of the clients for other material assistance varies with the survey. Surveys that study the most needy understandably reveal more serious, long-term client problems. One such study was of soup kitchens in the city of Baltimore (Chaiklin, 1983). Interviewed were 271 individuals in 17 of the roughly 30 soup kitchens in the city. The survey noted that rather large percentages of the clients appeared to have long-term mental health needs. Twenty-eight percent had been in mental hospitals in the last ten years. Fourteen percent had been outpatients in mental hospitals (these were usually the same individuals who were inpatients at one time). The author of the study believes that the results may indicate that some of the deinstitutionalized were simply "cut loose," with no follow-up outpatient care after release. The interviewers he used believed that 28% of the sample needed mental health treatment and that 15% were on the edge of need.

Another finding was that 13% had participated in alcohol programs, while an additional 17% claimed need for such a program. Based on admittedly unreliable interviewer judgments, the report concluded that roughly 40% appeared to have some type of alcohol problem.

The survey, unfortunately, did not ask respondents why they needed a soup kitchen. But it did ascertain some of their characteristics: 34% claimed to be homeless, and 41% claimed they had no income. Of those with an income, 80% received support from a government program rather than from employment.

Slightly over one-half were between the ages of 20 and 39, and about 60% were single. The author believed that this indicated a somewhat larger proportion of middle-aged or older individuals than many suppose. Roughly half of the respondents had children.

Comparing these statistics to the Minneapolis study, a much larger concentration of individuals with alcohol and mental health problems is apparent. The results probably indicate that certain specialized facilities attract clients with the most serious problems. Yet even in Baltimore, those with emotional and alcohol problems were in a minority. Though many had serious difficulties that could not be solved by a meal or a short-term material assistance program, this was not universally the case.

How Private Agencies React to Client Needs

Most of the fieldwork for this study was carried out during particularly hard times, the recession of 1980–1983. As unemployment rose and public welfare benefits were reduced, the pressures on private resources intensified greatly. An analysis of the responses of private agencies to the growing need demonstrates the extent to which the private sector may compensate for limits in public welfare and the flexibility with which it deals with new demands from those who need material aid.

Evidence concerning the private sector as a whole suggests that the potential for response is limited. In Chapter 5 an examination of the relation between community variables and the extensiveness of the emergency assistance network indicated that private emergency assistance is only slightly more available in communities with lower public welfare benefits. In addition, the total number of relevant private agencies apparently is not larger when need is greater. These results are only cross-sectional, but if private agencies do not offer much more aid in communities in which need is greater, it appears unlikely that increases in need will correlate with dramatic increases in private services for material needs within a given community.

Furthermore, a decrease in support of the private sector by the public sector was coterminous with the recession. While very little public support directly involves material assistance (as we have demonstrated), public funds affect the size of the entire private network, and thus a decrease may have an indirect bearing on material aid. When there are fewer agencies, the potential universe of those who may dispense material aid is smaller.

In a study relating the size of the budgets of private agencies to the amount of financial support available across states, Weisbrod and Schiff (1982) determined that when public financial support in a state is lower, private sources indeed provide larger contributions to private agencies. But this compensation only accounts for about 40% of the variance in support from government—60% of the "loss" is not compensated for. In addition, when compared to all state expenditures for welfare, the increase in private giving represents a minuscule amount. The evidence suggests that private agencies may not even be able to compensate for all of the reductions in support from the government.

CASE STUDIES

To gain more information, historical trends were investigated in each case-study county, both by asking about program changes at the original interview and by telephoning agencies one year after the original visit.

In West Virginia County, Information and Referral, the central intake agency, periodically totals client statistics. Most people requesting aid apply to this agency, so a relatively complete picture of the pattern of demand is evident. Between 1981 and 1983, reported need altered dramatically. The agency reported an increase from an average of 220 cases each month to about 650 cases a month 2 years later.

The new cases brought new problems to private agencies. In 1981 (just before our interviews took place), most clients were current recipients of AFDC—about 176 cases a month. Those not on the welfare rolls rarely applied. But 2 years later, 440 families a month who did not receive welfare applied for aid through the clearinghouse agency, six times the 1981 total. The number of AFDC families applying, which dropped, owing to restrictions in eligibility for public welfare, stood at 130. The tendency of the community to respond largely to AFDC recipients may also have changed, leading in part to the alterations in client characteristics. A small part of the increase might also be artifactual; one agency in town, Christian Food Bank, became more strict about referring all cases through Information and Referral in the intervening years (see Chapter 6). But this agency serves only about 100 families a month, and therefore its policy cannot account for the statistical patterns.

Even in this community, which had an unusually high interest in meeting material needs, the response to changing conditions was limited. No new agencies developed to deal with material needs. Budgets of existing agencies did not increase substantially as need expanded, and agencies thus generally could not significantly alter their programs. The Special Fund, the agency linked to a newspaper chain, continued to dispense aid only for rare, spectacular emergencies; the Red Cross simply was not heavily involved in meeting the emergency needs of families. A third agency, the Salvation Army, witnessed only a "small increase" in applicants, because Information and Referral assumed that the Salvation Army could not expand its caseload dramatically and therefore held referrals down. Christian Food Bank responded to increased demand by actually cutting back aid (see Chapter 6).

Two agencies, West Virginia Settlement House and the Rescue Mission, seem to have expanded their caseloads. But neither was able to meet need fully. The settlement house was simply forced to cut back on the average amount of aid offered. For example, food vouchers were reduced from $25 per family to $10 per family. The agency still claims to focus on AFDC recipients. The Rescue Mission experienced a 20% increase in the number of families it served, but the facility is nearly full. It also had to enforce rules on maximum length of stay more strictly.

The agencies in Texas County, limited to begin with, clearly could not respond in any large way to increases in demand—particularly since demand burgeoned between 1981 and 1983. Catholic Charities witnessed a doubling in applications for aid between 1980 and 1981 and another doubling in 1982, while the rural Christian Ministry noted an increase in demand from two or three applicants a week to two or three a day. No dramatic response occurred. Both agencies were forced to cut back on the amount of aid offered: vouchers for food were trimmed by more than half to an average of about $10 a family. A similar decrease occurred in the benefits dispensed by the Jewish Community Council.

No relevant new agencies developed, but some existing agencies were able to meet part of the increase in demand. The Religious Help Mission increased the number of individuals it took in, from 82 a day to 113 a day within 2 years. But because the facility has only 125 beds, further increases were clearly not to be expected. The Naval Relief Society, funded through payroll deductions of current military employees, was able to increase its budget by 27% as minimal salary increases and inflation made things more difficult for some members of the armed services. Only this relatively wealthy agency, catering to the needs of veterans and employees of the military, believes it was able to keep up with demand in Texas County.

In Pennsylvania County, the difficulty in meeting needs was somewhat mitigated by the growth in two large agencies over the last few years. (No other agencies grew or responded significantly to increased demand.) The Salvation Army noted a tripling of applicants for aid between 1980 and 1982, and apparently its budget grew enough for it to be able to meet the demand. As has been mentioned (see Chapter 4), part of the increase in aid included the addition of a food bank, supported with the help of the United Way. Looking at available 3-month totals for January through March of 1983, 2389 families and 692 transient men were served in the agency's material aid programs, up from 841 and 396 in the same period in 1981. The Rescue Mission was also able to increase the number of those in its meal program, from 30 to 50 a day from 1981 to 1983. However, the long-term housing it offered was constantly full and was not expanded. The Rescue Mission noted large increases in the number of homeless younger people applying, people who once had very good jobs. The director believes that the agency only "scratches the surface," meeting needs of a very small segment of those who no longer have homes.

Midwest is a large county, and, as such, it adapted in many ways to changing conditions. Some programs expanded; others contracted. Those that dealt with very special needs, such as the Red Cross or March of Dimes, did not increase their budgets or experience particularly large increases in demand; their missions were virtually unaffected by increased levels of poverty.

In other agencies, the increases in demand were dealt with in the usual way: by decreasing the amount of aid offered. For example, the demands on the emergency energy program tripled between 1980 and 1983. At the same time, federal funds for the program were reduced. To deal with shrinking resources, aid was cut for each applicant. A set amount of aid was dispensed for each trip a client made. This amount was reduced as resources grew tighter. Similarly, as has been mentioned, the Inner-City Churches Coalition cut back, like the Christian Food Bank, by creating a central intake agency to ward off demand.

Nevertheless, some response to the growing problems of unemployment were the result of concerted action by United Way, advocacy groups, and the county government. Much attention was paid to housing. The United Way chose to fund Advocates Incorporated to administer a Travelers' Aid program and an advocacy program for health maintenance. County government also funded advocacy efforts of the agency. With this budget, the agency attempted to coordinate an improved housing network. It helped to establish some additional small shelters and was also instrumental in the formation of an advocacy group to lobby for additional county support for the homeless. One outgrowth of lobbying has been an agreement on the part of the county to fund a new shelter. In 1982 the increase did not meet demand; over half of those applying for shelter were turned away each night. By the following year, however, only a very small proportion were turned away, although advocates believe that the shelters still service only a small proportion of the homeless and that some of the facilities are inadequate (see Chapter 8).

Food pantries also expanded, coordinated by another advocacy group, the Food Task Force. This agency is again closely tied to government, having received its original funding through Community Action agencies. It coordinates 70 food banks in Midwest County, collecting statistics to document needs while attempting to ensure that all neighborhoods have at least some program. The agency also helps conduct food drives, such as one held at baseball games each summer. The food that is obtained is dispensed to all food banks in the community. The agency stresses that resources are tight, and food assistance is limited. Yet apparently very few are turned away.

An occasional agency can also increase its program to some extent. Meal programs, for example, seem to have expanded. Catholic Meal Program increased the number of the people it served from 400 a night to 600. The agency never solicited new clients, nor did it advertise its services. It did not even solicit more volunteers. It was able to keep up with demand by expanding to a small degree the quantity of food the volunteers offer while keeping quiet about its availability.

In sum, the communities under study demonstrate somewhat different responses to increased need. In two—West Virginia and Texas counties—a lack of new resources greatly reduced the ability of agencies to respond, except through intensified rationing. Some tightened eligibility conditions, and some reduced the average grant. Only in housing did any expansion in services occur, and here the expansion was very small compared to the need. In the other two counties, some expansion took place, principally with the help of the United Way and the government. The United Way has encouraged some growth in resources in Pennsylvania and Midwest County. In West Virginia County, it has been active for a number of years but was not able to add more resources in the 1980s. In Midwest County funding from county government was used to promote advocacy and inevitably services. Much of the response of private agencies, ironically, is made possible by the active involvement of larger entities, particularly the government.

Obvious differences in the responses of individual agencies stem from their missions as well as from outside funding agencies. Those agencies that consider emergency aid a side program have tended to serve needs that are not closely tied to the overall degree of poverty, and the programs did not expand. Conversion-oriented agencies, while perhaps admitting more individuals to existing programs, appeared to have little interest in expanding to meet needs, or at least have a small ability to expand. Some church-related meal programs have even cut back. Perhaps churches are reluctant to be involved in emergency programs that diminish their capacity to deal with spiritual matters. The agencies that respond to increased need most often are good-works Christian agencies and community-oriented agencies. But many such agencies, having few additional resources to tap, were forced to ration aid further.

Client Responses

Given growing needs but limited resources, how do clients respond to private agencies? It is difficult to conduct in-depth discussions with clients for a number of reasons: They wish to maintain their privacy; it is difficult to predict when they will be at any agency; and the middle of a crisis is not a propitious time to conduct interviews. Nevertheless, to gain some understanding of the client perspective, eighteen such clients were interviewed in five agencies (fictitious names are used throughout). Four clients were interviewed in a group; the rest were interviewed individually.

Just as the private agencies must be placed in a community and societal context, so must the responses of clients. The attempt to obtain benefits from private agencies is part of a broader life situation involving one's culture, friends, relatives, and other agencies. In fact, we found that clients were more interested in talking about their lives in general than about their interactions with private agencies; no surprise, in retrospect, given the limited benefits private agencies dispense and the severe, long-term problems of most of those in need.

Past research suggests that even those in the most straitened circumstances are reluctant to approach private agencies. Harper (1982), in his study of transient men, reports a hierarchy among his subjects. Hobos have the highest status. They generally make their own way, riding the rails, taking temporary jobs, and borrowing from each other. The

"Army bums," those who use the Salvation Army, have the lowest status. It is stigmatizing to wear boots, shoes, or clothes that obviously come from charity. Stealing clothes seems more legitimate. Applying for food stamps—also called into question by some—results in a middle rank in the hierarchy.

There is a small amount of evidence that private agencies are also looked on as a last resort by the poor. In a group interview conducted for a parallel project,[1] women heading poor inner-city families on public welfare reported much contact with churches. But despite need, these women hesitated to ask for aid from their churches or even from others in the community. Asking for aid, they believed, "put them on the other side," that of those who take resources and do not provide them. It is a line that has many connotations for social status, once crossed.

One drawback in our interviews of clients of private agencies is that we spoke only to those who had already crossed this line. Not only had they applied for benefits, but, in most cases, they had obtained some type of award. The dislike of relying on charity, so obvious in other works and in the Minneapolis survey, may not, therefore, be as obvious in responses to our questions.

Carolyn Stack (1972), in her study of a poor black urban community, reports that sharing of resources is central to the life of the poor. Mutual obligation in a network of relatives and friends results in resources being mobilized to reach those who are in crisis. Those who share will receive resources, in turn, when they are in need. Welfare benefits are simply one more resource to be shared. According to Stack, the one-to-one relationship between agency and individual, assumed in most of the public and private sector, is sometimes a fiction. If this is so, the aid of private agencies may be seen as merely a supplement to a network and must be evaluated in the context of the client's social system.

PRIVATE AID AS A LAST RESORT

Because the public welfare network is said to be arbitrary, stigmatizing, degrading, and time-consuming, one might suspect that some people are discouraged from using it and rely on the private aid network as an alternative. But in the sample of 18 cases, this does not seem to be the case. Rather, the private material assistance network seems to be a last resort, used only in the absence of sufficient public funds. Clients generally seem to attempt to obtain the much larger public welfare benefits

[1] This study is being conducted by Sandra Danziger, Institute for Research on Poverty, University of Wisconsin, Madison, Wis.

when possible, and only to turn to the private sector when these are either unobtainable or not sufficient.

Of the 18 completed interviews, 14 of the respondents had contact with public welfare. Three received SSI benefits; three received AFDC benefits; three were receiving General Assistance; and three were at a shelter, on contract from a state division of corrections (a common practice in some Salvation Army units). Interestingly, in two other cases the contact with the public system was indirect. One single man lived with other people who were receiving AFDC; and in a final case, a husband whose wife received SSI benefits was interviewed.

Some of these respondents used private agencies because the public welfare benefits had proved insufficient for an emergency or special need. This was the case for our respondent who lived with his wife on an SSI check. Usually, he claimed, it was sufficient to cover basic expenses in a very run-down apartment. However, extra expenses arose: their dog ended up in a pound, and the funds needed to release it exhausted their food money. Thus he was forced to rely on a meal program for food.

There are also a number of situations in which the rigidity of the public system seems to be at fault. Mary, a recipient of SSI, normally lived in a local YWCA. However, she met a man and moved out to live with him. After 2 weeks the relationship dissolved; the man took the SSI check and absconded. Mary required temporary shelter from a private agency because all of her cash had been taken and SSI would not supplement her grant.

Six interviews took place in private shelters that received public funds. In these instances, the private agency was closely tied to the public system contractually, so that some who received General Assistance benefits or SSI could live in the shelter. The costs of care came directly out of the SSI or GA check. Mental health and alcohol problems determined the choice of these accommodations.

Some of those who were interviewed viewed private agencies as a regular supplement to insufficient public grants. This was particularly true of the meal programs that had no eligibility requirements. One couple received General Assistance benefits, but appeared for a meal every night except Saturday and had been doing so for 2 years. While it might appear that they were abusing the system, their need was real. They had no medical care and said that they probably could not afford to go to a doctor. To them the meal program was a necessary, permanent supplement to an insufficient income. (The grant for one person in this county was about $170 a month, and was slightly over $200 for a couple.)

CLIENT PROBLEMS

In addition to some presenting crisis, the large majority of the respondents had chronic problems, such as mental illness, little education, or long-term unemployment. Cause and effect are hard to measure, but a large majority of the clients had a style of dress, manner, or a life history that could make employment particularly difficult to obtain.

Perhaps one-fourth of them were deinstitutionalized from mental hospitals and continued to have related problems. One young man, for example, appeared to hallucinate during the interview. He would fade in and out of consciousness, repeating a story or answering a question that had not been asked. He had been institutionalized for schizophrenia until he was 18 (at the time of the interview, he was 23). He claimed he had only an eighth-grade education. He had no experience except as a "volunteer nurse," although he could not say where he had been a nurse, or when.

Other respondents had been out of work for years. Rosy, for example, had immigrated from Puerto Rico about fifteen years before. She received AFDC and had never been able to find a job. Although she desired to work, she had only 2 years of formal education and very little knowledge of English. Clearly, her life chances were not very good.

A few also mentioned long-term health problems—although no one we talked to received SSI for a physical disability. A bad back that lasted a number of years, a series of on-the-job injuries, or accidents also seemed to have made it temporarily difficult to obtain a full-time job.

Four others appeared to have no obvious special problems, but simply had been unable to find jobs owing to youth, perhaps racial discrimination, and the deteriorating economic situation for those without a special skill. Jolene, a 32-year-old black woman, had attended a 2-year college and was a licensed practical nurse (LPN). She had been working regularly since she was 16. She had been married, but had separated about a year before the interview and had many old debts. Unfortunately, she had lived in another state until shortly before her separation. She said that she had not been able to obtain a local job or even save enough money to certify her LPN status in her new state. Clearly, her need was real. She donated blood to obtain money for gasoline to go to the welfare department.

The three "true transients" in our sample used material aid when they were between the temporary jobs that had become their way of life. One claimed that he was a long-term alcoholic, although he underplayed the importance of this problem. He mentioned that he had had a long series of jobs as a baker, bus driver, bus mechanic, and foreman in a manufacturing plant. He had received General Assistance for the last few years and was temporarily staying in a shelter, paid for by public welfare. (Six of the 18 clients had lived on the streets on some occasions.)

One respondent reported a history of drifting, work, and alcohol. He was a self-employed farmer for 7 years and then was divorced. He had averaged six jobs a year since that time. He made enough money to get by, and spent any extra on drink. He claimed to have "pulled some bad things" on his family after his divorce so he was no longer welcome at home. He had no plans to contact his family again.

One respondent appeared to attend a meal program more as a social occasion than as a food supplement. Her social world centered on this once-a-week religiously based meal program. On Sundays she sang in the choir of the church providing the meals, and she also helped serve. Although her family visited her occasionally, the program appeared to provide her major human contacts.

Only one client seemed to have less than severe needs. This was a college student who relied on a free meal from a meal program to supplement an otherwise limited income. The student felt no compunction about receiving a meal, claiming that she lived on a limited budget, working her way through school.

NETWORKS

Studies of lower-class life-styles mention the importance of a friendship network in getting by, but most of our respondents did not feel that they had access to such a network. Many were on the outskirts of society, without friends; a few had used up their friends; and others only knew people who were as poor as they. It was rare for an individual both to rely on private agencies and to borrow from friends.

Dave, a married man with no children, had been unemployed for about 2 years. His problems were partly due to a back injury, which was improving. One of the few individuals who did not use public welfare in the sample, Dave also had few other resources. He claimed that most of his friends were on AFDC and had children and could lend him no money. His wife's friends were all alcoholics who were constantly broke. And his family had recently moved to Alaska and left him behind. His father, who had come to his aid in the past, had run out of patience and asked Dave to stay behind when the rest of the family moved to Alaska.

Others seemed to have friends and relatives who would not help.

Mary, who had a mental disability, received a check from SSI. She had four married children living in the area. When her emergency arose, she had asked her children for help. Although she had no place to stay, her children refused to take her in, claiming that they had no room. Mary excused their behavior, saying that "things were pretty tight for all of them." In fact, she had recently lent one son $30 to cover his rent.

All of those who appeared to be chronically mentally ill reported that they were almost totally reliant on the welfare system for support. A few even considered the caseworkers in public and private agencies as their only "real friends." Others reported that they had used up their friends and family by continual requests for lodging or money.

One man who appeared to be a transient said he only relied on the private agency because his other contacts were not yet operating. His story was that he came to town with a list of "friends" with whom he could stay, but he could not find them. He apparently presumed that he would eventually run into them. He relied on private agencies as a backup to a friendship network—a backup he claimed to be reluctant to use.

Even among those who said they had friends, the amount of sharing between them was limited. It appeared possible to borrow a few cigarettes and to trade baby-sitting, but not to trade food, clothes, or money. It may very well be that many of those in our sample, having been poor for such a long time, had no expectation of being able to return material aid, and thus could no longer participate in full in a sharing network.

There were two exceptions. One woman who received AFDC came to an agency with three of her friends. Her contribution was the automobile, which she often furnished to those in need. Apparently she occasionally received food or small gifts from her friends in repayment for the car. All of them went together to supplement their benefits with help from the private agency. This situation seems closest to the pattern of mutual aid and hustling mentioned in chronicles of ghetto life—but it is a minor theme among the clients of private agencies we interviewed. Only one other respondent reported receiving aid from another source—her son. It is notable that this is the same woman who attended a meal program largely for the social support it offered.

In two other cases, asking help from a private agency appeared to be preferable to turning to family. Stan, a young out-of-work respondent, said that he could have obtained "a few dollars" from his grandfather but did not like to ask often (perhaps because he had nothing to offer in return). Joan, who had recently broken with her boyfriend, revealed that she had some relatives in the area but no close friends. Her mother was willing to offer some emergency aid, but receiving aid from her mother would be tantamount to admitting defeat, because her mother had cautioned her away from the boyfriend.

Nevertheless, the overwhelming picture in this sample is one of critical needs for which the private sector is the only source. In response to a specific question, all but the two people mentioned above said that if they were not helped they would either try a different agency or go without. Some claimed that their alternative to a shelter was the street.

CLIENT ATTITUDES TOWARD PUBLIC AND PRIVATE AGENCIES

We hypothesized that, because public welfare is often viewed as a right and private aid as charity, individuals would feel more stigmatized and less positive about using the private sector. Although there is some evidence that people use private agencies reluctantly, only after other resources are exhausted, in many ways the original hypothesis was not confirmed. In fact individuals found private agencies more helpful and less degrading than public agencies. Despite the fact that many believe that private aid is more stigmatizing than public welfare, our respondents often professed the opposing view.

Why is this so? Stigma is largely something that occurs in an interaction. Even if a client feels there is nothing wrong with accepting charity, he or she often finds stigma reflected in the attitudes of other actors in the system. Our respondents thus claimed they were more stigmatized by the public sector because they were treated with less dignity.

In response to a direct question, all but 2 of the 18 respondents expressed a deep distrust and hatred of the public system, although most of their economic subsistence came from this source. One couple claimed that they were "hassled, surprised, and blackmailed" at city welfare. They never knew when their benefits would be cut, or why. They realized that if they did not follow the rules, they would be cut off—but it was unclear exactly what the rules were. Steve, who received General Assistance, was also very negative toward the agency. He believed that black people were treated with greater consideration and that his race was held against him. He also claimed that the money was too limited, the wait for benefits too long, and the questions too intense. He said he would not use the public system at all if there were any choice.

Most were somewhat more favorable toward AFDC—but only one respondent liked the system very much. All others were critical. Jolene said that her AFDC worker was "very concerned" and that she was able to use mail-in forms and thus avoid many hassles. But she still felt that the guidelines were too strict and that the questions were too detailed. She was asked about every bit of property and was penalized for owning a car. She was asked if she ever entertained guests. "They practically ask how many times you go to the bathroom." She had also been to city welfare and found this more demeaning—she was treated like a "freak" and a "statistic." She resented that the television evening news sometimes showed people waiting at the agency.

In contrast to this picture of the public sector, most were favorably impressed by private agencies, and, surprisingly, there was a universal preference for using the private over the public sector, if there were a choice. Whereas public agencies were described as uncaring, too interested in forms, and distrustful, the private agencies were usually seen as friendly, caring, and dispensing aid with very little "hassle." No respondent's comments were more negative than positive.

One notable meal program, at which no questions were asked, seemed to be universally loved. Clients felt that they belonged there and had control over the operation. One couple even felt a right to complain when they believed volunteer workers said the wrong things or were not polite enough. Indeed, the general impression of the clients was that this was a "special" agency, that the priest who ran it was special, and that it was best not to tell other people about it. There was fear that the "wrong type" of people would come if knowledge were more widespread, and such people would upset the priest. Nevertheless, even at this agency there were no children; those who were interviewed and had children had many excuses for not bringing them, including the desire to protect children from others who used the agency.

Many positive comments were heard at other agencies. Agencies that dispensed food, clothing, and vouchers were considered "very good," "understanding," and "fair." The efficient service, which took only 10 or 15 minutes as opposed to the hours or days at the welfare office, was widely acknowledged. One man, who believed that the public system had "too many hassles, too much impersonality and paperwork" found the shelter at which he was staying "generally good." He realized that the shelter operated within tight financial limits. His main criticism was a lack of activities, particularly for the older men.

The private agencies were trusted enough that they apparently had become part of the life-style of the majority of those who were interviewed. Consistent with the Minnesota study, very few respondents had used the agency only once or had been to no other agency. Few had used private welfare for a lifetime, but most had been using private aid for from 1 to 4 years. Out of the entire sample, only three of those who used one meal program had no other contact with the private sector.

The group interview provided the most positive impression of private agencies, as compared to public ones. Four men were interviewed at a Salvation Army shelter that received funds, on a contract basis, to provide housing. They felt that their stay was a highlight of their lives:

> When asked what they thought of the Emergency Lodge all four enthusiastically responded with praise. The facility was compared to the Hyatt Regency by Bob, and the others agreed that they had seldom lived in greater comfort. . . . The staff were depicted as concerned and helpful. Examples of personal efforts of individual staff members were given. Bob (who had been burned out) spoke of the efforts made by his social workers to reestablish his identification papers, which were lost in the fire. . . . Bob indicated that the staff exercised great sensitivity in motivating residents to get out and resolve their problems. Pressure to act was applied, but, according to Bob, that pressure was seldom enough to cause a resident to rebel. . . .
>
> When pressed for any complaints about the Lodge the respondents mentioned only the curfew. The Lodge has an eight o'clock curfew from Monday to Thursday and a ten o'clock curfew from Friday through Sunday. While all four agreed that the curfew hampered their social life they also agreed that it was tolerable after a period of adjustment. Bob and Bill even added that they were so intent on making a success of their lives that the curfew was a good thing, because it largely prevented them from dating, and women had been their downfall in the past.
>
> All four spoke of the same metaphor of "building a cushion" for themselves so that the next time they fell they "won't fall flat on the pavement." The tone in which this metaphor was offered suggested a repetition of advice received from staff, indicating some level of counseling.
>
> When I suggested a comparison between public social services and the Salvation Army all four just laughed. They described public social services as an agency where no one cared about the client. Workers were there only to collect their pay. Their opinion was that public social services did as little as possible for a client, whereas the Lodge provided all they could and personal concern as well.

Given the more favorable view of the private sector, why do clients go first to the public sector? Part of the answer must be that, although it was unstated, there is indeed a greater reluctance to use charity (as Harper [1982] and Stack [1979] claimed). As mentioned earlier, our respondents had already used private agencies and overcome this reluctance. It is also likely that public welfare is used because it is more widely publicized and thus more accessible. The chief reason is almost certainly that the benefits dispensed by the public agency are much larger.

It appears that once the barrier to using private aid is overcome, people keep coming back. Even those who mentioned that they only came owing to pressure from a spouse or friend admitted that they would come again if they needed help.

CRITICISM OF PRIVATE AGENCIES

There were some criticisms of private agencies. Some complained of restrictions on how frequently aid could be obtained. Others claimed that programs did not treat all people equally. No subjective discrimination was mentioned by any interviewee, but a large number referred to rules by which families were helped more than individuals. While some said that this was a sensible rule, others believed that it unfairly discriminated against those who did not, or could not, have children.

It should be remembered, however, that our interviews took place in agencies that had been selected by the clients, often on the basis of past experience. Furthermore, these agencies had given permission for the interviews to take place. It may be that the agencies refusing permission were much more restrictive. Indeed, all religious shelters with conditions refused to give us permission to interview. Though such agencies are in a minority, one can imagine that they would be viewed a good deal less favorably by their clients.

Indirect evidence indicated that this was the case. One man at a meal program reported that he had once visited the local rescue mission but had left immediately because religion was forced on him. He believed that the purpose of the mission was not to take care of him but to try to save his soul. He selected the meal program at which he was interviewed largely because few questions were asked and religion was not foisted upon him. He was allowed to keep his dignity and was treated like "family." Another respondent also reported dislike for a rescue mission, saying that he preferred to sit all night in a chair in a large room made available during the winter than to put up with rescue mission life.

Another respondent complained that a rescue mission he had used had required him to attend a church service before receiving a meal. He felt that the mission had no right to force religion on him.

One couple mentioned demeaning conditions imposed by the Salvation Army. To obtain shelter, the couple had to prove their identity and abide by a number of "house rules," such as when to go to bed, when to shower, and so forth. The agency had also forced them to apply for public aid. The couple felt that their "one-down position was taken advantage of" and that the workers were "too pushy" in attempting to get them to change their life-style.

Still others complained about eligibility rules at other agencies and the tendency to favor families over individuals. While complaints were not vociferous, some also objected to the number of questions that were asked. Generally, clients appeared to be ashamed to admit they had needs and felt comfortable in inverse proportion to the number of questions asked.

THE WORST AGENCIES

The shelters at which we conducted interviews tended to be small, somewhat personal, and favorably viewed by clients. Those who have studied life on the street paint a rather different picture of the large, urban shelters that transients use. Most are "mass" facilities, housing a large number of (usually) men in a single room. Insects, theft, violence, and filth are common. One such report notes:

> We much preferred our heat grate to any of the available shelters, either city-run or privately operated. We were familiar with all of them, well aware of the conditions and the regimen; the brutal guards, the disinterested or hostile staff, the theft, the filth, and the vermin, and the thoroughly degrading and dehumanizing environment. For example, ammonia would occasionally be poured in the middle of the dormitory floor; the men, awakened by fumes and gasping for breath, would rush from the room. This was simply a form of insurance so that the guests would not take too long in rising, dressing, and getting back on the street, even though there was nowhere to go for at least two or three hours. (Hombs and Snyder, 1982, p. 112)

Conditions appear to be related to the size, the number of staff, and the physical accommodations at a shelter, not to whether it is a public or private facility. Nevertheless, a view of the private sector cannot be considered complete without reporting this, the worst case. Perhaps the long-term single homeless—those with the most severe personal problems according to surveys—are dealt with by a less humane type of agency, the type other studies focus on in depth (Baxter and Hopper, 1981).

STIGMA IN USING THE PRIVATE SECTOR

Even though our respondents liked the way they were treated at private agencies, overall, they admitted some reluctance in using them. They claimed that asking for aid was "demeaning," that a person in need had a "terrible, low-down feeling" about asking for help, or that one felt "uneasy" about receiving aid. Perhaps the request, viewed as admission of an inability to cope, reduces one's self-esteem.

One of the most interesting findings of our interviews was that our subjects found public and private agencies equally "demeaning" on this point and compared the two on other traits (e.g., the number of questions asked). Thus, one woman claimed that she had worked for years without asking for help, and she saw the help she now received as a "right." She did not abuse the system and had put much into it. She thus expected aid back—from both the public and the private sector. She preferred the private agency because it was "less degrading" in its day-to-day contact. Individuals treated her on a one-to-one basis. Most "are volunteers or just a little above you in income." In the public sector, "some social workers are on an ego trip. 'I'm going to help the world.' "

Another couple claimed that all aid was "charity" and therefore demeaning. But, they reasoned, if the situation is demeaning, there is no reason to "make it worse" by relying too heavily on a public agency that simply points to the problem. Rather, it is better to receive aid from the private sector, where those who dispense aid are at least helpful.

While some might claim continual use of assistance leads to dependency, there was very little sense of hopelessness or dependence among all but perhaps two of the respondents. Most continued to view their plights as temporary and to believe that better times were ahead. Roughly half of the respondents spontaneously mentioned their desire, and expectation, that a good job was just around the corner. One client, for example, told us that her financial situation was temporary. She was optimistic that she could "weather the bad times." She said she was willing to work, if she could only find a job. Another told us that he "had pride" and did not want to convey a need for assistance. He saw himself as young and having potential. He said he was able to work and desired to improve his education. He was considering social work as a career.

Conclusion

The lives of many of those who use private agencies are extraordinarily harsh. According to broad surveys and our interviews, long-term difficulties usually exist. The typical client may have worked in the past but has suffered hardship for a number of years. Lack of a useful network of friends and relatives, inadequate or unavailable public welfare benefits, and some chronic physical or mental health problems may add to the difficulties.

Clearly private agencies cannot meet all of the material needs of such individuals. Given the nature of agencies, for some clients the aid offered may be not much better than no aid at all. This seems to be particularly true for the homeless, single "street people" who are turned away from the small shelters. Those who live on the streets may prefer a heat grate to a large shelter, not because they are proud, but because the larger shelters are practically unlivable.

The search for private aid also appears to be demeaning because in our culture poverty is virtually a crime. Stigma exists, and those who use private agencies may feel they are degrading themselves. A minority of private agencies add to the degradations, and many discriminate to the extent of sending a message that those with families are more deserving than others.

Nevertheless, private agencies meet crucial needs; the poor would go without food or shelter if they did not exist. Many of the studied agencies are even likely to mitigate problems in a humane manner. Unhampered by the complicated regulations that impede public welfare agencies, they act speedily and ask few questions. Those genuinely interested in the needy are able to turn a negative experience into a positive one. Scholars often believe that public welfare is superior because it is legally a right, while charity is more demeaning. But the distinction between charity and welfare, so important in social theory, apparently was not important to the poor in our sample; they were more interested in whether their needs were met and whether they were treated with dignity.

One key theme of this book is that the private sector is characterized by varying missions. Perhaps the only safe summary statement is that the way applicants are treated varies with the mission of the agency. According to our interviews, agencies committed to serving all in need, that ask few questions, and that dispense useful benefits, are perceived in a favorable light. Those that are suspicious or prefer "saving souls" to feeding and sheltering the poor are not regarded as highly. Our sense is that, except for the large shelters, the humane agencies are in the majority. Nevertheless, this is a debatable point; in any situation in which discretion is possible, great variance results.

CHAPTER 8

Political Roles of Private Agencies

Most of this book focuses on the tangible services private agencies provide. This is only natural. Though limited, this aid is crucial. But from a larger perspective, the political roles of private agencies are equally important. The agencies may, while providing benefits, serve as barriers to the formation of a more adequate public system. Their services may be perceived as obviating the need for public financial support, or they may actively promote values and behaviors in their clients that embody acceptance of inequities. However, the agencies may also actually encourage change by advocating for increased public benefits or other public policies.

As Chapter 2 pointed out, the private sector assumed all of these roles in the past. The Charity Organization Societies worked to reduce the role of government and to promote a form of social welfare that socialized workers into the advancing industrial economy. Their ideology may have dominated the private sector before the New Deal. But some private agencies also advocated for such change as increased governmental benefits (settlement houses), and specific social policies were core missions of certain agencies. (The Salvation Army, for example, was a prime advocate for Prohibition.)

The growth of government and the changing conceptualization of the private sector may have altered political roles. Agencies may no longer be as involved in social control, or they may advocate more frequently. While the data are far from definitive, the case studies and the 12-county survey provide insights into the extent to which private agencies play active political roles.

Private Agencies as Means to Socialize the Poor

One way in which private agencies may work against change is to convince clients that their problems are their own fault. Galper (1975), for example, claims that professional social workers impute problems to individuals, not to their environment, thereby reducing the possibility that clients will rebel. Workers may also convince clients that by adopting new attitudes and behaviors—particularly those the powerful would prefer—they can improve their lives. In the case of agencies that provide material assistance, this would translate into the utilization of counseling programs to transmit to clients a sense of personal insufficiency and a desire to change.

A small number of private agencies in our case studies appear to attempt to socialize the poor in these ways. Such conversion-oriented shelters as the Pennsylvania and Midwest rescue missions mandate that clients attend prayer meetings and perhaps demonstrate a desire to convert. The Pennsylvania facility, it may be recalled, demands conversion in exchange for an extended stay at the shelter. The agency also believes that clients are poor partly owing to deficiencies in religious training, and it attempts to convince clients of the validity of this position. Alcoholism, for example, is thought to cause much homelessness and is said to be the result of a religious deficiency that clients should recognize and change.

A few of the agencies that promote the formation of a religious community attempt to provide an alternative life-style that may decrease social awareness. One church-related meal program was exemplary:

> Maybe 30 people sat in attendance for the service in the old, large church. They appeared to be of all ages, quite poorly dressed and talking loud through the service. Children cried and played games; a new mother played with her tiny baby and made audible comments. The speaker began the hour service by reading a St. Patrick's Day card which he had been handed. He next said that the organist was very happy today as her son had come from Milwaukee for the weekend. . . . A group of five stood up to sing from the hymnal but only one woman could be heard. This same woman stood up again in a duet and drowned out the other singer in an out-of-tune, slurred rendition of "The Old Rugged Cross." . . . The speaker read from the Scripture and admitted it wasn't clear to him what the passage meant. The congregation responded to this and to other humorous comments with heart-warming laughter—a clear sign of their liking for this man. During the message, the speaker claimed that people and their inner worth far outvalue items of great monetary value. He criticized the city welfare system and social workers in general, saying that "the social workers are paid too much to care for the poor and can't understand them; their salaries of over $30,000 annually won't let them reach out to the needy." . . . The underlying theme was that only the church program was a friend. (Project Field Notes)

Some agencies have requirements for eligibility that may indirectly exert social control. In Texas County, Catholic Charities turns down few, but makes distinctions along a deserving-undeserving dimension. Among single men, those who appear ready to work are given priority, on the assumption that many who claim to be in need are simply unwilling to work. Many other agencies give priority to the elderly or to couples with children. Although the attempts to ration aid in this fashion are at least partly a result of scarce resources, it can be argued that the criteria serve to convince some of those in need that they are not as deserving as others or are largely to blame for their own problems.

The extent to which social control is successful may be questioned, however. The missions themselves admit that they convert very few, if any, of the homeless they serve. Our interviews also suggest that very few of those who are sheltered adopt the agencies' view of their problems. Instead, they go through the necessary motions to get served. Indeed, though the number of clients interviewed for this book is small, it is striking how many of them share the common American belief that their condition is temporary and a product of bad luck. Such a belief may not support social change, but neither does it reflect agency attempts to convince individuals that they caused their own problems.

Further, the number of agencies that appear to attempt to intentionally socialize the poor is small. Only seven of the agencies visited—about one in eight—had any counseling program. And with the exception of the program of the missions, counseling appears to be unrelated to social control. Both the Texas military program and the Inner-City Churches Coalition, for example, mandate budget counseling for those who repeatedly request aid. But counseling is a minor barrier to receiving benefits—the benefits are guaranteed if the needy person agrees to attend the session, whether he or she follows the recommendations of the counselor or not. Further, the counseling is generally of limited duration—often one long session—and may actually be of some use to those in need. Counseling of this sort is given only to those with some income, not to the destitute.

Radical politicians claim that private agencies, by the very act of providing aid to the needy, obscure the responsibility of the system for the plight of the poor. By helping the needy to eke out an existence, the private agencies enable their clients to continue to hope that good times are just around the corner. Such criticism convicts private agencies of protecting the existing system merely because they do not actively promote rebellion. It should be noted that those who receive aid feel free to complain about the public system and to remark that private aid is limited. The ability of private agencies to pacify the needy is thus insignificant.

Private Agencies as Barriers to Provision by Government

Because this research focused on the agencies and their communities, not on the public sector, we have somewhat less evidence on the extent to which private agencies serve as barriers to reform, limiting improvements in public welfare or changes in the social structure. Some people indeed point to the private sector as an alternative to public support. For example, when President Reagan cut social welfare services, he fully expected philanthropy to take over—not by "wastefully" duplicating the public sector, but by more selectively helping those who were truly in need. Many in the "new right" clearly share this vision (Berger and Neuhaus, 1977).

The research does call into question the extent to which private agencies are used by public officials to support this position, even if it does not speak to all of the broader political issues. The public welfare officials interviewed in the case-study communities, for example, clearly did not view the existence of the private sector as a reason to limit public aid. Most, while recognizing that private agencies back up the public system, note that its aid is limited and that it does not reduce the need for increases in public benefits, changes in employment policies, and so forth. In West Virginia and Pennsylvania counties, public welfare directors reported that private resources were so scarce that requirements that they be exhausted before public benefits are dispensed are often overlooked; in Texas County, the public sector often tried to package aid with private agencies to create a more adequate program, acknowledging the limits of both; in Midwest County, private agencies were not seen as a viable alternative for large-scale problems. In fact, private agencies were viewed by the public sector as more important as lobbyists than as providers of material benefits. Similarly, the heads of a large number of the private agencies that were visited made it clear that they do not believe that private support is adequate and that they say so at every opportunity.

Other sources of information paint a picture that is consistent with this. For example, in a survey of public emergency assistance programs, county public welfare executives were asked about the adequacy of the private sector to meet needs that the public sector cannot meet (Handler and Sosin, 1983). Forty-five percent of the executives reported that clients may turn to the private sector if public aid is inadequate, but only 13% reported that private charity provided a "large amount" of aid. The aid instead is assumed to be temporary and stop-gap. Its availability does not prevent the majority of executives from reporting that many problems require more public support. When surveyed, 75% claimed that more coverage of basic needs was required; 55% believed that more coverage was needed for special needs; while 53% claimed that additional coverage was needed to cover the breakdown of appliances or other one-time extra expenses.

Finally, while evidence is not definitive, a cursory reading of public responses to claims that the private sector can substitute for the public calls into question the extent to which this view is commonly accepted. The cuts in welfare have been successfully legitimated on the basis of protecting the "truly needy," not on the expectation that private agencies would pick up the slack. And most of the scholarly replies to attempts to replace the public sector by the private sector have also been negative. An Urban Institute study thus points out that the private sector is unable to meet needs on a large scale and will even shrink if public funding is reduced, because roughly half of all expenditures in the private sector apparently emanate from government (Saloman and Abramson, 1982). Looking at the private sector as a whole, the study points out that an increase of income of 30% would be needed simply to offset the effects of the 1982 budget cuts on private agencies, and that the needed increase is 60% for welfare and education. The researchers conclude:

> Ironically, however, while opening new opportunities for voluntary activity, the Economic Recovery Program may have the effect of weakening many of the private, voluntary organizations through which such activity occurs. Non-profit organizations are not simply an alternative to government; rather, they operate in many spheres as partners of government. As a result, the same policies that reduce the role of government—and, hence, increase the need for non-profit organizations—also reduce the ability of these organizations to meet the need. (p. 220)

If this position is common, the claims that the private sector can replace the public will not obtain much support.

To be sure, there are ways in which private agencies support some political interests over others. Witness, for example, the activities that the United Way supports and those it fails to support (see Chapter 3). But it appears unlikely that the existence and activities of private agencies will serve either to reduce the size of the public welfare system or to indicate that structural changes are not needed. It may very well be that the extent to which private agencies are viewed as alternatives to other types of social provision or social change depends far more on a balance of political forces than on the independent role of the private sector.

Advocacy in Agencies Providing Material Assistance

To what extent do private agencies advocate for change in public welfare or in society as a whole? In the 1980s a notable growth has occurred in coalitions of private agencies to attempt to increase resources.

Coalitions are common to three of the four case-study counties. Texas County has a coalition that meets to share information about clients and about the availability of new resources. In West Virginia County, Information and Referral coordinates services and also passes information to cooperating agencies. Neither county, however, advocates to change conditions for the poor. To be sure, Information and Referral collects information about changes in the levels of need that could be used for advocacy, but it does not appear to use this information. Perhaps most of those who are involved in the service network in West Virginia County are aware that assistance is inadequate, but they also believe that few additional resources can be brought to bear on the problem.

In Midwest County, the one large urban case-study county, coalitions indeed advocate. The Food Task Force, for example, is attempting to bring about change in the distribution of food. The agency, which has its roots in a 1969 organization that was successful in its fight to obtain breakfast for inner-city children, is currently housed in a church and receives a small amount of religiously based funding. But, as appears to be common among agencies that advocate, most of its resources come from the local Community Action agency.

The Food Task Force's charge from its government-funding source is to improve the access of individuals to public benefits. It assists applicants in appealing food stamp decisions and in filling out assistance applications. It also uses whatever influence it has to put pressure on welfare administrators to alter idiosyncratic rules that restrict benefits. It has a particularly close, if sometimes antagonistic, relation with the local Department of Public Welfare. Problems are ironed out in monthly meetings.

As mentioned in Chapter 7, the Food Task Force also coordinates 70 emergency food pantries in the county. Coordination is designed to improve the procedures of food banks and ensure that all areas of the city are covered. In addition, the task force has been involved in citywide drives for food donations, which are then distributed to pantries. It has successfully increased private donations of food.

The agency also advocates for wider reforms. It collects data on the number of individuals in need, the reasons for need, and the effect of government budget cuts on individuals and families. Although this effort, which began in 1982, is too new to evaluate, the agency believes that it can use the statistics to challenge government policies, particularly local ones involving food and food stamps.

A second example, Advocates Incorporated, was summarized in part in Chapter 4. This agency, which also is supported through public funds, is expected to be a general advocate. It is involved in landlord–tenant disputes and appeal procedures in income maintenance programs. It is financially supported by local government because one of its other functions is to take pressure off the local General Assistance program by appealing denials in the SSI program and in AFDC.

The agency is also active in advocating for the provision of new benefits and services. It was instrumental in establishing a statewide coalition to deal with emergency shelter, the Midwest Council for the Homeless. The organization helped to organize a meeting of all interested public and private agencies in the state and to develop a steering committee from the participants. The steering committee is collecting statistics about the need for housing and is advocating for state and local financial aid for shelters on the basis of the statistics. So far, the county has responded by agreeing to build one additional shelter, and as Chapter 7 noted, this and other changes dramatically reduced the number of individuals without access to a shelter. Nevertheless, many of the new facilities are inadequate. One is a large room in a local hospital. Because it would be illegal to offer sleeping quarters, the room is furnished with rows and rows of chairs. During the winter, perhaps 100 people spend the night sitting on the chairs.

Data from other sources reveal other state and local coalitions that have helped to develop new resources. In Boston, Vine Street Inn has been expanded with the help of aid from public sources for which it advocated. It now has 55 full-time staff members and provides shelter for 300 men and 50 women each night (Leepson, 1982). Some new shelters opened in New York and in many other large cities, occasionally as a result of court cases pressed by coalitions, but more often owing to publicity generated by coalitions.

Some support for services to the poor comes from lobbying groups that do not dispense material aid but have gathered information from coalitions of those who do. The Community for Creative Non-Violence has published a number of volumes on the lives of those who are without shelter. On the basis of the information, it has sponsored protests in Washington over the plight of the homeless, including a hunger strike, which resulted in the development of new, federally supported shelters in Washington, D.C.

It is clear that information from local agencies helped the Community.

Its writings are filled with data from private agencies. One of its publications reports on the increase in homelessness after 1980, as documented by local shelters (Hombs and Snyder, 1982). This study relies on locally provided information to trace the number of deaths due to exposure in 12 cities, and to relate how state and local coalitions helped to increase the capacity and quality of shelters.

Nevertheless, the Community for Creative Non-Violence has had to report failures as well as successes. In Phoenix, two shelters have been condemned; a 1981 ordinance prohibited soup kitchens and shelters downtown; and lying down or sleeping on public property has become a misdemeanor. The local newspaper argued, "We didn't tolerate prostitutes—why tolerate bums?"

The Community for Creative Non-Violence has used the data it obtained to lobby for federal legislation. Finding that there were 2 million homeless people in the country (we will later comment on the validity of the figure), the coalition testified on the need for additional shelters before the U.S. House of Representatives, Committee on Banking, Finance, and Urban Affairs, Subcommittee on Housing and Community Development. The National Coalition for the Homeless, which represents many of the state and local groups, also testified. As a result of a general public outcry, the testimony of a large number of advocacy groups and shelters, and pressure from local governments as well as from the National Coalition, a 1982 jobs bill appropriated $100 million for emergency shelters. The provision was repeated in the following year. Although funds are limited and temporary, the bill was an important step in meeting short-term, emergency needs.

LIMITS AND CONDITIONS OF ADVOCACY

Judging by these case studies and brief descriptions of coalitions, advocacy occurs and succeeds only under a limited set of conditions. In all of the documented instances, advocacy groups are supported by forces external to the network providing material assistance. In the case of the Community for Creative Non-Violence, the major source of support is the activism of progressive Catholics who are similar in their outlook to the Catholic Workers. In many of the other cases, funding from the government is crucial to advocacy. A third possible source of advocacy might be legal aid projects, whose employees often join coalitions for change in welfare (Sosin, 1984).

Generally, it appears that agencies advocate for changes that are quite closely allied to their own service programs. The Food Task Force had an interest in food that stemmed from its own role in pantries and food provision. And many of the organizations that were at least partly active in the Midwest Coalition, such as the Salvation Army and Red Cross, were already involved in the provision of beds to the homeless. The success of the coalition meant reduced pressures on these agencies.

Advocacy was also limited to issues about which private agencies had information and legitimacy. Private agencies had the ability to document the need for housing because they served the homeless. Legitimacy may have resulted from public sympathy, which arose as increases in need in the early 1980s became obvious. Where public sympathy did not exist, such as in Texas County, or where little aid could be provided, such as in West Virginia County, activism did not occur.

One of the implicit assumptions of the analysis is that advocacy occurs when it is in the interests of those advocating. It may increase their resources, legitimate their mandate, or help to support a specific mission. But this also implies limits to advocacy. At the broadest level, it affects the goals for which advocacy develops. Coalitions demand resources for the homeless or the unemployed if the number of homeless and unemployed put pressure on agencies, but very few coalitions also directly consider long-term solutions to problems causing inadequate housing or income. The National Coalition for the Homeless has been unable to develop a coalition to attack broader issues. The issue of homelessness touched a common chord among communities only when placed in terms of charity to the desperate and seen as a short-term goal. Attempts to consider structural problems leading to homelessness did not achieve legitimacy (Stern, 1984).

AGENCY FAILURES TO ADVOCATE

Other information from the case studies reveals that advocacy often ceases as quickly as it develops in many private agencies. Such was the case with the United Migrants Association of Midwest County. A few years ago, when the agency received funds from a Community Action project, advocacy was a prime activity—both for individuals and to change laws. But funding now comes from the U.S. Department of Labor, whose regulations forbid advocacy by organizations using its funds. The agency now gives job training to migrant farm workers who have moved to the local area.

Another example is Catholic Workers' House, a Catholic Worker organization in Midwest County. Early in its history, the agency attempted to combine advocacy with the provision of material assistance and with hospitality. But the combination of service and advocacy was not stable. After the Vietnam era, during which protests flourished, the early leaders of the movement were replaced by the second generation, and advocacy was greatly reduced. Catholic Workers' House continues to believe in the importance of advocacy but does not practice it; for example, when a coalition of emergency shelters recently developed to attempt to aid the homeless, the organization neither sent a representative to the original meeting nor became involved in the steering committee.

The reasons for the reduction in advocacy in this agency are clear. Its director mentioned that, especially in difficult economic times, dispensing material aid is quite time-consuming and leaves little time for advocacy. Furthermore, it was pointed out that the agency is run by a small group of volunteer "members," whose motivation depends upon group solidarity and the rewards of belonging to an organization with a philosophy they share. The time spent in small-group communication to ensure this solidarity leaves little time or energy to advocate. It also seems likely that funding may not be in tune with attempts to advocate, because the agency now receives much of its support from members of the community who see its role as the giving of relief.

This also appears to be the case with the Catholic Meal Program, a highly legitimate agency with stable funds, a potential to advocate in the community, and an ideology favoring advocacy. This agency also failed to join the coalition for more housing. While the director has a strong commitment to the poor, his advocacy is usually confined to making speeches before religious groups. Again, the director seemed to imply that the energy devoted to supplying material needs and maintaining a spiritual community "drives out" political coalition building. And although he did not say so, perhaps members of a religious order feel uncomfortable entering a political forum in which most actors do not share the basic goals of the order.

In sum, pressures from funding sources, from internal missions, and from the need to maintain internal integrity apparently can result in a failure to advocate. And, of course, it is obvious from previous chapters that the majority of agencies that supply material aid simply do not view advocacy as part of their mission. Charity, and not reform, is central to the mission of agencies as diverse as Catholic Charities and the Salvation Army, the Red Cross and the March of Dimes.

Factors Related to Advocacy

The advocacy that occurs in agencies dispensing material assistance is less than one would generally expect of private agencies. According to the 12-county data set, whereas roughly 11% of all private agencies advocate, only 5% of the agencies that provide material aid engage in this activity. Using a simple *t*-test, the difference in the extent of advocacy between material assistance providers and other private agencies is statistically significant.

Why is this so? The case studies, as presented above, suggest some answers in that they point to the constraints placed on the agencies by such factors as missions and funding sources. But it may be useful to present a more formal, if also preliminary, examination of the possible differences between agencies that advocate and those that do not, to reveal how agencies that provide material aid fit in.

Although there are many other possible approaches (Olson, 1965; Grodzgins, 1966; Smith and Freedman, 1972; Gamson, 1975; Piven and Cloward, 1977; Handler, 1978; Moe, 1980; Oberschall, 1980), the theoretical approach of this book suggests that engaging in advocacy might depend upon the nature of the community, the missions of agencies, and funding arrangements. While more specific hypotheses would be useful, the literature does not provide a very strong base from which to develop them. Based on the results of previous chapters, it can be expected that advocacy, like the provision of material aid, is less common in professional, client-changing organizations. Given the historical review in Chapter 2, it may also be the case that advocacy is less often an activity of religious affiliates. In addition, perhaps agencies that serve the poor or are located in communities having large-scale social problems are more likely to advocate. But these are general ideas, and it is necessary to conduct an exploratory study to find more specific relationships.

MISSIONS AND COMMUNITIES COMPATIBLE WITH ADVOCACY

One way of understanding why some agencies advocate and some do not is to develop a model of determinants of advocacy from the 12-county data set, just as we developed a model of determinants for dispensing material assistance in Chapter 5. This involves separating community variables, attributes of the public welfare system, and variables representing mission into groups, looking at the bivariate relations between these attributes and whether or not agencies advocate, and then developing a discriminant analysis, based on the groupings and the bivariate relations. (See Chapter 5 for details of the procedure.) While the measures consider only some, selected traits of agencies, the results may help reveal differences in characteristics between agencies that advocate and those that commonly provide material aid.

Table 8.1 reports the results of such a discriminant analysis. Nine variables enter the final equation predicting advocacy. Together they correctly predict whether an agency advocates or does not for about 76% of the sample. One of the nine involves a measure of the community context, with advocacy tending to be more common for agencies in communities containing a higher percentage of blacks. When the black proportion of the population is higher in the 12-county sample, the community also has (to a statistically significant degree) a larger population, higher AFDC benefits, and a greater population density. These other variables also demonstrate statistically significant relations with the propensity of an agency to advocate, although they do not enter the final equation once the percentage of the population that is black is entered. Perhaps, then, the results imply that agencies are more likely to advocate in large, heterogeneous communities in which there are more conflicting interests, more conflicts among groups, and in which there thus is more legitimacy for advocacy (Sosin and Caulum, 1983).

The eight other variables involve the mission of the agency. One mirrors the equation predicting material assistance programs: agencies that advocate are not as likely as other agencies to specialize in an age group. Since specialization appears to be a characteristic of more professional agencies, the relation may indicate that such agencies are less likely to view advocacy as a legitimate activity, for the reasons Cloward

TABLE 8.1
Discriminant Analysis: Determinants of Advocacy in Private Agencies (N = 1025)

Variable	Standardized coefficient	Wilks lambda ratio to enter equation	Level of statistical significance
Problems of the handicapped	.414	.972	.001
Problems of discrimination	.411	.950	.001
Age specialization	−.442	.935	.001
Religious affiliation	−.384	.923	.001
Landlord–tenant problems	.306	.915	.001
Alcoholism	−.162	.912	.001
Problems of the developmentally disabled	.177	.909	.001
Drug abuse	−.100	.909	.001
Percentage of community nonwhite	.365	.897	.001

These variables group 76.7% of all cases correctly.

and Epstein (1967) developed in their analysis of agencies that do not provide material needs.

Agencies that deal with alcoholism or drug abuse are also less likely to advocate, according to the analysis. These relations may also reflect professionalization. Alcoholism, for example, has come to be seen as a medical problem, best dealt with by individual treatment (and such social control measures as keeping alcoholics off the highways). This orientation may be inimical to attempts to improve the social environment of alcoholics by advocating. (We are of course assuming that agencies advocate for the same population groups they serve in other ways.)

It is also notable that agencies with a religious affiliation are less likely to advocate. It may be that many religious philosophies involve attempts to change individuals rather than society. As was true at the turn of the century, perhaps it is rare for agencies that are interested in conversion or good works to also believe that an effort should be made to change laws, policies, or the case decisions of other agencies.

What missions are consistent with advocacy? Two involve dealing with landlord–tenant relations and discrimination. These problems almost by definition involve advocacy, so that their inclusion in the final equation needs little comment.

The final equation also suggests that agencies that deal with the developmentally disabled and the handicapped are more likely to advocate. This may reflect the fact that many nationally affiliated local groups are now advocating for better services and more resources for those with handicaps and other disabilities. Perhaps these groups maintain an advocacy stance because they are able to attract members who agree that the handicapped and disabled are not at fault for their problems, are not served very well by the public sector, and thus deserve more public resources. In addition, advocacy for the handicapped and the developmentally disabled has been something of a success story. It has resulted in massive increases in resources (Erlanger, 1978). As sociological theorists point out, advocacy groups are more likely to attract members when the probability of success is high.

AFFILIATION AND FUNDING COMPATIBLE WITH ADVOCACY

Although accurate data exist for only half of the 12-county sample, it is also possible to determine how funding arrangements and affiliation relate to the propensity to advocate. Results of such an analysis are reported in Table 8.2.

It is commonly claimed that the role of large governmental agencies in the welfare state reduces advocacy, because agencies that receive public

TABLE 8.2
Advocacy and Patterns of Organization in Private Agencies

Characteristic	Percentage of agencies that advocate ($N = 62$)	Percentage of other agencies ($N = 508$)
National organization affiliation	24.2%	19.7%
Federal funding	24.2	18.3
State funding	25.8	17.1
County government funding	17.7	12.8
Funding from foundation	3.2	1.0
Funding from donation	46.8	34.1*
Funding from memberships	25.8	5.7*
United Way funding	8.1	10.4

* $p < .05$ in the two-tailed test.

funds are forced to be less critical of government. The table, however, reveals no statistically significant relations between any measure of obtaining support from government and advocacy. While certain government programs ban advocacy that makes use of federal funds, and there are pressures in Washington to extend such policies, as of yet, advocacy and obtaining funds from government are not inconsistent at the agency level. If anything, the direction of the relations is positive. As Kramer (1981) implied, agencies receiving public funds may have some incentive to advocate in order to maintain or increase funding. We also know from the case studies that certain government grants or contracts to private agencies are directly designated to promote advocacy.

While the data indicate no relation between support from the United Way or from foundations and advocacy, Table 8.2 does suggest that agencies that advocate rely much more frequently than other agencies on membership fees and voluntary donations (the relations are statistically significant). Perhaps advocacy depends on the existence of a group of people who share the political concerns of the agency and who supply the funds.

ADVOCACY AMONG AGENCIES PROVIDING MATERIAL ASSISTANCE

These results and explanations make it apparent why agencies that provide material aid advocate less often than other private agencies. Beginning with more conceptual issues, the preceding analysis suggests that agencies advocate less often when they view problems as the fault of the individuals they serve. As has been demonstrated throughout this volume, most agencies that dispense material assistance seem to interpret the issue partly as a problem of individual adjustment. Unlike the handicapped and the developmentally disabled, those in need of material aid are not considered to be particularly deserving of further support from the government.

Further, advocacy for the needy may involve a more challenging view of the social order than other types of advocacy, thus making it more difficult to find adherents or to convince possible members that there is a high probability of success. This is not always the case. Advocacy for those who have been denied food stamps, for example, seems to demand little in the way of broad structural changes. But some advocacy for material problems may involve such sweeping changes as the provision of more jobs, alternate housing arrangements, or drastically altered public welfare programs.

Looking more narrowly, the specific variables included in Table 8.1 demonstrate that agencies that advocate often have different characteristics from agencies that provide material aid. Most notably (see Chapter 5), many agencies that are involved in meeting material needs have a religious orientation, but agencies that advocate tend not to be religious in orientation. Similarly, Chapter 5 revealed that agencies providing material assistance are slightly more common in communities in which welfare benefits are lower, while data on advocacy suggest that agencies that advocate tend to be in communities with slightly higher welfare benefits (counties with a higher proportion of black residents). In addition, social problems that are common in agencies that advocate are different from those that characterize agencies that provide material aid. Advocacy is common in agencies that serve the handicapped and disabled; material assistance is less likely to be provided by such agencies. Perhaps the groups for which it is deemed particularly appropriate to advocate are ones for which the provision of material aid is not viewed as a high priority.

There are also small differences in sources of funds of agencies that advocate and agencies that provide for material needs. Agencies that advocate often rely on membership fees and direct donations; membership fees are not as common in agencies that provide material assistance. In addition, the United Way is not as prone to support agencies that advocate as it is to provide at least some support to certain agencies that provide for material needs (see Chapter 5 for details). Having somewhat different sources of funds, perhaps agencies that engage in one of the activities are less likely to obtain support to engage in the other one.

There is one characteristic that is typical among both types of agencies: the tendency to deal with all age groups rather than specializing. Age specialization may imply an interest in professional counseling, which is inimical to both advocacy and the provision of material needs. However, this one common element is overwhelmed by the extent to which providing material aid responds to different contexts and motives than does advocating.

Given the possibility that the difference in agency missions might explain why so few agencies that offer material aid also advocate, it is useful to test this relation. If the propensity to deliver material assistance is entered into an equation predicting advocacy, it should drop out after these other factors are considered. However, Table 8.3, which presents a discriminant analysis that adds the measure of dealing with material needs to the variables that have relations with advocacy and then selects those with statistically significant relations, does not support this conceptualization. Rather, agencies that provide material aid are less likely to advocate, even when placed in an equation that includes the other factors. Why is this so? Perhaps the basic ideology involved in dispensing material aid is of itself counter to advocacy. In the existing frame of

TABLE 8.3
Discriminant Analysis: Determinants of Advocacy in Private Agencies, Material Aid Variables Added (N = 1025)

Variable	Standardized coefficient	Wilks lambda ratio to enter equation	Level of statistical significance
Problems of the handicapped	.366	.972	.001
Problems of discrimination	.390	.950	.001
Age specialization	−.576	.935	.001
Material aid	.376	.920	.001
Landlord–tenant problems	.289	.911	.001
Religious affiliation	−.273	.905	.001
Alcoholism	−.148	.903	.001
Problems of the developmentally disabled	.146	.900	.001
Problems of individual and family life	.107	.899	.001
Problems of drug abuse	−.101	.898	.001
Percentage of the community nonwhite	.371	.884	.001

reference of private agencies, dispensing material aid must be accompanied by views of clients as inferior, time commitments, or resource commitments that make advocacy more difficult to carry out. No wonder the case studies suggest that agencies that advocate for the needy either do not directly deliver material assistance, or obtain funds from the government and thus tend to be rather different from the typical agency in the network.

Conclusion

At the turn of the century, private agencies played a crucial role in American ideology. The Charity Organization Societies, and even the settlement houses, were looked upon by many as the solutions to the problems created by poverty and immigration. The agencies were counted on for many social control purposes, such as to socialize Eastern European immigrants into American culture. At first some of the agencies even claimed they could replace the public sector by dealing with the individual-level problems that were said to be at the root of poverty.

During the 1920s and beyond, most private agencies admitted that they could not handle such a burden. Since that time, private agencies have expanded at a very slow pace compared to the public sector, and their legitimacy is no longer as well established. The general public has come to expect public welfare to deal with poverty—whether punitive or permissive policies are endorsed. Few desire to turn the clock back.

The tentative data at our disposal suggest that, perhaps due to changed expectations and a reduced role, the agencies that dispense material aid do not play a very strong social control function. It is true that some of them imply that poverty is the fault of the individual and attempt to change individuals or at least distinguish between the deserving and undeserving. But many of these agencies do not take their ideology farther than the provision of budget counseling. Moreover, the amount of aid offered is so limited that even when an agency expects religious conversion in exchange for assistance, few clients seem to take the demand seriously. Most important, the vast majority of agencies do not try to convert individuals or change their behavior, even if they believe—and many do not—that individuals cause their own economic problems. The mission of service is stronger than the desire to change individuals.

According to our data, agencies that provide material aid are also less likely than other agencies to advocate. This lack of advocacy appears to be directly associated with the characteristics of the material aid effort (values, time, resources), and partly caused by the fact that different contextual factors characterize agencies that are able to develop the resources needed to advocate. Material assistance agencies deal with clients who have little public sympathy. These agencies often have missions and types of financial support that are not consistent with advocacy.

Nevertheless, it appears that the advocacy role is more important than social control. In some communities, advocates ensure that clients receive their legal entitlements. Advocacy has also been helpful in expanding resources to deal with increases in financial need. A few agencies use their special knowledge of the poor at least to document need, and some actively join coalitions that advocate.

There are areas in which such advocacy is less likely. Very few agencies take a leadership role in promoting structural change in society. Even though many believe that their clients face poor housing and inadequate employment opportunities, these are not their primary concerns. Moreover, much of the leadership for advocacy often comes from the borderlines of the private sector—agencies with some public funding. Just as the major advocacy efforts at the turn of the century came from agencies that did not dispense material aid, it also appears that current leadership comes from political actors who make use of information provided by direct service agencies but who do not provide services themselves.

CHAPTER 9

The Evaluation of Private Programs

The Current Picture

In one were to summarize the findings of this book in a line, it would be that the contribution of the private sector to meeting the material needs of the poor is modest. But while private agencies do not help clients as much as may be desired, they do less harm than some fear. This can be demonstrated by summarizing the extent to which they supplement the public system, advocate for the needy, or support the status quo.

SUPPLEMENTING THE PUBLIC SYSTEM

Sufficiency

The evidence suggests that the changes in society over the last half-century have reduced the ability of the private sector to sufficiently meet material needs. The growth of government programs has taken some attention away from the private sector, reducing the legitimacy of private agencies. Because the proportion of the GNP this sector receives has not grown along with the public effort, its resources are limited. And while there is little evidence that the public refuses to support most types of services through private agencies if they are also public responsibilities (see Chapter 3), most people hold that the provision of material assistance should be primarily a public responsibility.

As a result of this situation, private agencies are only able to provide supplementary benefits, such as temporary shelter, food for a few days, help with utility bills, or aid to recover from a disaster. They do not cover continuing needs. Most who make use of the programs must treat them as additions to public benefits or as an alternate means of support for very specific situations within limited time frames.

Our data also suggest that the private network currently is not able to provide sufficient resources even in this supplementary role. It is limited by competition with other private agencies, by the middle-class emphasis of United Way and national organizations, by a lack of interest in material aid found in most private agencies, and by constricted sources of donations. Our interviews with clients thus revealed that although aid was generally seen as some help in meeting needs, it was only a stopgap. Chapter 7 pointed out that as needs increased during the last few years, few agencies could alter their service network to respond adequately.

To be sure, the data in Chapters 4 and 6 suggest some coordination between the two sectors that might demonstrate supplementation. Most private agencies deal with short-term needs government programs do not cover well, and many intentionally coordinate their services with the public sector. However, this coordination is only superficial. As Chapter 4 suggests, the limits imposed by economic conditions and community ideologies may mean that no extra effort is made to meet needs when the public sector is less generous. Accordingly, gap filling (a subject of Chapter 5) occurs only to a limited degree and in specific locales. In addition, agencies do not alter types of service to fill gaps in the public system. Other factors determine what type of aid is distributed. Shelters, food pantries, general service agencies, and what have you, are almost randomly distributed.

Though the role of private agencies is therefore limited, it is nevertheless significant. As the evidence suggests, private agencies exist in every community and save many from starvation and homelessness. Often they provide the only source of shelter to hundreds of thousands of people—some the victims of disaster, others facing a sudden loss of income or a change in family circumstances, still other chronically homeless for a number of reasons. Private food programs provide for many who would otherwise go hungry. General programs often cover utility payments, rent, and needs for furniture; side programs cover important health-related expenses; and single-mission agencies provide what they are organized to distribute, whether shoes or shelter. Although public programs may in theory meet the same needs, overlap is only theoretical owing to limited budgets; the private agencies indeed fill needs.

The few interviews with clients completed for this study, along with reported surveys, confirm the importance of private agencies in meeting needs. A large proportion of the clients interviewed believed they had nowhere to turn if the private agencies did not aid them. The main point, then, is that there is a lack of sufficiency, not of importance. Private aid certainly does not substitute for public welfare, long-term aid, a good job, or relatives and friends, but it is seen by clients as vital when these sources are not adequate.

Equity

Equity may be defined as the extent to which individuals with similar needs for services are provided similar benefits. Procedures to ration aid test equity, and our question might be how private agency procedures affect their ability to provide supplementary benefits.

As Chapter 6 suggests, most agency policies favor dispensing aid widely across the needy population. But some agencies do limit aid to groups, either excluding or exclusively assisting public welfare recipients or single individuals. Further, funding limits and ideology cause some clients in private agencies to be given more benefits than others. In what seems an ironic twist, agencies sometimes give more money to persons who have full-time jobs lined up than to those without hope of employment, under the assumption that the former are a better investment. Certain agencies weed out all but the heart-rending cases. Many shelters serve only men, which means that facilities to house families are, by comparison, greatly restricted.

Because the type of aid that is provided is often predetermined by the mission of the agency, each program tends to provide for a small set of needs it views as legitimate. Thus clients with unpopular needs are less likely than others to receive aid. And not only is the aid an individual receives dependent on the predisposition of an agency to dispense it, but there is no guarantee that the range of community services will match the range of community needs.

Most of the private agencies also appear to have great leeway in deciding whom to serve. Students of such discretion (Handler and Hollingsworth, 1971; Handler, 1973) worry that this leads to individuals making moral distinctions between deserving and undeserving clients and imposing conditions on some. The data clearly indicate that a few agencies demonstrate a degree of subjective selectivity. But this problem must be kept in perspective. Many of the private agencies studied here appear to be surprisingly free from such individual-level vices. Agencies may dispense more aid to families than to single individuals, but most try to dispense some aid to nearly all who request it and use very basic need-related criteria. Service to a particular community, a good-works philosophy, and even fear of backlash from a church congregation seem to work against making distinctions between clients. Instead, the more equitable technique of limiting benefits per visit or limiting the number of repeat visits is used.

Given the lack of national policy and lack of consistent values from place to place, the size of the network and the nature of the problems served differ with community preferences and resources. Perhaps the most severe inequity this book uncovered is thus that communities with more resources provide more benefits; they tend to have more agencies, and they may also have larger agencies. Our data also reveal that communities concentrate on specific needs: Texas County focuses on migrants; West Virginia County has many agencies that cover the expenses of current recipients of public welfare; and Pennsylvania County appears to have a slightly above-average interest in dealing with food needs of displaced workers.

Character of Service

Do private agencies deliver services in a way that compensates for the impersonality of public programs? Our interviews with clients suggest that a lack of rules—and thus few questions about eligibility—increases satisfaction. Private agencies face few pressures to develop rules; as a result, the clients we interviewed generally believed that benefits were provided with sympathy and warmth. Most preferred the attitudes of private agency employees to those of public employees. Quick service, few demeaning questions and requirements, and a sympathetic, nonstigmatizing attitude seem often to prevail. Some private agencies even seemed to furnish a sense of belonging to a community. Helping out in a kitchen or participating in neighborhood meal programs may not be much, but it provides a point of reference for the poor in an increasingly impersonal world. To be sure, most encounters with private agencies are brief and result in only limited emotional responses from clients—but these responses are often positive.

Of course some programs have rigid rules. Certain religious shelters make demands on applicants that seem uncalled for in the context of the bleak prospects of many of the poor. One agency employee actually tried to convert me during an interview, having read me verses from the Bible out loud. I found the encounter annoying; it provided much anxiety because I believed that I could not obtain the information I needed if I did not cooperate to some degree. How those who do not have shelter must feel in a similar situation!

One other criticism of the private agencies studied here is their failure to provide the social services most needed by the poor. Agencies in the sample rarely give employment counseling, medical care, help in finding an apartment, crisis counseling, and so forth. Though there are obvious exceptions, such as budget counseling in many agencies and special services offered by some Traveler's Aid offices, the Red Cross, and Salvation Army, normally agencies that provide material aid do not have a professional service orientation. Indeed, the two goals are actually inconsistent according to a common view (Cloward and Epstein, 1967).

One other characteristic of the sampled agencies is their tendency to provide in-kind rather than cash benefits (see Chapter 6). This is also true of many of public welfare's emergency assistance programs. But it certainly is a far cry from the cash system normally adopted in basic income maintenance grants in the public sector and does not demonstrate an accepting attitude. Many reasons for the in-kind character of benefits exist. Some are practical, such as when a special discount is given for a voucher by Greyhound or the local gas station. Others are dictated by the donors, who may wish to provide in-kind benefits only. Some relate to the mission of the agency, as in the case of food and meal programs. But programs provide vouchers or in-kind benefits even when no such reason is apparent. Most respondents told us that in-kind aid assures that the grant is used for the intended purpose. In other words, private agencies desire to maintain control over how the aid is spent, because they view their role as providing limited benefits, not dispensing cash for general purposes.

Cultural Pluralism

To what extent do private agencies contribute to cultural pluralism by supporting communities, ethnic groups, religious groups, or individuals with similar values? Many consider this an important criterion for evaluating private agencies, under the assumption that modern societies, and modern government, tend to suppress cultural differences. Grønbjerg (1982), for example, worries that the United States is becoming a "mass society," in which equal political rights are linked to governmental programs that ignore cultural differentiation. She considers private agencies one counterbalancing force, in a sense supplementing the public sector by providing alternate identifications.

Because this work is primarily aimed at assessing the effect of organizations on clients, little attention was paid to cultural pluralism. However, one of the few things we can say with certainty is that a spectrum of religious values is indeed to be found among private agencies: the Salvation Army's interest in one sort of fundamentalist religion, a different version of fundamentalist religion in missions, the emphases of Catholic Charities and Catholic Workers on a religious community all contrast with the secular missions of the Red Cross.

Notably missing are sets of values that mirror anything else about local communities. A few Community Action agencies attempt to represent community values, as do some agencies run by ethnic groups. But in all cases, these are publicly funded organizations, ones that many believe are not indigenous in the sense of expressing a cultural tradition. Something of a truncated range of cultural views is thus expressed.

Two possible explanations for this apparent lack of pluralism come to mind. One is that communities have less solidarity than in the past, so that cultural pluralism is not desired (and financially supported) by many. I have argued this position elsewhere (Sosin, 1979), although the argument remains speculative. A second possibility is that, given the reduction in poverty since the turn of the century, the material assistance network is no longer looked on as a repository of pluralism. Material needs are probably not a central concern to most cultural groups, except in poor communities, where the groups cannot support many agencies.

ADVOCACY

Advocacy entails support for interest groups with different political goals from those that are dominant—in particular, perhaps different from those found in government. Evidence is this book suggests that agencies dispensing material aid often do not advocate with persistence. In fact, the material aid agencies studied here are less likely than others in the private sector to engage in any sort of advocacy. As has been mentioned, religious affiliations, the time-consuming nature of the material aid effort, the sources of funds (from direct donations), and possibly a belief that those in need are experiencing individual problems and not social ones all militate against advocacy. In addition, advocacy for the poor may be seen as criticism of the social order, of those in power, and of the belief that those in need are to blame for their situations.

There is, nevertheless, some advocacy in the studied agencies. Most notably, the leaders of the advocacy movement often come from private agencies that receive public funds. Sometimes government even supports advocacy agencies to attack other levels of government. In addition, publicly funded agencies with community-related missions often advocate for economic issues. These advocates can organize other private agencies, particularly when many are overwhelmed with requests for aid and desire help from government (either directly, or indirectly through expansions of public programs).

Coalitions of agencies that document need can claim special expertise, which makes them effective lobbyists. Lobbies were responsible for the 1983 legislation providing federal support for shelter and food (Public

Law 98-8). They may also have been useful in pointing out the problems of the poor as benefit programs have been cut. The long lines at food pantries, seen on news programs in every community, might also have helped convince legislators to stop cutting programs (although not to increase many of them). At present, advocacy by private agencies seems part of a holding action to retain the basic institutions that help the poor.

SUPPORT FOR THE STATUS QUO

There is very little evidence that private agencies support the status quo, either by convincing clients that they are at fault for their own problems, or by making it appear that new services, benefits, or structural changes are not needed. Few counsel clients, let alone try to change their basic attitudes. The agencies generally do not claim that they meet needs to such an extent that public programs are irrelevant. And although certain public figures point to the private sector to prove that there will be little damage done by cutting public programs, such claims do not seem to affect policy.

To the extent that private agencies alleviate misery, it can be argued that without them, the social order would be more vulnerable to challenge. But private agencies provide such a tiny fraction of benefits for the poor that this seems unlikely. The private sector's material aid programs simply reflect a number of traditional values and concerns of communities and particular ethnic and religious groups. They do not argue for or against reform. The existence of private agencies is for the most part a historical accident, conditioned by the dictates of religion, ethnic solidarity, and past, more extensive public sanction. They are thus what is often called "loosely coupled" with the public system, existing in some sort of balance, with some degree of cooperation and antagonism, but largely with a very independent set of objectives and practices.

Private Agencies as Some Envision

These findings do not uncover a dramatic role for private agencies, at present, and they also severely question some of the recent claims about what the private agencies might accomplish. Some scholars say that private agencies may potentially operate as "mediating structures," forming a buffer between mass society and individuals and thus reemphasizing the role in society of individuals and their local communities

(Berger and Neuhaus, 1977). While it is always possible to find an exceptional agency that meets this criterion for a small group of people, at least as far as can be demonstrated from an examination of agencies that provide for material needs, the mediating role is far from evident. As has been mentioned, the private agencies at best display a set of religious missions that might express the sentiments of part of the community, along with some very specific secular interests in certain social problems or issues. In a sense, this implies only a narrow range of community sentiments, particularly given neighborhood religious heterogeneity. More telling, the agencies do not seem to actively involve their communities. Even those that view themselves as community centers, in which boards of directors represent the community, operate almost independently of their boards. The few agencies that provide a cultural experience for their clients or a sense of community to their volunteers have little impact.

At least one commentator has called for the dismantling of the public welfare system (Murray, 1984). While his basic claim is that benefits do recipients more harm than good, a secondary argument is that private agencies can meet the needs that public agencies currently handle. Those who are interested in the mediating role of private agencies actually make the same case. They state that handing more power to the private sector would result in an outpouring of energies and thus the creation of more adequate mediating structures.

In contrast, I believe that the private sector is limited to a supplemental role in anything that might approach an adequate income maintenance system. The private sector as a whole is only a seventh the size of the public sector, and only a small portion of it is actively engaged in furnishing material aid. Income maintenance programs in the public sector cost over $200 billion a year, whereas donations to private social welfare agencies are about $4 billion a year (Kramer, 1981). It is unlikely therefore that the private effort can ever hope to replace public programs that serve the poor. Indeed, the current public system, as we have seen, does not reach all of the poor.

A host of pressures will limit the private sector under practically any conditions. Existing evidence thus suggests that, if there were no governmental programs, individual contributions would not take up very much of the slack; our statistical evidence demonstrates that there is only a slightly larger material assistance effort in counties with a more limited public system, and that there are more agencies in richer communities.

The case studies also suggest little compensation by private agencies for limits in the public system. When economic conditions deteriorated and basic income maintenance grants were reduced, there were no noticeable increases in the provision of material goods in two of the four localities studied. One result of drastically increased demands was a restriction of aid through changes in rules or the dispensing of fewer goods to those in need. The two wealthier counties demonstrated a bit more compensation, though it was unclear to what extent they succeeded in meeting need. In general, aid appears to be a function of the willingness to contribute to unfashionable causes. The legitimacy of these causes does not closely reflect economic need.

CHAPTER 10

Epilogue: Proposals for Reform

What, then, can we expect the private sector to accomplish? I would argue that we should begin with the assumption that the supplemental role is the most likely one and find ways to improve it. These improvements, however, must take the constraints on the private sector into account. Thus I discuss here proposals that will not only better serve the needy, but are within the realm of possibility, given the structure of the private sector. Reforms that meet these two criteria are divided into those that can be implemented in the immediate future and long-range plans.

Short-Term Reforms

The present is not a propitious time for monumental reforms in the private sector. Resources are tight, competition for them is keen, and no new conceptualization of the role of private agencies seems to be gathering support. To be sure, the present administration is encouraging an increased private role, but this is unlikely to occur without increases in financial aid, which are not forthcoming. Private agency executives offered us few suggestions of their own for change, generally considering their agencies unable to take on increased responsibilities. It thus seems useful to develop strategies for the short term that alter the behavior of private agencies to a small degree.

I believe that private agencies should be encouraged to give greater support to those with material needs. Reports of increases in the poverty rate, as well as the information from agencies and reports presented throughout this book, document the growing need. At the same time, public welfare benefits have been reduced, and states have demonstrated little willingness or ability to compensate. As I read the economy, the return of economic prosperity will not improve conditions for many of those at the bottom of the economic ladder. A major private material assistance effort is thus vital to alleviate the large number of personal economic crises. Since even the HUD study suggests that three people are living on the street for every one in a shelter, the number of facilities for emergency housing must be greatly increased (even if long-run solutions to homelessness might require a host of other policies). The doubling and tripling of the number of clients who make use of other agencies, along with resulting rationing strategies, demonstrates a need for additional food, clothing, and payments for utilities. Social services, to help those in a crisis to build a more secure future insofar as that is possible, are also important.

Who should provide these additional resources for agencies to dispense? The United Way, which now supports material assistance efforts only sparingly, could increase its donations to existing agencies and perhaps fund new agencies. Agencies that stress counseling and other labor-intensive services should contribute something to meet the material needs of their clients. Agencies that deal with the chronically mentally ill, for example, might be advised to deal with the financial problems of these very dependent individuals, problems that SSI benefits do not completely solve. States may be able to use the AFDC-Emergency Assistance program to support emergency housing for families, and efforts should be devoted to ensuring that they do so. This source of funds can be used at a savings because it is matched at a 50% rate by the federal government.

There is also a short-term need for continuing advocacy. Chapters 7 and 8 overview attempts to hold food drives, to document the needs that exist in communities, and to attempt to obtain additional funds. These efforts must continue to focus public attention on the problems of the poor.

Can these suggestions be implemented? They demand a change of outlook. Professionally oriented organizations are apparently reluctant to dispense material aid, and the United Way also often demonstrates reluctance. I believe that, if they desired to do so, the agencies and the United Way could shift some of their resources to the needy. Those who provide funds, particularly individual donors, do not seem to demand a strict accounting of every dollar; a moderate redistribution of resources should be possible.

Part of the reluctance of private agencies to provide material aid and to advocate stems from the belief that these activities are not professional. But this belief is now being challenged. A recent school of thought in social work stresses that individuals can only be appropriately served if workers take into account both environmental pressures and individual problems (Pincus and Minahan, 1973). Ideologically, this perspective is widely accepted in the academic community. It also appears to be more successful in solving clients' problems, according to evaluation studies (Wood, 1978). It seems consistent with widening the focus of agencies to providing tangible resources and advocating. We cannot be absolutely sure, however, that this point of view will be readily accepted by those in a position to devote more attention to the poor.

Long-Run Reforms

In light of this uncertainty about achieving minimal reform, it might seem inappropriate to consider more substantial, long-run reform. From the point of view of need, however, there is a good reason to suggest a much expanded supplemental role for private agencies. The small size of basic income maintenance benefits, the increase in poverty, and the large number of people living on the streets all attest to the inadequacy of current provisions.

Why not attempt to alter the public sector directly, without involving private agencies in any major capacity? Because the day of universal, adequate, income maintenance benefits is distant and may never arrive. To briefly summarize a complicated argument that has been made elsewhere (Sosin, 1979), the growth of large interest groups advocating for business and for lower taxes, distrust of the "undeserving poor," lack of political power of inner cities, and the balance being struck between civilian and military spending militate against any large-scale increases in social welfare. While it may be worthwhile to continue to increase comprehensiveness, this approach is not a sufficient one, in itself, to reduce need.

Even if large increases in public support occur, there still would be problems in meeting emergency needs in the public sector. Natural disasters, lost checks, illnesses, appliance breakdowns all require additional aid that government agencies are loath to provide.

To be sure public systems can adopt specialized programs to deal with individualized needs outside of the basic grants, and it can even be claimed that such separation may enable agencies to balance standardization and discretion. But the public emergency programs have many problems at present in meeting needs (Handler and Sosin, 1983). These programs tend to specialize in only one emergency need, such as energy assistance, rent arrearages, or natural disasters, so many needs are not met. Coverage is spotty. Rules are strict. Applicants must meet stringent income and asset tests, must have a qualifying emergency, and must settle for limited aid.

Clearly, many such restrictions result from the need to ration limited resources. But part of the problem with public special needs programs is that standardization has come to represent an ideology. Administrators and policymakers have come to value equity and simplicity over sufficiency, and the control of error over flexibility. This ideology has spread beyond basic grants, to cover emergency programs. Concern over error and fraud and the desire for administrative simplicity and horizontal equity result in procedures that create standard, rigid benefits. I believe that it is now nearly impossible for government agencies to maintain a standardized basic grant system without feeling pressure to rigidify their specialized programs (Sosin, 1984).

In light of the problems the public sector has in meeting certain needs, it is only natural to turn to the private sector as an alternative. But we have already documented some of the limits of private provision. What is the solution? If there is any at all, it might lie in a combined effort in which government (at various levels) *contracts* emergency services to private agencies. Contracts of services, if they can be implemented, have at least some chance of expanding benefits, increasing advocacy, and also ensuring a somewhat higher quality of service than exists at present.

ADVANTAGES OF THE PRIVATE SECTOR

One of the advantages of contracting is that it counters the most severe defect of the private system, the inequities across community and state. It has been argued that community networks vary directly with wealth, and that each community focuses on certain types of clients to the exclusion of others. With public support, this could change. Funding could be equalized—at least within the geographic region covered by the relevant unit of government—and local priorities could be balanced by those of a higher level.

Not only might inequities be eased, but it is even conceivable that the private agencies might be able to provide aid in a manner that is superior to that of current public emergency programs. This is due to the difference in political environments. Private agencies simply do not face the same pressures to avoid fraud and error and to account for every penny, as do public agencies. As we have argued, the general public and those who provide funds have only a general notion about what the private agencies should do, while many of the specifics depend upon internal missions.

In addition, because they do not dispense basic grants, private agencies are less likely to be viewed as subverting equity by dispensing material aid for special purposes. Many have been concerned that dispensing such benefits in a discretionary, flexible way leads to the social control of clients (Handler, 1973; Cloward and Piven, 1974). That is, when social workers have the power to say yes or no to a particular request, they can use their power to force compliance to a large set of norms involving life-style, how money is spent, and demeanor. But if basic grants remain the province of the public sector while special-purpose grants are handled by the private sector, then no matter how discretionary the special-purpose grants become, the basic grant will remain unconditional. Thus social control will be kept to a minimum for at least the bulk of support. In fact, the data presented in this book imply that private agencies do not exercise much social control. They rarely impose conditions or even counsel clients.

Another advantage of such programs is that the private sector should be able to respond quickly. Private agencies have less paperwork than public agencies, and, if funds are distributed to many private agencies, workers will have relatively small caseloads. Indeed, most clients interviewed for this book even now find the private sector more responsive to them than the public sector.

I would also argue that, if public funds were contracted, advocacy would increase. As Chapter 8 notes, publicly funded private agencies are the most likely to advocate, particularly when they find that the supply of services does not equal the demand. By increasing the role of the private sector as well as their access to government funds, one would thus be likely to increase their propensity to advocate.

Given the fact that so few such agencies currently advocate, a counterargument might be that private provision would result in a reduction of advocacy, because governmental agencies that now deal with material needs would reduce their efforts to increase benefit levels and services. However, evidence suggests that supplemental programs that are provided by the public sector are so constrained that they do not provide an impetus to advocacy (Handler and Sosin, 1983). Because the programs are so rigid, workers are not necessarily aware of increased need. Furthermore, workers also often informally turn down clients, so increased demand never even reaches the application stage, where it becomes obvious and can mobilize support.

Of course private agencies are unlikely to advocate for sweeping change in the social structure if they become the main service providers. But they will be useful in pointing up the deficiencies of income maintenance grants and perhaps may lobby for a bit more funding than would otherwise be made available for supplemental programs.

SHORTCOMINGS AND SOLUTIONS

Some might object that, given current characteristics of private agencies, contracting may make for more problems than it solves. But I would argue that appropriate policies could limit the deficiencies of the private sector. Opponents might, for example, point to evidence that access to private agencies will be limited because many feel more stigma in using the private sector than they do using public programs. But according to our respondents, stigma due to the attitudes of workers is the more important phenomenon, and this type of stigma is found less frequently in many private agencies than in public agencies. Funding could be limited to those agencies that have been found to be particularly free of stigma—such as small agencies with few conditions, and Community Action projects (Morris, Lescohier, and Withorn, 1975).

This call for support for private aid may seem a bit suspect given the rather negative picture we painted of some urban shelters. But the inadequacies of these shelters have nothing to do with whether they are public or private. The major problem is size. The large dormitory-style facilities are clearly inadequate. The logical proposal is to rely on the smaller, more intimate shelters.

Some may also claim that owing to a lower level of accountability and the ability of agency workers to evade rules, individual inequities occur in private agencies. But I would argue that inequities are inevitable in emergency programs, whether public or private. It is difficult if not impossible to develop a set of rules that eliminates the need for judgments and thus bias. Indeed, the definition of inequity is a matter of controversy. Suppose a family comes in with a need for a large amount of cash to replace stolen tools used for work. The family is usually self-sufficient and can, with the cash, obtain new tools that might enable the breadwinner to return to work. Should special time or money be spent on such a family? One view of equity says no, because needs should determine resources. Another might say yes, because flexibility demands common sense decisions. Thus decisions depend upon values and cannot be completely controlled unless complicated ethical choices have been made in advance.

A funding strategy of broad rules to limit discretion, and trust in the judgment of agency workers is the only way to deal with the equity problems. By funding agencies whose structures support a client orientation and whose missions are good works and community service, the government should be able to minimize inequities.

PROBLEMS OF CONTRACTING

New problems might be generated by public support. Again, I believe that administrative strategies can reduce difficulties. Thus, one fear might be that, if too closely tied to one governmental agency, the material assistance agencies may not advocate for fear of losing funding. Even though other researchers have noted that support from the government is not inconsistent with advocacy (Kramer, 1981)—a finding confirmed in Chapter 8—perhaps an agency totally dependent upon this one source of funds would hesitate to lobby. This seems to be the case for energy programs.

However, this book consistently demonstrates that the behavior of private agencies is closely tied to their missions. Those with general interest in good works, or service to the community, or solving a certain problem, have material assistance programs that are consistent with their aims. Therefore a reduction in advocacy will be less likely if government-funded programs are established among agencies that have compatible, general missions.

Another useful administrative strategy might be to fund the agencies from a different level of government than the one that provides the basic welfare benefits. For example, if a state-run AFDC program is found wanting by material assistance programs in the private sector, federal funding might encourage some degree of autonomy and thus some amount of lobbying. A federal SSI program might be best matched with state or local funds for private agencies dealing with the same client population. The issue is not the final source of funds—they may all stem from the federal government—but the administrative structure in which they are dispensed. Federal block grants for material assistance programs for the elderly thus might provide enough local control to assure autonomy.

Some may also argue that, if given public responsibilities, private agencies would begin to face the same pressures the public agencies encounter. Concerns over accountability could cause private agencies to become as rigid as public agencies. But I believe that private agencies, because they are not directly under the control of government, should come under less scrutiny. And they will not be expected to provide horizontal equity.

Finally, part of the rigidity of public emergency assistance programs stems from their close contact with other public programs that tend to be standardized. I have argued elsewhere (Sosin, 1981), as have others (DiMaggio and Powell, 1983), that agencies tend to develop similarities in structure to others with whom they feel some degree of affinity. The emergency assistance programs are rigid because the basic income maintenance programs are rigid. Not having the same reference group, particularly if funds are dispensed in the ways we have discussed, private agencies are less likely to become rigid.

Another set of criticisms involve cultural pluralism. Ralph Kramer (1981) is particularly concerned about the reduction in pluralism caused by dispensing public funds to private agencies. He argues that, while it is important to ensure accountability in private agencies when they receive public funds (to help reach his goal of universal, equitable services), accountability might increase dependency and thus reduce the pluralistic, autonomous benefits of the private sector.

At the onset, it should be noted that his analysis is clearly tied to the cultural pluralism framework. If one does not have such a framework, some of the problems do not seem as serious. To me cultural pluralism should not be heavily stressed. While I have no quarrel with agencies that manage to maintain a sense of cultural identity while dispensing benefits, I believe the benefits are most important. When the two are disparate, the needs of the poor should come first. Other private concerns may indeed be directed most toward promoting cultural pluralism—such as social clubs, the Shriners, groups supporting the symphony or the ballet, and so forth. Indeed, the limited types of cultural pluralism currently supported in the agencies providing material aid brings into question the extent to which there is a cultural tradition that may be compromised.

Further, public funding of certain private agencies might not reduce existing pluralism in the private system as a whole. Many private material assistance programs exist in agencies with broad religious or ethical aims. Some such agencies made it clear in our interviews that they will not accept funds from government. I believe that these units will not reduce their efforts if public funds are dispensed to other agencies. These units may maintain pluralism. Indeed, any material aid program will have eligibility criteria that are bound to reject some of the needy. An independent private sector will still be needed.

In addition, there is little evidence that public funds actually decrease the autonomy (and thus pluralism) of private agencies. Two empirical studies carried out about fifteen years ago (Lambert and Lambert, 1970; Perlmutter, 1971) demonstrate very little impact of public funds on autonomy. While the agencies altered their clientele to become eligible to receive the public funds, they actually felt more autonomous, rather than less so, because they were freed from the demands made by local sources of funds. One study (D'Agostino, 1974) appears to demonstrate a larger loss of independence, but the study focuses on the types of clients served, not the nature of services. A New York study concludes that the major burden is additional paperwork (Hartogs, 1978). To be sure, very restrictive rules can reduce autonomy; but if governmental funds are dispensed within the framework of contracts that allow leeway, past studies suggest little impact on autonomy.

It is even possible that contracting will encourage additional forms of pluralism. Many neighborhoods and special interest groups must desire to establish their own material assistance programs in their local communities but cannot now do so; we have seen that poorer communities tend not to have the resources necessary to support many agencies. It may very well be that minority communities in a county like Texas County or poor communities in general will be able to increase their organizational capacity and solidarity if the contracted services are available. Indeed, the great inequity in offered emergency aid between counties and between communities within counties can be addressed by making adequate funding available.

One final possibility is that, if emergency aid were distributed by private agencies, increased support would be easier to obtain. At present public administrators are partly responsible for limiting these programs. Many executives apparently believe that emergency programs subvert the goal of standardization. Thus, they desire to keep the programs small (Handler and Sosin, 1983). Obviously, there may be less such pressure if private agencies disbursed the funds.

THE PUBLIC CONTRIBUTION

It is important to stress that I am not advocating a simple, direct supplementation of all private material assistance efforts. Rather, I am suggesting that the public sector develop a thoughtful, selective process to use private agencies to meet special material needs. This involves careful consideration of which agencies to fund as well as how to fund agencies.

How much will this program cost? This of course depends upon the extent to which needs are met. But our previous work with the public system suggests that relatively adequate emergency assistance programs in this sector cost about 3 or 4% of the totals for the basic income maintenance program. I assume that this represents approximately what it would cost to fund the private program, although how much of the cost will represent new funds depends upon the size of the current public income maintenance supplementary programs in a given state or locality. Because the new funds will supplement private contributions, will not go to all private agencies, and will be used flexibly, it is possible that the funds will go farther in private agencies than they currently do in public agencies. This is speculative, however, and it ignores the possibility of rising costs as salaries within private agencies increase with the infusion of new funds.

The above estimate does not include shelter. It is clear that public funding for shelter is inadequate and new money is necessary. The cost depends upon the number of homeless who will use the new shelters. Extrapolating from the previously mentioned Milwaukee studies, there may be two million homeless people in the country in any year. From Milwaukee estimates provided to the author for these purposes, the average length of homelessness is about 2.6 weeks. Further, Milwaukee officials claim that shelters range in cost from $8 to $32 a night, and we can assume a cost of $15 ($32 represents the cost of a highly intensive service program for a proportion of the homeless in Milwaukee). Putting these figures together, the program might cost about $550 million.

However, the program will be adding to additional private funds. Using the $4 billion estimate of the total size of the private network, along with the estimate from our sample (discounted for programs with more than one purpose) for the proportion of agencies that dispense services to the homeless, it may be that roughly $100 million are currently spent on such services from private sources. As a rough estimate, then, $450 million may be needed to create a comprehensive program.

One other method of estimating is to rely on the national survey (U.S. Department of Housing and Urban Development, 1984; see Chapter 7). This report estimates 190,000 individuals living on the street each night (minimum) and calculates the average shelter cost (including meals) at $19 per night for each person. Multiplying through to obtain a daily figure and projecting across the year, the cost of adding sufficient new beds may be $1.3 billion per year. Naturally, a reliance on the higher HUD or coalition estimates greatly increases cost estimates.

The Extension Ladder View

These reforms involve more than a series of administrative changes; they also imply a redefinition of the relation between the public and private sectors, reconceptualizing the role each plays in meeting material needs. They posit a greater, more active role of private agencies and do not accept the ideology that the public sector should completely dominate. One must therefore ask the practical question: To what extent can such a conceptualization gain sufficient political support to be implemented.

This notion of a sharing of responsibilities has historical roots. Nearly a century ago, Webb (1914) suggested that private agencies might best be an "extension ladder." They build upon the benefits provided by the public sector, extending them to provide additional help. Webb believed that such help should not include a basic standard of living but should involve more flexible, individualized aid that is beyond what a public system can provide.

My policy suggestions involve precisely such a view. Private benefits are meant to extend public benefits. The latter should provide basic income maintenance, and the former should supplement it. My view differs from Webb's in that I support an important role for private agencies in advocating for sufficient basic benefits. My view also differs in suggesting contracting mechanisms. But the core of the proposal is similar.

I believe that when placed in terms of the extension ladder view, my proposal is capable of obtaining legitimacy. Since the New Deal, many have become comfortable with the notion that basic material needs should be provided by government (at least for certain groups). At the same time, the role of the private sector in providing for more specialized needs is gaining legitimacy because private agencies are often viewed as providing high-quality services for specific needs and situations demanding discretion (Wilensky and Lebeaux, 1958). Instituting such a conceptualization in practice is not at all inconsistent with our basic values. The dispensing of income maintenance grants demands equity and can best be legitimated by public programs. Supplementary aid requires flexibility; it should be provided by private agencies.

At present there are clearly many unmet financial needs. The public sector probably will not meet the most individualized ones; the private sector cannot meet them. Private agencies respond to private interests. Benefits are determined by community values and the missions of the agencies rather than by the needs of the poor. Resources are limited. Public agencies, despite having more funds, seem to respond more to potential political pressures than to clients. Perhaps by creating a division of labor between the public and private sectors, it will be possible to meet more fully the needs of the impoverished: to combine humane treatment, equity, and a potential for social change in a complex, impersonal, persistent social order.

References

Abbott, Grace. 1941. *From Relief to Social Security: The Development of the New Public Welfare Services and Their Administration*. Chicago: University of Chicago Press.

Aldridge, Howard. 1979. *Organization and Environment*. Englewood Cliffs, N.J.: Prentice-Hall.

Alexander, John K. 1980. *Render Them Submissive: Responses to Poverty in Philadelphia 1760-1800*. Amherst: University of Massachusetts Press.

Arce, A. Anthony; Tadlock, Marilyn; Vergare, Michael; and Shapiro, Stuart H. 1983. "A Psychiatric Profile of Street People Admitted to an Emergency Shelter," *Hospital and Community Psychiatry, 34*, 812–817.

Axinn, June, and Levine, Herman. 1975. *Social Welfare: A History of the American Response to Need*. New York: Harper and Row.

Bakal, Carl. 1979. *Charity U.S.A.* New York: Times Books.

Baxter, Ellen, and Hopper, Kim. 1981. *Private Lives/Public Spaces*. New York: Community Service Society.

Berens, Robert. 1967. *The Image of Mercy*. New York: Vintage Press.

Berger, Peter L., and Neuhaus, Richard John. 1977. *To Empower People: The Role of Mediating Structures in Public Policy*. Washington, D.C.: American Enterprise Institute for Public Policy Research.

Bremner, Robert H. 1980. *American Philanthropy*. Chicago: University of Chicago Press.

Brittain, Jack W., and Freeman, John. 1980. "Organizational Proliferation and Density-Dependent Selection." Pp. 291–338 in John R. Kimberly and Robert H. Miles, eds., *The Organizational Life Cycle*. San Francisco: Jossey-Bass.

Brodkin, Evelyn, and Lipsky, Michael. 1983. "Quality Control in AFDC as an Administrative Strategy," *Social Service Review, 57*, 1–34.

Buckley, Weltra. 1972. *Modern Systems Theory*. Englewood Cliffs, N.J.: Prentice-Hall.

Chaiklin, Harris. 1983. *The Service Needs of Soup Kitchen Users*. Baltimore: University of Maryland School of Social Work and Community Planning.

City of Madison. 1982. "Survey of Need for Emergency Housing," Madison, Wis. (mimeo.).

Cloward, Richard A., and Epstein, Irwin. 1967. "Private Social Welfare's Disengagement from the Poor: The Case of Family Adjustment Agencies." Pp. 40–63 in George Brager and Francis Purcell, eds., *Community Action against Poverty*. New Haven, Conn.: College and University Press.

Cloward, Richard A., and Piven, Francis F. 1971. *Regulating the Poor*. New York: Pantheon Books.

Cloward, Richard A., and Piven, Frances F. 1974. *The Politics of Turmoil: Essays on Poverty, Race, and the Urban Crisis*. New York: Pantheon Books.

Cohen, Michael D.; March, James G.; and Olsen, Johan P. 1972. "A Garbage Can Model of Organizational Choice," *Administrative Science Quarterly, 17*, 1–25.

Coleman, James. 1974. *Power and the Structure of Society*. New York: W.W. Norton.

Colier, Richard. 1965. *The General Next to God: The Story of William Booth and the Salvation Army*. London: Collins St. James Press.

Cooley, William, and Lohnes, Paul R. 1971. *Multivariate Data Analysis.* New York: John Wiley.

Coughlin, Bernard J. 1965. *Church and State in Social Welfare.* New York: Columbia University Press.

Crystal, Stephen, et al. 1983. "New Arrivals: First-Time Shelter Clients," New York Human Resources Administration (mimeo.).

D'Agostino, Peter. 1974. "Purchase of Social Services: A Prepayment Approach?" Ph.D. Dissertation, University of Wisconsin-Madison, School of Social Work.

Danziger, Sheldon. 1982. "Poverty and Inequality under Reaganomics," *Journal of Contemporary Studies, 5,* 17–30; also available as Institute for Research on Poverty Reprint 457, University of Wisconsin-Madison.

Danziger, Sheldon, and Smolensky, Eugene. 1983. "Abrupt Changes in Social Policy: The Redistributive Effects of Reagan's Budget and Tax Cuts," Institute for Research on Poverty Discussion Paper 725-83, University of Wisconsin-Madison.

Davis, Allen F. 1967. *Spearheads for Reform: The Social Settlements and the Progressive Movement, 1890–1914.* New York: Oxford University Press.

DiMaggio, Paul J., and Powell, Walter W. 1983. "The Iron Cage Revisited: Institutional Isomorphism and Collective Rationality in Organizational Fields," *American Journal of Sociology, 48,* 147–160.

Edelman, Murray. 1977. *Political Language: Words That Succeed and Policies That Fail.* New York: Academic Press.

Epstein, Irwin. 1981. "Advocates on Advocacy: An Exploratory Study," *Social Work Research and Abstracts, 17,* 5–12.

Erlanger, Howard. 1978. *Strategies for Action: Developmental Disabilities and State Government.* Madison, Wis.: Center for Public Representation.

Evan, William. 1966. "The Organizational Set: Toward a Theory of Interorganizational Relations." Pp. 173–192 in James D. Thompson, ed., *Approaches to Organizational Design.* Pittsburgh: University of Pittsburgh Press.

Filer Commission. 1977. *Giving in America: Towards a Stronger Voluntary Sector.* Washington, D.C.: Commission on Private Philanthropy and Public Need.

Freeman, John, and Hannan, Michael T. 1983. "Niche Width and the Dynamics of Organizational Populations," *American Journal of Sociology, 88,* 1116–1145.

Friedman, Milton. 1962. *Capitalism and Freedom.* Chicago: University of Chicago Press.

Galper, J. H. 1975. *The Politics of Social Services.* Englewood Cliffs, N.J.: Prentice-Hall.

Gamson, William. 1975. *The Strategy of Social Protest.* Homewood, Ill.: Dorsey Press.

Goodrick, David, and Howden, Michael. 1978. "Survey of Residents of City of Milwaukee Rooming Houses, Boarding Houses, and Second Class Dwellings," Milwaukee, Wis. (mimeo.).

Grodzgins, Morton. 1966. *The American System: A View of Government in the United States.* Chicago: Rand McNally.

Grønbjerg, Kirsten. 1982. "Private Welfare in the Welfare State: Recent U.S. Patterns," *Social Service Review, 56,* 1–26.

Gross, Edward. 1968. "Universities as Organizations: A Research Approach," *American Sociological Review, 33,* 518–544.

Handler, Joel F. 1973. *The Coercive Social Worker.* Chicago: Rand McNally.

Handler, Joel F. 1978. *Social Movements and the Legal System: A Theory of Law Reform and Legal Change.* New York: Academic Press.

Handler, Joel F., and Hollingsworth, Ellen Jane. 1971. *The Deserving Poor: A Study of Welfare Administration.* Chicago: Rand McNally.

Handler, Joel F., and Sosin, Michael. 1983. *Last Resorts: Meeting Emergency Needs in Public Welfare.* New York: Academic Press.

Harper, Douglas. 1982. *Good Company*. New York: Harper and Row.
Harrington, Michael. 1976. *The Twilight of Capitalism*. New York: Simon and Schuster.
Hartogs, Nelly. 1978. *Impact of Government Funding on the Management of Voluntary Agencies*. New York: Greater New York Fund/United Way.
Hombs, Mary Ellen, and Snyder, Mitch. 1982. *Homelessness in America: A Forced March to Nowhere*. Washington, D.C.: Community for Creative Non-Violence.
Huntsberger, David. 1967. *Elements of Statistical Inference*, 2nd ed. Boston: Allyn and Bacon.
Jacobs, David. 1974. "Dependence and Vulnerability: An Exchange Approach to the Control of Organizations," *Administrative Sciences Quarterly, 19*, 45–59.
Jacoby, Henry. 1973. *The Bureaucratization of the World*. Berkeley, Calif.: The University of California Press.
Janowitz, Morris. 1976. *Social Control of the Welfare State*. New York: Elsevier.
Kaplan, Barry J. 1978. "Reformers and Charity: The Abolition of Public Relief in New York City, 1870–1898," *Social Service Review, 52*, 202–214.
Kasinitz, Philip. 1984. "Gentrification and Homelessness: The Single Room Occupant and the Inner City Revival," *Urban and Social Change Review, 17*, 9–14.
Katz, Daniel; Gutek, Barbara; Kahn, Robert; and Barton, Eugenia. 1975. *Bureaucratic Encounters*. Ann Arbor, Mich.: University of Michigan Press.
Katz, Daniel, and Kahn, Robert. 1966. *The Social Psychology of Organizations*. New York: John Wiley.
Kornhauser, William. 1959. *The Politics of Mass Society*. Glencoe, Ill.: Free Press.
Kramer, Ralph. 1973. "Future of Voluntary Service Organizations," *Social Work, 18*, 56–69.
Kramer, Ralph. 1981. *Voluntary Organizations in the Welfare State*. Berkeley, Calif.: University of California Press.
Lamb, H. Richard. 1984. "Deinstitutionalization and the Homeless Mentally Ill," *Hospital and Community Psychiatry, 35*, 899–907.
Lambert, Camile J., and Lambert, Lea R. 1970. "Impact of Poverty Funds on Voluntary Agencies," *Social Work, 15*, 53–61.
Lampman, Robert. 1983. "The Effects of Social Provision on the Economy," Institute for Research on Poverty, Notes and Comments, University of Wisconsin-Madison.
Lavine, Sigmind A. 1970. *Evangeline Booth: Daughter of Salvation*. New York: Dodd Mead and Company.
Leepson, Marc. 1982. "The Homeless: A Growing National Problem," *Editorial Research Reports, 11*, 759–812.
Leiby, James. 1978. *A History of Social Welfare and Social Work in the United States*. New York: Columbia University Press.
Lipsky, Michael. 1980. *Street Level Bureaucracy: Dilemmas of the Individual in Public Services*. New York: Russell Sage.
Lubove, Roy. 1980. *The Professional Altruist: The Emergence of Social Work as a Career, 1880–1930*. Cambridge, Mass.: Harvard University Press.
Lurie, Harry L. 1961. *A Heritage Affirmed: The Jewish Federation Movement in America*. Philadelphia: Jewish Publication Society of America.
McGerigle, Paul; Hunt, Paul; and White, Susan. 1979. *Management of the Family Housing Crisis in the City of Boston*. Boston: Urban Community Planning Corporation.
McMillen, Wayne. 1945. *Community Organization for Social Welfare*. Chicago: University of Chicago Press.
McNeil, Kenneth G. 1978. "Understanding Organizational Power: Building on the Weberian Legacy," *Administrative Science Quarterly, 23*, 65–90.
Manser, Gordon, and Cass, Rosemary Higgens. 1975. *Voluntarism at the Crossroads*. New York: Family Service Association of America.
March, James, and Simon, Herbert. 1958. *Organizations*. New York: John Wiley.

Michels, Robert. 1915. *Political Parties: A Sociological Study of the Oligarchical Tendencies of Modern Democracy*. New York: Tr. Eden and Cedar Paul.

Miller, William D. 1973. *A Harsh and Dreadful Love: Dorothy Day and the Catholic Worker Movement*. New York: Liveright.

Mills, G. B. 1981. "Quality Control in Welfare Administration: An Analysis of Payment Error in Aid to Families with Dependent Children." Ph.D. Dissertation, Harvard University, John F. Kennedy School of Government.

Moe, Terry M. 1980. *The Organization of Interests: Incentives and the Internal Dynamics of Political Interest Groups*. Chicago: University of Chicago Press.

Morris, Robert; Lescohier, Ilana; and Withorn, Ann. 1975. *Social Service Delivery Systems: Attempts to Alter Local Patterns, 1970–1974*. Waltham, Mass.: Brandeis University.

Moynihan, Daniel Patrick. 1969. *Maximum Feasible Misunderstanding: Community Action in the War on Poverty*. New York: Free Press.

Murray, Charles. 1984. *Losing Ground: American Social Policy, 1950–1980*. New York: Basic Books.

Oberschall, Anthony. 1980. "Loosely Structured Collective Conflict: A Theory and an Application." Pp. 45–68 in Louis Krisberg, ed., *Research in Social Movements, Conflicts, and Change*, Vol. 3. Greenwich, Conn.: JAI Press.

O'Grady, John. 1931. *Catholic Charities in the United States*. Washington, D.C.: National Conference of Catholic Charities.

Olson, Mancur. 1965. *The Logic of Collective Action*. Cambridge, Mass.: Harvard University Press.

Pennings, Johannes M. 1980. "Environmental Influences on the Creation Process." Pp. 134–160 in John R. Kimberly and Robert H. Miles, eds., *The Organizational Life Cycle*. San Francisco: Jossey-Bass.

Pennings, Johannes M. 1982. "Organizational Birth Frequencies: An Empirical Investigation," *Administrative Science Quarterly, 27*, 120–144.

Perlmutter, Felice. 1971. "Public Funds and Private Agencies," *Child Welfare, 50*, 264–270.

Pfeffer, Jeffrey, and Leong, Allan. 1977. "Resource Allocation in United Funds: Examination of Power and Dependence," *Social Forces, 55*, 775–790.

Pfeffer, Jeffrey, and Salancik, Gerald R. 1978. *The External Control of Organizations*. New York: Harper and Row.

Pincus, Allen, and Minahan, Anne. 1973. *Social Work Practice: Model and Method*. Itasca, Ill.: F.E. Peacock.

Piven, Francis F., and Cloward, Richard A. 1977. *Poor People's Movements: Why They Succeed, How They Fail*. New York: Pantheon Books.

Platt, Marjorie B. 1980. "Emergency Assistance Impact Study." Boston: Massachusetts Department of Public Welfare.

Plotnick, Robert B., and Skidmore, Felicity. 1975. *Progress against Poverty: A Review of the 1964–1974 Decade*. New York: Academic Press.

Rochefort, David A. 1981. "Progressive and Social Control Perspectives on Social Welfare," *Social Service Review, 53*, 568–592.

Ross, Edyth. 1978. *Black Heritage in Social Welfare, 1860–1930*. Metuchin, N.J.: Scarecrow Press.

Saloman, Lester M., and Abramson, Alan J. 1982. "The Nonprofit Sector." Pp. 219–243 in John L. Palmer and Isabel V. Sawhill, *The Reagan Experiment*. Washington, D.C.: The Urban Institute.

Selznick, Philip. 1949. *TVA and the Grass Roots*. Berkeley, Calif.: University of California Press.

Simon, Herbert. 1964. "On the Concept of Organizational Goal," *Administrative Science Quarterly, 9,* 1–22.

Smith, Constance, and Freedman, Ann. 1972. *Voluntary Associations: Perspectives on the Literature.* Cambridge, Mass.: Harvard University Press.

Sosin, Michael. 1979. "Social Welfare and Organizational Society," *Social Service Review, 53,* 392–405.

Sosin, Michael. 1981. "Juvenile Court Commitment Rates: The Role of Organizational Factors," *Social Service Review, 55,* 284–299.

Sosin, Michael. 1984. "Legal Rights and Welfare Change: 1960–1980," paper presented at conference, "Poverty and Policy: Retrospect and Prospects," Williamsburg, Va., December 6–8.

Sosin, Michael, and Caulum, Sharon. 1983. "Advocacy: A Conceptualization for Social Work Practice," *Social Work, 28* (May), 12–17.

Stack, Carolyn. 1979. *All Our Kin: Strategies for Survival in a Black Community.* New York: Harper and Row.

Starbuck, William. 1983. "Organizations as Action Generators," *American Sociological Review, 48,* 91–102.

Stern, Mark J. 1984. "The Emergence of the Homeless as a Social Problem," *Social Service Review, 58,* 291–301.

Stinchcombe, Arthur L. 1965. "Social Structure and Organizations." Pp. 142–193 in James March, ed., *Handbook of Organizations.* Chicago: Rand McNally.

Swift, Linton B. 1934. *New Alignments between Public and Private Agencies in a Community Family Welfare and Relief Program.* New York: Family Welfare Association of America.

Taussig, Michael. 1976. "Trends in Inequality of Well-offness in the United States since World War II," in *Conference on the Trend in Income Inequality in the U.S.,* Institute for Research on Poverty Special Report 11, University of Wisconsin-Madison.

Teele, J. E., and Levine, S. 1968. "The Acceptance of Emotionally Disturbed Children by Psychiatric Agencies." Pp. 103–126 in Stanton Wheeler, ed., *Controlling Delinquents.* New York: John Wiley.

Terrell, Paul. 1979. "Private Alternatives to Public Human Services Administration," *Social Service Review, 53,* 56–74.

Thompson, J. D. 1967. *Organizations in Action.* New York: McGraw Hill.

Trattner, Walter I. 1984. *From Poor Law to Welfare State,* 3rd ed. New York: Free Press.

Trolander, Judith Ann. 1982. "Social Change: Settlement Houses and Saul Alinsky, 1939–1965," *Social Service Review, 56,* 346–365.

United Way of America. 1977. *A History of the United Way.* Alexandria, Va.: United Way.

United Way of America. 1980. *United Way Measurements: Survey Data and Analysis of Performance, 1979 United Way Campaigns.* Alexandria, Va.: United Way.

Urban Coalition of Minneapolis. 1982. "Hardship in Hennepin County," Urban Coalition, Minneapolis.

U.S. Congress, Subcommittee on Public Assistance. 1977. "Hearings before the Subcommittee on Public Assistance of the Committee on Finance." *Congressional Record,* U.S. Senate, Ninety-Fifth Congress, First Session, H.R. 720, July 12, 18, 19, and 20.

U.S. Department of Commerce (Bureau of the Census). 1970. *Census of Housing: General Housing Characteristics: U.S. Summaries, 1970.* Washington, D.C.: GPO.

U.S. Department of Commerce (Bureau of the Census). 1980. *Census of Housing: General Housing Characteristics: U.S. Summaries, 1980.* Washington, D.C.: GPO.

U.S. Department of Housing and Urban Development. 1984. *A Report to the Secretary on the Homeless and Emergency Shelters.* Washington, D.C.: U.S. Department of Housing and Urban Development.

U.S. Department of Labor (Bureau of Labor Statistics). 1981. *Consumer Price Index, Detailed Report for 1980.* Washington, D.C.: GPO.

Watson, Frank. 1922. *The Charity Organization Society Movement in the United States: A Study in Philanthropy.* New York: Macmillan.

Webb, Sidney. 1914. "The Extension Ladder Theory of the Relation between Voluntary Philanthropy and State or Municipal Action," *Survey, 31,* 703–707.

Weber, Max. 1947. *The Theory of Social and Economic Organization.* New York: Oxford University Press.

Weick, Karl E. 1976. "Educational Organizations as Loosely Coupled Systems," *Administrative Science Quarterly, 21,* 1–19.

Weisbrod, Burt, and Schiff, J. 1982. "Collective Provision of Social Services: The Role of the Private Nonprofit Sector," University of Wisconsin-Madison (mimeo.).

Werner, Ruth M. 1976. *Public Financing of Voluntary Agency Foster Care: 1975 Compared to 1957.* New York: Child Welfare League of America.

Wilensky, Harold L., and Lebeaux, Charles N. 1958. *Industrial Society and Social Welfare.* New York: Free Press.

Wilson, James Q. 1973. *Political Organizations.* New York: Basic Books.

Wisconsin Information Service. 1982. "Summary of Emergency Shelter Care: Demand vs. Resources, Utilization Trends, and Population Characteristics," Milwaukee, Wisconsin Information Service (mimeo.).

Wisconsin Information Service. 1983. "No Place to Go: Emergency Shelter Referral Network Annual Report, 1982," Milwaukee, Wisconsin Information Service (mimeo.).

Wood, Katherine. 1978. "Casework Effectiveness: A New Look at the Research Evidence," *Social Work, 23,* 437–458.

Young, Dennis R., and Finch, Stephen J. 1977. *Foster Care and Non-Profit Agencies.* Lexington, Mass.: Lexington Books.

Yuchtman, Ephraim, and Seashore, Stanley E. 1967. "A System Resource Approach to Organizational Effectiveness," *American Sociological Review, 32,* 891–903.

Zald, Meyer. 1970. *The Political Economy of the YMCA.* Chicago: University of Chicago Press.

Zander, Thomas K. 1980. "Why Milwaukee County Needs a 'Home for the Homeless,'" Wisconsin State Public Defender, Milwaukee (mimeo.).

Index

A

R

S

T

Institute for Research on Poverty Monograph Series

Published

Michael Sosin, *Private Benefits: Material Assistance in the Private Sector.* 1986

George J. Borjas and Marta Tienda, Editors, *Hispanics in the U.S. Economy.* 1985

Joel F. Handler and Michael Sosin, *Last Resorts: Emergency Assistance and Special Needs Programs in Public Welfare.* 1983

Irwin Garfinkel, Editor, *Income-Tested Transfer Programs: The Case For and Against.* 1982

Richard V. Burkhauser and Karen C. Holden, Editors, *A Challenge to Social Security: The Changing Roles of Women and Men in American Society.* 1982

Jeffrey G. Williamson and Peter H. Lindert, *American Inequality: A Macroeconomic History.* 1980

Robert H. Haveman and Kevin Hollenbeck, Editors, *Microeconomic Simulation Models for Public Policy Analysis, Volume 1: Distributional Impacts, Volume 2: Sectoral, Regional, and General Equilibrium Models.* 1980

Peter K. Eisinger, *The Politics of Displacement: Racial and Ethnic Transition in Three American Cities.* 1980

Erik Olin Wright, *Class Structure and Income Determination.* 1979

Joel F. Handler, *Social Movements and the Legal System: A Theory of Law Reform and Social Change.* 1979

Duane E. Leigh, *An Analysis of the Determinants of Occupational Upgrading.* 1978

Stanley H. Masters and Irwin Garfinkel, *Estimating the Labor Supply Effects of Income–Maintenance Alternatives.* 1977

Irwin Garfinkel and Robert H. Haveman, with the assistance of David Betson, *Earnings Capacity, Poverty, and Inequality.* 1977

Harold W. Watts and Albert Rees, Editors, *The New Jersey Income–Maintenance Experiment, Volume III: Expenditures, Health, and Social Behavior, and the Quality of the Evidence.* 1977

Murray Edelman, *Political Language: Words That Succeed and Policies That Fail.* 1977

Marilyn Moon and Eugene Smolensky, Editors, *Improving Measures of Economic Well-Being.* 1977

Harold W. Watts and Albert Rees, Editors, *The New Jersey Income–Maintenance Experiment, Volume II: Labor-Supply Responses.* 1977

Marilyn Moon, *The Measurement of Economic Welfare: Its Application to the Aged Poor.* 1977

Morgan Reynolds and Eugene Smolensky, *Public Expenditures, Taxes, and the Distribution of Income: The United States, 1950, 1961, 1970.* 1977

Fredrick L. Golladay and Robert H. Haveman, with the assistance of Kevin Hollenbeck, *The Economic Impacts of Tax–Transfer Policy: Regional and Distributional Effects.* 1977

David Kershaw and Jerilyn Fair, *The New Jersey Income–Maintenance Experiment, Volume I: Operations, Surveys, and Administration.* 1976

Peter K. Eisinger, *Patterns of Interracial Politics: Conflict and Cooperation in the City.* 1976

Irene Lurie, Editor, *Integrating Income Maintenance Programs.* 1975

Stanley H. Masters, *Black–White Income Differentials: Empirical Studies and Policy Implications.* 1975

Larry L. Orr, *Income, Employment, and Urban Residential Location.* 1975

Joel F. Handler, *The Coercive Social Worker: British Lessons for American Social Services.* 1973

Glen G. Cain and Harold W. Watts, Editors, *Income Maintenance and Labor Supply: Econometric Studies.* 1973

Charles E. Metcalf, *An Econometric Model of Income Distribution.* 1972

Larry L. Orr, Robinson G. Hollister, and Myron J. Lefcowitz, Editors, with the assistance of Karen Hester, *Income Maintenance: Interdisciplinary Approaches to Research.* 1971

Robert J. Lampman, *Ends and Means of Reducing Income Poverty.* 1971

Joel F. Handler and Ellen Jane Hollingsworth, *"The Deserving Poor": A Study of Welfare Administration.* 1971

Murray Edelman, *Politics as Symbolic Action: Mass Arousal and Quiescence.* 1971

Frederick Williams, Editor, *Language and Poverty: Perspectives on a Theme.* 1970

Vernon L. Allen, Editor, *Psychological Factors in Poverty.* 1970